Social Work Theory and Psychoanalysis

for Clive

Social Work Theory and Psychoanalysis

Margaret Yelloly
Department of Applied Social Studies
University of London Goldsmiths College

VNR *VAN NOSTRAND REINHOLD COMPANY*
New York — Cincinnati — Toronto — London — Melbourne

**Published by Van Nostrand Reinhold Company Ltd.,
Molly Millars Lane, Wokingham, Berkshire, England**

*Published in 1980 by Van Nostrand Reinhold Company,
A Division of Litton Educational Publishing Inc.,
135 West 50th Street, New York, NY 10020, USA*

*Van Nostrand Reinhold Limited,
1410 Birchmount Road, Scarborough, Ontario, M1P 2E7,
Canada*

*Van Nostrand Reinhold Australia Pty. Limited,
17 Queen Street, Mitcham, Victoria 3132, Australia*

Library of Congress Cataloging in Publication Data

Yelloly, Margaret.
  Social work theory and psychoanalysis.

  Based on the author's thesis, University of Leicester,
1975, which was presented under title: Professional
ideologies in British social work.
  Bibliography: p.
  Includes index.
  1. Social work education — Great Britain. 2. Psychoanalysis — Great
Britain. 3. Social service — Great Britain. I. Title. [DNLM: 1. Social work,
Psychiatric. 2. Psychoanalysis. WM30.5 Y43s]
HV11.Y44 1980 361 79-21978
ISBN 0-442-30166-9
ISBN 0-442-30167-7 pbk.

Printed and bound in Great Britain at
The Camelot Press Ltd, Southampton,

Preface

The subject of this book, psychoanalysis in its relation to social work, is an emotive one. No topic attracts either such passionate commitment or such bitter antagonism as this area of human psychology. Dispassionate study of a theme so absorbing is therefore difficult, though I have done my best. The book is based on my Ph.D. thesis, *Professional Ideologies in British Social Work*, University of Leicester 1975, where greater detail as to sources can be found.

The first chapter sketches in the main features of the psychoanalytic paradigm on a very broad canvas as a prelude to the arguments which follow. This is succeeded by an historical account of the growth of psychoanalytic influence in Britain — necessary because this is beset by many misconceptions, and there is as yet no comprehensive history of British social work which corrects and sets them in perspective. Despite this historical excursion, the main intention of the book is to examine some of the issues that are raised for contemporary social work education and practice (both in Britain and elsewhere) as a consequence of this relationship, and this forms the substance of the final chapters. I am conscious that the book is incomplete and presents few definitive conclusions; this is inevitable when the field of study is itself changing rapidly.

My thanks are owed to many people who have generously helped at various stages, among them Miss R.M. Braithwaite, the British Association of Social Workers, Miss Sybil Clement Brown, Miss Irmi Elkan, Miss J.M.L. Eyden, The Family Welfare Association, Mr. Don Gregory, Miss P. Hardiker, Miss P.E. Harwood, Dr. Martin Herbert, Miss Noel Hunnybun, Mrs. K. Mc-Dougall, Mr. Herschel Prins, Mrs. B.M. Rogers, Miss J.M. Snelling, Miss Margaret Tilley, Miss Enid Warren, Mrs. C. Winnicott and Dame Eileen Younghusband.

Acknowledgement

The author is grateful to the following publishers for their permission to reproduce extracts from their publications.

Academic Press Inc. (NY) Ltd.
George Allen & Unwin Ltd.
Associated Book Publishers Ltd.
Basic Books Inc.
The Estate of Lord Beveridge.
British Association of Social Workers.
Carnegie United Kingdom Trust.
Columbia University Press.
Constable & Co. Ltd.
Faber and Faber Ltd.
Family Service Association of America.
Greenwood Press.
Hogarth Press Ltd.
University of Chicago Press.
Longmans Group Ltd.
McGraw-Hill Book Co.
National Association of Probation Officers.
National Association of Social Workers, Inc.
New York Times Book Co.
James Nisbet & Co. Ltd.
Pelican Books Ltd.
Random House Inc.
Sage Publications.
Smith College Publications.
Stanford University Press.
United Nations.
Dr. B. Wolman.
Yale University Press.

Glossary of Some Psychological Terms Used

Behaviour therapy: The modification of maladaptive behaviour through experimentally validated techniques based largely upon learning theory.

Dynamic psychology: Any psychological theory concerned with causal relationship or which stresses the interaction of forces within the mind and focuses especially on drives and motives. Psychoanalysis can be regarded as one of the dynamic psychologies.

Psychiatry: A medical specialism concerned with the care and treatment of mental disorders.

Psychoanalysis: The study of human mental functioning originated by Sigmund Freud. Psychoanalysis refers to: (1) a systematic body of theory; (2) a particular method of psychotherapeutic treatment; (3) a method for investigating the workings of the mind. A major assumption is that of unconscious mental process, and psychoanalytic treatment is largely concerned with the analysis of transference and resistance, and the elucidation of unconscious motives.

Psychoanalyst: One who is trained in the theories and techniques of psychoanalysis, and who holds a qualification from a recognized psychoanalytic institute or society. A psychoanalyst is not necessarily medically trained, though in practice a large proportion are psychiatrists.

Psychodynamic: Although widely used, this term does not appear in Wolman's *Dictionary of Behavioural Science*, and it is used with considerable indefiniteness.

The term usually refers to classical Freudian theory and subsequent theories derived from it which claim that behaviour is determined by the equilibrium achieved between the dynamic forces acting on the individual. Behaviour often appears incomprehensible to the subject or observer because he is not usually conscious of all the motives and conflicts influencing him*.

It is used in this book in a comprehensive sense to refer to all those theories and therapies which originated with or have derived from the work of Freud and his followers, and which assume the existence of unconscious motives, and the phenomena of transference and resistance; it thus includes but is broader than psychoanalysis. Forms of

* Meyer, V. and Chesser, E.S. *Behaviour Therapy in Clinical Psychiatry*, p. 15.

therapy based upon psychodynamic principles can be distinguished from both physical and behavioural methods of treatment.

Psychotherapy: A somewhat loose term to designate the treatment of mental or psychological distress through psychological (as opposed to chemical or physical) means. Psychotherapy may or may not be based upon psycho-analytic principles (i.e. psychoanalytically oriented); other important orientations are behavioural and client-centred (Rogerian) psycho-therapies.

Psychotherapist: One who practices psychotherapy. Psychotherapists may or may not be medically trained. Although various forms of training for psychotherapy exist at present in Britain, there is no form of registration of psychotherapists, and no agreement as to what psychotherapy is, nor what qualifications should be regarded as acceptable for its practice. Its practice is therefore at present entirely unfettered by professional or legal restrictions.

Further Reference

RYCROFT, C. *A Critical Dictionary of Psychoanalysis*. London. Nelson, 1968.
WOLMAN, B.B. *Dictionary of Behavioural Science*. MacMillan Press, 1973.

Contents

Introduction

The extent to which the theories and concepts of psychoanalysis have affected the development of social work in Britain is a major and so far unresolved issue. It is of far more than academic interest and has long been a source of fascination for practising social workers, as well as a happy hunting ground for their critics. Nevertheless, despite its theoretical and practical importance, there have been no studies of the relationship between psychoanalysis and social work that might help to establish the nature of this influence, its degree, or the precise ways in which the theories and concepts of psychoanalysis have gained acceptance and influenced social work practice. That this influence has been extensive seems to be unquestioned. Heraud, a British sociologist, affirms that social work 'is marked by a mainly therapeutic ideology which stresses that work must be done with the individual irrespective of the reform of the social structure in which the individual is placed', and that 'a psychological, and in particular a psychoanalytic, framework has been adopted as the vital model for professional practice'[1]. Lees regards it as a widely accepted interpretation of the history of social work that 'during the inter-war years social workers became largely absorbed with psychodynamic concepts to the exclusion of concern with wider social influences'[2]. This is a view he goes on to challenge strongly, contending that concern with wider social influences and the need for social reform was never excluded, despite the new interest in techniques of psychotherapy. Despite the stress by some authors[3] on the positive benefits that have accrued to social work through this influence the effects have been regarded by critics as predominantly negative, involving a disengagement from problems of poverty and the wider social environment, a disinclination to tackle issues of social policy, an over-concern with technique, and an inflexibility in relation to the development of other theoretical approaches of a nonpsychodynamic, and even a nonpsychological, nature.

These assertions raise many interesting questions. How real has this influence been? Was it in fact as extensive as is widely believed? At what historical points, for what reasons, and through what channels has it found its way into social work? Have psychoanalytic theories been absorbed in a wholesale and indiscriminating way, or have the borrowings been selective? What has been the nature of this borrowing, what use has been made of it, and in what specific ways has it had effects on the theory and practice of social work? In general, a somewhat exaggerated picture seems to have gained currency, in particular as to the extent to which psychoanalysis influenced

1

social work during the inter-war years. The present study suggests that this influence in those years was very slight, except among a small number of psychiatric social workers; the main body of social work remained little affected.

It may be that the lack of British literature has tended to encourage the use of British and American historical accounts in a somewhat undifferentiated way, despite the marked and significant differences between the development of social work in their very different historical and cultural contexts. In particular Woodroofe's phrase 'the psychiatric deluge' has been widely taken out of context, and applied equally to British as to American social work, of which alone she used it; she was in fact at some pains to point out that in Britain this influence, though detectable, was 'little more than a trickle'[4]. That several of the historical accounts of British social work have been especially concerned with psychiatric social work, or have been written by psychiatric social workers with experience in the child guidance movement where this influence was undoubtedly strongest, may further have contributed to a conception of social work as a whole as being much more 'psychiatric' than in fact it was.

It is important to note that the 'psychiatric inundation' thesis has been vigorously challenged in relation to American social work, and recent studies point to considerable discrepancy between the primary sources and secondary accounts of the history of social work[5]. If the view that psychoanalytic theory influenced an elite minority fringe rather than the main body of theory and practice is correct, then it would seem that this influence in American social work too, at least in the 1920's, has been greatly exaggerated and is little more than a myth whose persistence is due in large part to its dramatic appeal.

There is evidence, however, that after the Second World War marked changes took place in British social work. The impetus towards professionalisation (evident in the growth of professional associations and the movement towards a unified body, in the emergence of a professional casework identity and in the attempts to establish standards of training and competence that would win public acceptance) was associated with the development of a body of theory in which that of a psychodynamic nature played a significant part; the influence of psychoanalysis on social work theorising was at that time considerable and transmitted through various channels (one of which was the child guidance movement) though it was only one of a number of intellectual and theoretical strands which together wove the fabric of the new professional culture emerging in the mid-1950's. The present study draws mainly on documentary sources: it is not possible to say how far psychoanalysis affected social work *practice* as distinct from writing, but there is little doubt that it profoundly affected the values and perspectives of social work. Further, the widespread adoption of a clinical or medical stance towards human disorders, which psychoanalysis has reinforced, has led to a therapeutic perspective the appropriateness of which has been seriously questioned in the light of the complex tasks with which the practitioner today is confronted. For many

2

practitioners (those more especially who are employed in nonclinical settings) such a perspective fails to make sense of the functions they see themselves as performing and to that extent is felt to be unsatisfactory as an explanation and justification of their practice. In recent years social work practice has broadened out into more varied and functionally diffuse roles; social workers today may act as therapists, as advocates on behalf of their clients, as resource mobilisers channelling resources of various kinds, as resource generators, as enablers, educators, and coordinators. Psychotherapeutic work, if it is undertaken at all, is for most a peripheral rather than a central feature of practice; and in the light of the complex and varied professional tasks in which they are actually engaged, a clinical stance is felt by many social workers to be limiting and insufficient, and to act as a restraint upon other promising avenues of professional development.

Allied to this can be seen a renewed sensitivity to the effects of social and structural factors in creating and maintaining problems and stresses for the individual, and new attempts to find ways of mitigating these, whether at an individual, a community or, perhaps more exceptionally, a political level. Changes of this kind are taking place all over the world though the forms are different: in some countries social workers are adopting a radical stance in relation to social change which has virtually eclipsed the more familiar professional focus on the individual in his interpersonal relationships. In Britain, where social work is not generally noted for its radicalism, a view of social work and its professional role seems to be emerging which does not altogether reject but is far more broadly conceived than that of a treatment orientated casework; this allows for the possibility of intervention at several different levels, and for the use of a wide range of helping methods. This conception is illustrated by the widespread adoption of the unitary approach, cutting across the traditional casework, group work, community work classifications. Add to this the challenge to traditional social work thinking from the left, and a certain scepticism towards 'therapy' as the personalisation of public ills, and it is scarcely surprising that social work today finds itself confused — indeed, in some ideological turmoil. Thus it seems an opportune moment to examine the contribution psychoanalysis has made to social work and to reassess it.

1
The Psychoanalytic Perspective

The importance of Freud's discoveries in the field of psychology can hardly be overstated; it has been observed (by authors whose work lies in the very different field of learning theory and behaviour modification) that 'almost all subsequent theories of man's behaviour derive from Freud, deviate from Freud, or are in opposition to Freud'[1]. His influence on social life in general — on education and childrearing as well as on psychiatry, psychology and the newer professions such as counselling and social work — has been immense, and few have escaped its effects. His theories were revolutionary in terms of the major emphases of 19th century psychiatry; as against its somatic cast he sought for psychological explanations of certain forms of illness, and in contrast to the prevailing rationality he searched for the hidden and unconscious aspects of psychic life.

The term 'psychoanalysis' is itself used variously, sometimes in a restricted, sometimes in a comprehensive way, and it is therefore necessary first of all to clarify the term. I shall then endeavour to convey some of the main characteristics of the psychoanalytic perspective by reference to the basic postulates of the unconscious mind, psychic determinism, infantile sexuality, and mental conflict, but without any attempt to summarise the theories of psychoanalysis; for these the reader is referred to Freud's major works such as the *Introductory Lectures* and *New Introductory Lectures,* and *The Interpretation of Dreams*; and to introductory texts such as those of Brenner and Wolman[2]. Finally I shall survey some of the more recent directions in psychoanalytic work which are of particular significance for social work.

1.1 Definitions

Psychoanalysis can refer to a theory of the mind and its workings, to a special form of psychotherapy, and to a specific research methodology, all developed by and associated with the name of Freud. It is only with the first of these that we shall be concerned at this point although all three aspects are closely inter-related and contribute to each other. In the strict sense, psychoanalysis refers to the work of Sigmund Freud, and to that of analysis in the direct classical tradition, and it is in this sense that it will be used here. The orientations covered by the term are those recognised by and included within professional psychoanalytic institutes and societies such as the British Psychoanalytical Society; a psychoanalyst is one trained under the auspices of such an institute

4

and holding a recognised qualification. Thus as it is used here the term 'psychoanalyst' is restricted, and does not include those trained within the Adlerian or Jungian professional societies, nor those analytically oriented therapists (who may have undergone a didactic analysis) who do not hold a recognised psychoanalytic qualification. The term 'psychodynamic' will be used in a more extensive sense to refer to those theories that derive from Freud, which stress the importance of unconscious mental processes and which involve acceptance of such central psychoanalytic concepts as transference and resistance.

Any definition has its difficulties. Rycroft, for example, uses the term psychoanalysis to refer to 'all those theories and therapies — whether Freudian, Jungian or existentialist — which assume the existence of unconscious mental processes, which concern themselves with the elucidation of motives and which make use of transference — and which can be differentiated from the organic school of psychiatry and from behaviourism by the fact that they regard subjective experience as a central object of study and not as an awkward contaminant which has to be either ignored or eliminated'[3]. In other words, he uses the term 'psychoanalytic' in a comprehensive way approximating to that in which other authors use 'psychodynamic'. It is true, as Rycroft[4] observes, that the distinctions between the different psychodynamic schools have never been appreciated by the lay public, and that the situation is further complicated by the presence of Kleinian analysts within the British Psychoanalytic Society, although the theories of Melanie Klein are regarded by some Freudians as quite unorthodox and outside the psychoanalytic tradition. Nevertheless, to reserve the term psychoanalysis for the theories and methods devised by Freud and his successors has the advantages of definiteness, distinctness and accepted usage, and for these reasons I have not followed Rycroft's much broader definition.

A distinction may be made between classical psychoanalysis and later revisions and developments. Not only did Freud's own work develop over time, but significant developments and modifications were made by later analysts, leading to the emphases which psychoanalysis is now developing and which differ in many important respects from those of the classical theory. Important revisions of this kind were made, for example, in the 1950's by the Neo-Freudians (Fromm, Horney, Sullivan) who stressed the impact of social and cultural factors and de-emphasised the instinctual and biological aspects of the theory, and by ego psychologists (Hartmann, Kris and Loewenstein in particular) who have focussed attention on the psychology of the ego and its development through object-relationships, thereby elaborating and extending that area explored by Freud in his later work. In some ways these newer emphases reflect great changes in psychoanalytic orientation and are far more important to an appreciation of the contribution of psychoanalysis to contemporary social work than are the classical theories, so that particular attention must be given to them.

A further distinction should be made between Freud's clinical observations and the explanatory theories developed to account for them; not all the latter have been accepted to the same degree as the former. Thus, while Freud awakened interest in human nature, in infancy and childhood, in the irrational in man, in motivation and the unconscious — in psychology 'it is for the most part his *conceptions* of these fields of study and his *observations* in them, not his *concepts* and *theories* about them, which have been accepted'[5].

Moreover, the use of psychoanalytic terminology does not necessarily indicate a true acceptance of Freudian ideas, and may even be misleading as an indication of influence. Psychoanalytic concepts have been particularly liable to modifications, both within the psychoanalytic movement itself and in the course of their transmission into other fields. Many of Freud's concepts were provisional and were later modified or superseded so that they may have different meanings at different stages of his work; sometimes however the original use (given up by the author himself) had already passed into general currency. Thus he abandoned the term 'subconscious' before 1900, but this still frequently occurs (as recently as 1971 in a book on counselling[6]) and its use has perhaps been perpetuated by the references to it in Hart's popular *Psychology of Insanity*. Further modifications may have been made by later analysts, and even within the clinical literature terms such as 'insight' may have a number of different meanings[7].

In the course of their transmission into other fields, concepts devised for use within a specialised clinical context are often diluted or transformed into commonsense versions, thereby losing their original specificity. For example, one social work writer discribes repression as a means of dealing with anxiety 'by unconsciously willing to stop whatever was causing the anxiety' and goes on to say that 'it can work quite well, particularly in the short term, and is frequently used by social workers as a first-aid procedure until a long-term resolution of a personality problem may be achieved'[8]. This has nothing whatever to do with the psychoanalytic concept of repression, and shows the kind of distortion to which psychoanalysis has been peculiarly susceptible. When, as is often the case, the social worker's knowledge of psychoanalytic concepts is gained through secondary sources rather than from first-hand acquaintance with Freud's own work, such distortions the more readily occur and can easily be perpetuated and disseminated through the literature. As Shakow and Rapaport have observed, it is probably in general the case that Freud's work has had more impact than genuine influence based on real understanding[9].

1.2   Some Major Psychoanalytic Postulates

1.2.1   The Unconscious

Freud's theories rested on a number of basic postulates. Of these, the four most important are: the concept of the unconscious mind and of unconscious mental processes; psychic determinism; the fundamental role of sexuality (particularly infantile sexuality) as a driving force in human behaviour and in the development of personality; and the presence of conflict as an essential and ineluctable characteristic of human life.

The first major postulate is that what is psychical is not necessarily equivalent to what is conscious, and indeed that the major part of mental life is unconscious. The most important discoveries of psychoanalysis relate to the unconscious workings of the mind, and the laws that govern them. Unconscious mental processes, however, cannot be directly observed, but only inferred, and the techniques Freud devised for investigating these areas of hidden mental activity (the analysis of dreams, fantasies and associations) assume that they do in fact exist and can thus be studied, albeit indirectly.

> The existence of the unconscious is an assumption that forced itself upon psychoanalytic research when it sought a scientific explanation and a comprehension of conscious phenomena. Without such an assumption the data of the conscious in their inter-relationships remain incomprehensible: with such an assumption, that which characterises the success of every science becomes possible: to predict the future and to exert systematic influence.[10]

It has become almost a truism to say that Freud's most original work relates to his investigation of the unconscious mind — those aspects of thought, feeling or ideas that influence behaviour, but in ways not apparent to the actor, nor accessible to his rational or cognitive understanding and control. Initially, Freud was brought to a realisation of the importance of unconscious factors by Bernheim's experiments in hypnotism. In this the strange workings of the mind are displayed with exceptional clarity. Under hypnosis, a subject may be given instructions to perform certain actions when he awakes. These he will carry out, but without knowing why he does so or being aware of the instructions he has received. Such experiences provide a convincing demonstration that the mind is not a unity, nor is it coterminous with what is at any moment in time present to our awareness; it was Freud's conviction that what is unconscious may powerfully influence behaviour, and that the rational elements in human action and decision had been greatly overestimated in 19th century psychology.

Freud did not 'discover' the unconscious mind, as Whyte[11] has shown. The concept has a long history and was part of European intellectual thought for several centuries, though without the clinical connotations it acquired in psychoanalysis. For Goethe and Schiller, the unconscious was the origin of creative and imaginative ideas and the source of the springs of poetic imagination. But if literary and philosophical thought attempted to redress the Cartesian equation of mind with awareness, the study of psychology was concerned essentially with the study of *conscious* mental processes and the phenomena with which Freud as a physician was especially involved — neurotic and hysterical symptoms — were not regarded as proper subjects of

7

scientific study[12]. These phenomena, and those such as parapraxes, unaccountable lapses of memory, dreams and other irrational aspects, could in Freud's view be explained only by postulating unconscious processes which were not directly observable but could be inferred. The nature of these unconscious processes, and how they worked, was the crucial problem which was to occupy him for most of his professional life. It is perhaps surprising, seen from our perspective, that the concept of unconscious mental activity should have occasioned such bitter opposition. 'By thus emphasising the unconscious in mental life' Freud wrote, 'we have called forth all the malevolence in humanity in opposition to psychoanalysis'[13]. He believed this opposition to have its root in a narcissistic wound; humanity was having to come to terms with a view of human nature in which no-one was master in his own house, 'but must remain content with the veriest scraps of information about what is going on unconsciously in his own mind'[14]. Although later psychoanalytic schools have differed from Freud in their conceptualisation of the unconscious, it was nevertheless the rock on which all later work was built and remains the essential and inalienable core of the psychoanalytic paradigm. The stripping away of illusions, and the baring, with almost surgical precision, of the hidden inner nature of the mind was the task Freud set himself. Freud's historical contribution, wrote Jung, lay in the fact that 'like an Old Testament prophet, he overthrew false idols and pitilessly exposed to the light of day the rottenness of the contemporary psyche'[15]. The major method for exploring the unconscious was the analysis of dreams and their meaning, the *via regia* to the unconscious.

Freud used the term unconscious in two different ways — sometimes in a commonsense descriptive sense, and in his later work in a dynamic sense. In its descriptive sense Freud's use of the term does not differ from that of everyday. For example, an idea may disappear from consciousness subsequently to be recalled; this is a fact of everyday experience. While absent (for example while other thoughts are occupying our minds) the original idea has not been erased but is simply latent. But hypnotic experiments showed that this account was insufficient. The hypnotic subject remembers that an act has been performed but all the associated ideas (who told him, when, and why) remain unconscious. From this, Freud suggested, we are led from a purely descriptive to a dynamic view of the unconscious. Such ideas may not be conscious, but are none the less active in that they have observable behavioural effects. This was especially the case with hysterical patients, whose symptoms were to be understood in the light of such unconscious ideas — for instance, a woman who vomits because she unconsciously believes that she is pregnant.

Contained within the dynamic view of the unconscious there is a further differentiation. These ideas are of two kinds — those that can become conscious with relative ease and those that remain unconscious and split off in spite of their intensity and activity. In *A Note on the Unconscious*, Freud briefly indicated the kind of process which he believed to take place, and this was described more fully in his 1915 paper[16]. The central concept here was

8

resistance: some ideas are so incompatible with the conscious outlook of the subject that they meet with strong resistance and are not permitted to enter conscious awareness; that is, they are repressed. A large part of the unconscious mind consists of contents which are subject to repression, though the unconscious is more than simply what is repressed. Freud distinguished between ideas that are unconscious but not dynamic (preconscious) and those that are unconscious and dynamic — mainly (thought not wholly) sexual in character and repressed. In terms of structural theory, the id is unconscious, and the ego largely preconscious; none the less, there are large portions of the ego and the superego which remain unconscious[17]. For the psychoanalyst the term unconscious usually means 'accessible to consciousness only with difficulty, or not at all', while preconscious means 'readily accessible to consciousness, though not conscious at the moment'[18].

The major distinction made in the later work related to the processes operating in the id (the unconscious) and the preconscious ego, termed respectively the primary and secondary processes.

> Behind all these uncertainties there lies one new fact whose discovery we owe to psychoanalytic research. We have found that processes in the unconscious or in the id obey different laws from those in the preconscious ego. We name these laws in their totality the primary process, in contrast to the secondary process which governs the course of events in the preconscious, in the ego.[19]

Ernest Jones regarded Freud's greatest achievement as consisting in the discovery and elucidation of these processes. The primary process is not logical; the unconscious, as Wolman puts it, 'works by its own prelogical language', irrational, contradictory, full of allusions, distortions and symbolic meanings. The task of unravelling its language resembles that of the cryptologist decoding a strange and unfamiliar cypher. This is in contrast to the secondary process operating in the conscious and preconscious, which represents the more orderly, structured logical processes usually implied by the term 'thought'.

1.2.2 Psychic Determinism

In Freud's view, behaviour is never accidental or haphazard but is purposeful and occurs as part of a process of mental activity, much of which may not be conscious; but if the underlying process can be understood, even apparently random behaviour can be seen to have meaning. In *The Psychopathology of Everyday Life*, Freud set out to show how slips of the tongue, lapses of memory and unaccountable errors were, on clearer analysis, explicable in terms of unconscious determinants. The central message of the final chapter of that work is that 'certain shortcomings in our psychical functioning ... and certain seemingly unintentional performances prove, if psychoanalytic methods of investigation are applied to them, to have valid motives and to be determined by motives unknown to consciousness'[20].

Theoretically, it should be possible to trace the determinants of every behavioural event, and to reconstruct the causal connections preceding it, so that apparent discontinuities are shown to be part of a continuous causal sequence. Although *The Psychopathology of Everyday Life* focusses on normal functioning, exactly the same principle can be applied to neurotic symptoms, and in the reconstruction of these links lay the possibility of a rational approach to their resolution.

1.2.3   Infantile Sexuality

In Freud's own day, sexuality was a taboo subject, even within the medical profession itself, and, as is well known, the sexual nature of his theories does much to explain the resistance they encountered. Freud himself came under severe censure for his frank discussion of both normal and abnormal sexuality and of the role it played in neurotic illness. But an essentially new feature of his theory (and one which Freud himself did not adopt readily) was that sexuality was to be found not only in the adult, but also in the child, and characterises the life of the human from birth. A child, Freud considered, had sexual instincts and activities from the very first, and the normal sexuality of the adult is coloured and shaped by the early sexual life of the infant. To childhood with its 'powerful wishful impulses', essentially erotic and instinctual in nature, many later sexual disturbances (and neuroses without obvious sexual origin) could be traced. Thus the first years of infancy came to have a special importance, because they contain the first expression of sexuality, 'which leaves behind decisive determinants for the sexual life of maturity'[21].

It should be noted that sexuality has a wider connotation in psychoanalysis than it has in ordinary usage. 'Sexuality, in psychoanalysis, refers not merely to matters pertaining to copulation or preparatory to it but includes all sensual strivings and satisfactions'[22]. Thus in the *Outline* Freud distinguishes between the concepts of 'sexual' and 'genital': 'The former is the wider concept and includes many activities that have nothing to do with the genitals'[23].

1.2.4   Mental Conflict

Implicit in his view of mental processes is the assumption that conflict is an inevitable and inalienable characteristic of mental life. The mind was not conceived as a unity, but as consisting of warring elements: his conception of the structure of the psyche represents an attempt to show how intrapsychic conflict comes about and the mechanisms for dealing with it. These mechanisms (sublimation and repression pre-eminently) occur in everyone, and in the normal no less than the neurotic personality, but a neurosis can be seen as an unsuccessful or maladaptive attempt to deal with conflict in a way which has seriously disturbing or dysfunctional effects for the individual. Freud's views on the origins of neurosis are dependent upon the notion of conflict. Neurotic symptoms are always acquired in the early years and arise through the incapacity of the immature ego to cope with instinctual demands which are too great for it.

> Neuroses (writes Waelder) have their genesis in conflicts arising from the sexual instinct, and to the psychoanalyst it is always in such inner conflicts, and not in externally imposed conditions and events (though these may be contributory or precipitating factors) that the origins of a neurosis must be sought.[24]

Psychoanalysis, it has been said, 'is human nature viewed as conflict'. Conflict itself, however, is not abnormal nor necessarily neurotic, but an inescapable fact of human existence; what matters is how it is dealt with and the adaptive or maladaptive nature of its resolution.

1.3   Recent Directions in Psychoanalysis

Freud died in 1939, and in the last three decades psychoanalytic work has developed along other avenues, the significance of which is not always appreciated, particularly perhaps by its critics. Many of the older concepts such as the notion of psychic energy (and indeed the basically mechanistic model of the psyche) which were characteristic of Freud's early work have now quietly disappeared, and the attention of psychoanalysts has moved away from purely intrapsychic factors to a focus on the person as he is shaped by his biological inheritance, in the crucible of his early interpersonal relationships, and by the cultural milieu within which he lives. Much of the conceptualisation and language of earlier psychoanalytic work finds little resonance today, and it is to the newer developments we must look for work that is currently influencing social work education and practice. Important among these developments are the work of the Neo-Freudians, ego psychology, object relations (which can be viewed as a particular aspect of ego psychology), existential analysis, and the application of psychodynamic concepts to the understanding of groups and families. There is also considerable literature in which psychoanalytic insights are applied to the study of organisations, but this will not be reviewed here.

1.4   The Neo-Freudians

This term has been used of a group of analysts (among whom are Fromm, Horney and Erikson) who were critical of the narrowly biological orientation of psychoanalysis and what they regarded as its neglect of cultural factors in the development of personality and in the aetiology of neurosis. Particularly influential has been the work of E.K. Erikson and his conception of psychosocial stages in the development of identity; this emphasises the social and cultural nature of the tasks which the ego has to master on the road to maturity. His eight maturational stages with their typical crises (trust vs. mistrust, autonomy vs. shame and doubt, initiative vs. guilt, industry vs. inferiority, identity vs. role diffusion, intimacy vs. isolation, generativity vs. stagnation, integrity vs. despair) are similar to Freud's own psychosexual stages, but stress the impact of cultural rather than instinctual factors in the process of emotional development. Although Erikson's *Childhood and Society* is widely used on social work courses in this country, the work of the Neo-Freudians has probably been more influential in America than in Britain, and for this reason is given somewhat brief mention.

1.5 Ego Psychology

The ego psychologists built upon the later emphases of Freud's work, concerning themselves particularly with the synthesising role of the ego in the personality. While ego psychologists do not discount the instincts nor reject the drive-determined nature of behaviour, their work represents a shift of primary interest to other aspects of the personality — the ego rather than the id, and the secondary rather than primary processes.

The ego concept was present in Freud's theorising from the first, but underwent a number of changes in meaning and emphasis. In the 'Project for a Scientific Psychology' (1895), the ego was seen as a structural means of directing the effective discharge of instinctual tensions, in accordance with reality and environmental conditions. Between 1900 and 1923 his main work centred on the dynamics of illness and less on normal adaptive functioning, and his primary focus of interest lay in the role of libidinal drives and of conflict in the aetiology of the neuroses. His interest in the ego concept seems therefore to have diminished; the ego was present in relation to the central concept of repression, but seems to have been seen primarily as a repressive and inhibitive force[25].

In the later period (1924—1938) themes embryonically present in the 'Project' were picked up and developed. The ego was now conceived as concerned not merely with the control of drives but as having an active adaptational and integrative role; it was seen as operating in accordance with the reality principle, whereas the id was associated with the pleasure principle. The key change, it has been said, was the recognition 'of an active principle independent of libidinal drive energy, which involves the turning of *enforced* responses into *ego-initiated* processes'. With this conception came the development of a new field of psychoanalytic study concerned particularly with ego development through object relations.

The development of ego psychology has been especially associated with

Hartmann, Kris, Loewenstein and Rapaport. For Hartmann, the key feature is the synthetic or organising function of the ego. It is seen in the role of problem-solver, and its functions have to do not only with conflict, and ways of dealing with conflict, but with adaptation to the environment in a more general sense. Thus, for Hartmann, many ego functions are relatively independent of drives, and develop through stimulation by and interaction with the environment; this theory therefore allows for the integration of such work as that of Piaget on cognitive processes, with the general psychoanalytic theory of development. It gives attention preeminently to those aspects of the ego which derive from its reality orientation — cognition, rationality, perception, attention, memory, planning, foresight — that is, the secondary processes.

Ego psychology with its emphasis on the integrative and adaptive aspects of personality has brought about radical changes in psychoanalytic thinking, not always reflected in the teaching of psychoanalytic theory given on social work courses. These changes have been summarised as follows:

From conflict to crisis resolution. While classical theory was mainly concerned with conflicts arising from instinctual tensions, ego psychology has turned its attention to other types of conflict which pose problems for the ego; in particular, developmental crises which arise when earlier adaptational modes cease to 'fit' new maturational conditions and the social expectations which are associated with them.

From defence to adaptation. The earlier interest in the defensive functions of the ego arising from analytic concern with pathology and illness has given way to a broader conception of the ego as concerned with the solution of adaptive problems, of which its defensive functions are only one aspect.

From instinctual drives to motivational diversity. Though it does not ignore or reject the role of the sexual and aggressive instincts in motivation, ego psychology recognises other noninstinctual motivators. While libido theory is not rejected, its status within the newer emphasis must be problematic to say the least, and what ego psychology is moving towards is a more comprehensive theory of motivation in which sexuality and aggression are viewed as of major but not sole significance.

From explanatory priority of unconscious wishes to explanatory parity of conscious purpose. Classical theory laid emphasis on unconscious wishes, primarily of a sexual nature, in the genesis of illness; ego psychology allows for the appreciation of the causal significance of consciousness and of affective states which may themselves be seen as important determinants of behaviour[26].

Ego psychology has been sharply criticised by those in the classical tradition; it is regarded as heretical and reactionary in throwing aside the central and crucial Freudian insights with regard to the significance of sexuality and agression in human life. The ego psychologist, however, would reply that he does not underrate their significance; only that he is seeking to align psychoanalytic theory more closely with theoretical developments in other disciplines. Further, if new dimensions of behaviour emerge which are not adequately accounted for within the classical theories, the scientific nature of the psychoanalytic enterprise demands that the theory develop to take account of them. The classical concepts must be seen as incorporated in a larger and more comprehensive framework.

1.6 Object-Relational Theories   → attachment?

In British psychoanalysis the object-relational theories concerned with the earliest growth of the ego through the development of relationships with those in the infant's immediate environment (among whom the mother is the earliest and most important) have been especially influential. Analysts in this tradition include Klein, Balint, Bowlby, Fairbairn, Guntrip and Winnicott, and their work has mainly concerned the early development of the ego in personal relationship with significant others. Although much of this work is concerned with psychopathology (for example Fairbairn's work on the schizoid problem[27]), and has arisen from the attempt to understand the origin of distorted or defensive reactions to childhood experiences which persist into adult life and cause later psychological illness or malfunctioning, it has also stimulated a large and important body of research focussing on the reactions of those of normal personality to loss, such as occurs in bereavement or in childhood separation experiences[28].

Guntrip[29] has pointed to a struggle in Freud's thinking between two kinds of ideas; those which reflect the natural science, mechanistic way of thinking in which he was schooled, and those concerned with interpersonal relationships and psychodynamics. The first is reflected in the classical psychobiology; the second in the Oedipus complex and the phenomena of transference and resistance encountered in treatment. In this second stream of ideas lay the origins of a psychodynamic psychology concerned with the development of personality through early object-relationships, which partly determine the pattern of interpersonal relationships in later life, and have much to do with the development of a sense of identity and self-worth[30]. By psychodynamics Guntrip means 'the study of the motivated and meaningful life of human beings, as persons shaped in the media of personal relationships which constitute their lives and determine to so large an extent how their innate gifts and possibilities will develop ...'[31]. Object-relational theory owed much to the creative stimulus of Melanie Klein's work[32], and is also associated strongly with the work of Fairbairn.

Klein was concerned primarily with the intense inner experiences of the very young infant and, in the Kleinian view, the infant's relationship with the environment takes place on the basis of projection and introjection. The infant projects on to the environment his own inner loving or destructive fantasies

14

and the environment, invested with those feelings, is then introjected as a good or bad internal object. The environment thus 'confirms' the baby's anxieties and inner conflicts, but the source of these anxieties is primarily an internal and not an external one; it has something to do with the baby's actual environment and its real qualities, but this is of lesser importance.

Klein postulated two 'positions' or stages of development. In the paranoid-schizoid position the baby feels persecuted by his aggressive and destructive fantasies reflected back to him by part objects in his environment (the bad or frustrating breast). At this stage these are seen as quite separate objects, rather than as different aspects of the same object, and hence the phenomenon of 'splitting'. Splitting can be seen as a way of dealing with incompatible affects by projecting them on to different people; thus the witch and the peasant mother in the fairy-story Hansel and Gretel can be viewed as representing the hated and loved aspects of the same 'object', the mother. In the depressive position, the infant becomes aware of his ambivalence — that he wishes to hurt and destroy the person whom he also loves; the consequence is depression and guilt and the need to make reparation for his destructive fantasies. A further important Kleinian concept is that of 'projective identification'. This is said to occur when a feared or disliked part of the personality (for example, aggression) is psychologically invested in another person, and is thereby lost to the self, resulting in a feeling of depletion and emptiness.

For Fairbairn[33], the infant was to be seen as basically object rather than pleasure seeking — a radical departure from the classical Freudian view. Unlike Klein, for whom the infant psyche was from the start a battleground between the warring instincts of libido and death, Fairbairn postulated a unitary ego; the infant is naturally whole, but the unfolding of the development of ego may be damaged or interrupted by early experiences. Fairbairn was especially concerned wth the phenomenon of 'splitting of the ego' which could occur as a result of the infant's efforts to cope with unhappy experiences and to relate to both the benign and the frustrating or rejecting aspects of the mother. In his view the unmet needs of the infant became split off into a frustrated need-system, which remained relatively primitive and impervious to growth, and could constitute an impelling influence on behaviour. Such a split could result in a loss of vital parts of the ego, and a failure to develop the self, or central core of the ego, on the basis of which satisfying and mature object-relationships normally develop. Fairbairn's work derived from his practice as an analyst of adult patients and he was especially interested in the 'schizoid problem' — the failure of the ego to develop the capacity for mature relationships (the concept of 'mature dependence') through early failures in object-relations. He thus worked reductively from those current problems in emotional relationships that his patients brought into analysis, assuming that in transference was to be found a faithful re-enactment of the events of infancy.

D.W. Winnicott[34], for 40 years a paediatrician at the Paddington Hospital, had a unique opportunity to observe mother-infant relationships in a natural environment, and his work therefore adds a new dimension. He was concerned not only with the pathogenic aspects of infant development, but with the ways in which the ordinary mother sensed and responded to the needs of her infant in the early years, allowing him both dependence and growing independence. To Winnicott, emotional development began during pregnancy and in the first hours and days of life; it was viewed as a maturational process which takes place within a special environment — first and most fundamentally the mother-child nexus. Normal emotional development depends on the extent to which the mother is able to sense the infant's changing needs empathetically, and to provide a safe, responsive and facilitating environment. The capacity to provide this Winnicott calls 'good-enough mothering'. In first days of life this capacity is reflected in 'primary maternal preoccupation', a total devotion to and identification with the infant which enables the mother to become aware (as an outside observer never can) of the infant's needs.

Failure to provide the secure environment which is needed (not-good-enough mothering) may lead to failure in emotional maturation, and to the development of a 'false self' on the basis of compliance — of trying to be the person others expect or wish one to be — which has little to do with a real sense of identity or self-worth. The development of a false or defensive structure in the early years has been a central and basic theme in the work of many British analysts, and can be found in that of Laing and Balint, no less than in those in the mainstream of object-relations thinking.

Object-relations represents a very major change in focus and in conceptualisation. Freud's earlier work was deeply influenced by neurophysiological models, and he conceptualised psychological events in terms of physical concepts such as energy. Conflict was seen essentially in terms of instinctual drives which were frustrated by the inhibitions imposed by the ego or the superego. This somewhat mechanistic mode of thought could not provide an adequate language for conceptualising psychodynamics, and, in his later work, Freud himself was moving towards a more psychological and personal theory. For this the superego acted as a bridge. For the superego is in essence a psychological (or, more properly, a psychosocial) rather than a biological construct; it represents the social environment mediated through an internal image of a personal parental kind. Although it is still clearly within the psychoanalytic tradition, it does represent a major development from the classical theories in terms of its primary preoccupations and the concepts and language it uses. These changing concerns are inevitable. As a distinguished analyst has recently observed[35], the problems with which psychotherapeutic treatment is concerned are in part cultural artifacts; if the Viennese middle classes at the turn of the century suffered primarily from sexual repression, the modern equivalent is the loss of a sense of identity.

1.7 Existential Analysis

A further development has been the merging, in the work particularly of

16

Ronald Laing and David Cooper, of the psychoanalytic and existential traditions. This deserves special note, because Laing's work is widely known among British social workers, and may be assumed to have had considerable influence.

The modern existential tradition developed strongly during the 19th century, particularly in Germany, and later made considerable impact in Britain and America; the lateness of its British flowering is, according to the theologian Paul Tillich, to be related to the survival of orthodox religion in this country; for he sees the background of existentialism in the void left by the breakdown of the religions tradition in the last century, and in the new search for meaning and creative living experience in an alienating and depersonalised industrial world[36].

The term 'existentialist' is used of a philosophical stance which emphasises immediate subjective personal experience. The term is used in its Latin meaning of 'standing out' and applies to man alone. Only man is aware of his own being (*dasein*) and can respond to the fact of his existence. Two major characteristics of existence are its dynamic quality, and the uniqueness of each person. First, it is dynamic in that man is always in process of becoming, always passing beyond what he is at this moment, and thus always transcending himself. He only learns what he is through the process of experiencing himself. Sartre writes:

> ..man first of all exists, encounters himself, surges up in the world — and defines himself afterwards. If man, as the existentialist sees him, is not definable, it is because to begin with he is nothing. He will not be anything until later, and then he will be what he makes of himself. Man is nothing else but that which he makes himself. That is the first principle of existentialism[37].

Second, the sense of 'I-ness', of being a unique and irreplaceable self, the centre from which the world is perceived, seems to be a basic fact of human experience. Existence as a unique self involves the acceptance of autonomy and responsibility for oneself. To live according to external pressures is to become nothing more than an object; it is to be inauthentic and unfree. Authentic existence, on the other hand, is to live according to one's true self, which is like no other. But the self which is affirmed is simply what it makes of itself: it is defined by the ends it pursues.

The stark reality of the existential position is that there are no dreams, no unrealised potentialities, no alibis. There is no reality except in action. 'You are nothing else but what you live.'

> Man is nothing else but what he purposes, he exists only in so far as he realises himself, he is therefore nothing else but the sum of his actions, nothing else but what his life is.[38]

or again:

> What we mean to say is that a man is no other than a series of undertakings,

that he is the sum, the organisation, the set of relations that constitute these undertakings.[39]

The idea of existence presupposes a world, an environment which derives its order and its significance from the concerns of man. To the existentialist the world is an instrumental system; but man cannot exist apart from it: he is deeply engaged in it, and the close concrete ties by which he is related to his everyday world are expressed by the phrase 'being-in-the-world'. Being-in-the-world also implies an interpersonal environment, 'being-with-others'. While in the thinking of some existentialists such as Sartre the individuality — and, indeed, the solitariness — of the human condition is stressed, for others (particularly Martin Buber) the idea of relationship is central. Buber[40] speaks of two primary words, I—Thou and I—It, which reflect the two ways in which we relate to people and to things. The I—Thou relationship is a total one, which involves us in becoming open to the other, who is there as himself, and not just as a means or an instrument. The I—Thou language is spoken with the whole being. But the tragedy of human life is that the I—Thou frequently degenerates into an I—It relation — the other becomes merely an object, a thing, an instrument to be used or exploited. Thus the dialectical quality which Buber sees as characteristic of the I—Thou relationship is lost. In its genuine form, relationship is not controlling, not dominating, not possessive; it involves an acceptance of the other, and allows him the freedom to be as himself, as he is. Implicit in this is the idea of distance; a true relation 'perceives the other in his otherness, in his uniqueness. It leaves him room to be himself, so to speak'[41]. To control the other, to try to make him conform to our idea of what he should be, is antithetical to the respect which is inherent in Buber's conception of a true I—Thou relation.

There are certain central and characteristic themes which run throughout existential writing, despite the differing viewpoints which the term embraces. First, freedom, responsibility, decision are seen as at the root of existence; it is the exercise of freedom, and the responsible acceptance of the consequence of his actions, which make man human and distinct from all other forms of life. If God does not exist, argues Sartre, man has nothing to depend on, inside or outside of himself; there are no given values, no rules, no commands to legitimise his behaviour. He is his own legislator, and must take on himself his anguish of decision and commitment. In the famous phrase, 'man is condemned to be free'.

Second, there is an emphasis on the emotional and affective life of man; on the primacy of experience rather than of cognition or intellectual activity. Thus existentialist thinking has close links with psychology, and a psychological tradition has grown up which had been markedly influenced by existential writers.

Third, there is a preoccupation with the tragic aspects of human experience — alienation, despair, death. Anxiety itself is ontological and a necessary part of the human condition; but while, for some, the acceptance of anxiety and despair is part of a courageous act of self-affirmation (what Tillich calls 'the courage to be'), the writing of others, particularly Sartre, is permeated by a deep pessimism, though Sartre himself would prefer to see it as 'stern optimism'.

1.8 The Existential Critique of Psychoanalysis

Within psychiatry there has grown up an important tradition which has been influenced by the work of existential philosophers such as Heidegger and Jaspers (himself a psychiatrist). But although it has represented in some respects a reaction against psychoanalysis, this tradition has also been deeply influenced by it, especially the work of Jung, and several of its most outstanding figures have been psychoanalytically trained. Among these are Binswanger, Medard Boss, Rollo May and, in Britain, Ronald Laing. In some sense, therefore, existential psychiatry represents a merging of the existential and psychoanalytic traditions. Existentialists have tended to distinguish sharply between psychoanalytic theory and therapy. Binswanger, for example, though he viewed psychoanalytic theory as limited, made use of Freudian therapy as an effective form of treatment. And Boss, who discussed the procedure of psychoanalytic therapy in some detail, concluded than Freud's own therapeutic work was far more existentialist than his rather mechanistic theory might suggest. Existentialists have reacted against two particular features of psychoanalysis; what from an existential point of view is seen as its mechanistic and depersonalising language, and its determinism.

Depersonalisation seems to have been a necessary consequence of Freud's attempt to construct a scientific psychology and of the concept of 'homo natura' which underlay his whole psychoanalytic enterprise. The language and concepts of psychoanalysis split up the person into parts — id, ego, superego, drives, systems and so on. In terms of such a language it is not possible to develop a conception of man as a unitary whole. For Freud, psychology was essentially a biological science, and the whole idea of a psychic apparatus with its related systems is to be understood in biological terms. In attempting to give an account of man as a biological organism, psychoanalysis fails to deal adequately with him as a person; more than that, it takes away his very humanness and depersonalises him. Binswanger put it:

> This depersonalisation has by now gone so far that the psychiatrist (even more than the psychoanalyst) can no longer simply say 'I', 'you' or 'he' wants, wishes, etc., the only phrases that would correspond to the phenomenal *facts*. Theoretical constructs dispose him, rather, to speak instead of *my*, *your*, or *his* Ego wishing something. In the depersonalisation we see at work that aspect of psychiatry's founding charter that is most at odds with every attempt to establish a *genuine* psychology.[42]

For Binswanger, the very scientific constructs in which psychoanalysis was embodied were of themselves antithetical to subjective personal experience, which was the core of the therapeutic process. Natural-scientific psychology, he wrote,

> ignores the entire structure of ontological problems that surrounds the question as to the genuine who that so relates itself, the question as to the human self. When this self is objectified, isolated and theorised into an ego, or an Id, Ego and Superego, it is thereby driven out of its authentic sphere of being, namely existence, and ontologically and anthropologically suffocated.[43]

Or as Laing has put it: 'the theory of man as a person loses its way if it falls into an account of man as a machine or man as an organismic system of it-processes'[44].

Secondly, psychoanalysis is highly deterministic. Psychoanalytic theory is not necessarily erroneous or invalid, but it is limited because it deals with only one mode of being — that of man in his unfreedom, in those aspects of his life which are determined by his biological inheritance or the effects of his early experience. Its language and constructs, however adequately they explain certain aspects of behaviour (and certain limitations of freedom) are unable to express or do justice to the larger endeavour which psychotherapy has become, an endeavour which cannot exclude any aspect or mode of being. The categories in which psychoanalysis deals are thus felt by existentialists to be too restrictive to encompass the reality of the psychotherapeutic process — and to this extent to further limit rather than open up the patient's road to freedom. Its determinism sharply contrasts with the existential idea of freedom, which is the core of existence.

The difference between the psychoanalytic and existential attitudes can be seen in their treatment of anxiety. To the existentialist, anxiety is not always pathological, nor does it arise only from concealed and unconscious sexual or destructive wishes; it can also be ontological and stem from a sense of meaninglessness, fear or inability to be oneself. Anxiety, in this sense, is an ontological condition of existence. Similarly, guilt is not necessarily neurotic; it may arise from a sense of violation of self, a sense of self-betrayal. The only way out of existential anxiety and guilt is by mastering loneliness and despair and finding the courage to be, in a new and powerful self-affirmation. Rollo May writes:

> The existential approach in psychotherapy, as I understand it, is that only in a *heightened consciousness* of the problems of guilt, anxiety and conflict — an awareness that leads to some form of either/or choice — can these problems be met... The existential approach is the achieving of individuality, not by avoiding the conflictual realities of the world in which we find ourselves ... but by confronting these directly, and through the meeting of them, to achieve individuality and meaningful interpersonal relations.[45]

20

A central concept in Laing's thinking is that of ontological insecurity. This can best be expressed in his own words, which convey the flavour of the existentialist approach:

The individual ... may experience his own being as real, alive, whole; as differentiated from the rest of the world in ordinary circumstances so clearly that his identity and autonomy are never in question; as a continuum in time; as having an inner consistency, substantiality, genuineness, and worth; as spatially coexistent with the body; and, usually, as having begun in or around birth and liable to extinction with death. He then has a firm core of ontological security.

This, however, may not be the case. The individual in the ordinary circumstances of living may feel more unreal than real; in a literal sense, more dead than alive, precariously differentiated from the rest of the world, so that his identity and autonomy are always in question. He may lack the experience of his own temporal continuity. He may not possess an overriding sense of personal consistency or cohesiveness. He may feel more insubstantial than substantial, and unable to assume that the stuff he is made of is genuine, good, valuable. And he may feel his self as partially divorced from his body ...

If a position of primary ontological security has been reached, the ordinary circumstances of life do not afford a perpetual threat to one's own existence. If such a basis for living has not been reached, the ordinary circumstances of everyday life constitute a continual and deadly threat.[46]

In such a situation of ontological insecurity the individual has to protect himself against recurrent threats to his identity and indeed his very existence as a person; thus his every act becomes, as Binswanger puts it, 'a device for keeping out the dreadful', the fundamental existential anxiety.

A further limitation of psychoanalysis — at least for Binswanger — was the failure of Freud to take account of the spiritual aspects of man's nature, and he regarded this as a major weakness. Freud's own view was forthrightly and characteristically expressed in a letter thanking Binswanger for sending him a copy of his paper, *Freud's Conception of Man*. He wrote:

Of course, I don't believe a word of what you say — I've always lived only in the *parterre* and basement of the building. You claim that with a change of viewpoint one is able to see an upper story which houses such distinguished guests as religion and art, etc. You're not the only one who thinks that, most cultured specimens of homo natura believe it. In that you are conservative, I revolutionary.[47]

It is undoubtedly of significance that many of those whose philosophy of life has been influenced by existentialism have been those who found in it something more compatible with a religious or spiritual dimension of living than the strict scientific rationalism of Freud; for example, Binswanger, Frankl, Laing and Tillich.

In sum, therefore, for the existential psychiatrist the concepts and language of psychoanalysis somehow fail to give an adequate account of man as a person, and make the task of understanding him, in his whole and unique being, more and not less difficult. The very words and categories become barriers to knowing another in his personal and subjective reality.

Psychiatry has been influenced not only by existential philosophy but by its distinctive approach to the problem of knowledge. For the scientist, knowledge is knowledge of an object by observation; for the existentialist, it is knowledge by participation. The existentialist's mode of knowing is phenomenological; he directs himself to trying to understand (rather than explain) the particular mode of being-in-the-world of a person; and he tries to enter into the subjectively experienced meanings which structure the world of the other. This involves a readiness to lay aside preoccupations and prior categories, and to accept the experience of the other in his own terms, in terms of his particular mode of being. As Laing puts it, the task of existential phenomenology is 'to articulate what the other's 'world' is and his way of being in it'.[48] When that other is a patient, then

> existential phenomenology becomes the attempt to reconstruct the patient's way of being himself in his world, although, in the therapeutic relationship, the focus may be on the patient's way of being-with-me.[49]

Laing has particularly applied the phenomenological approach to the family patterns of schizophrenic patients. He holds that schizophrenia becomes intelligible in terms of the confused interpersonal environment in which it occurs: seen in this context, it is explicable, and is a kind of strategy for survival in a situation which can be coped with in no other way.

Existential psychotherapy is not a system as such, but rather implies a particular kind of attitude or stance towards the psychotherapeutic enterprise and towards the patient. Key aspects are the phenomenological mode of observation, the experiential mode of knowing , the emphasis on the present, and the centrality given to the notions of choice and decision.

First, the phenomenological mode of observation. There must be a readiness on the part of the therapist to 'perceive the patient in terms of his phenomenological reality and not in terms of the therapist's theoretical models'[50]. This involves participation and a willingness to be involved in, and committed to, a genuine encounter with the other. The existential attitude is one of involvement, not of detachment; it goes beyond mere observation:

> You may have a precise detached knowledge of another person, his psychological type and his calculable reactions, but in knowing this you do not know the person, his centred self, his knowledge of himself. Only in participating in his self, in performing an existential breakthrough into the centre of his being, will you know him in the situation of your breakthrough to him. This is the first meaning of 'existential', namely existential as the attitude of participating with one's own existence in some other existence.[51]

22

Further, the existential approach is more concerned with understanding the phenomenal world of the patient than it is with finding causal explanations; it is concerned with the 'what' of experience rather than the 'why'. The task of the therapist is to enter the perceptual world of the patient, to understand the meanings his experience has for him, rather than to explain it.

Second, the experiential mode of knowing. Not only does the therapist come to know the patient through a dialectical relationship which changes both, but the patient can only come to know himself through experience. 'A psychotherapy on existential-analytic bases ... proceeds *not* merely by showing that patient where, when, and to what extent he has failed to realise the fulness of his humanity, but it tries to make him experience this as radically as possible...' [52].

Third, the emphasis on the present; the existentialist is concerned with the past only in so far as that can shed light on the issues of the present. This is mentioned elsewhere as a characteristic of other psychotherapeutic schools; for example, ego psychology and behaviour modification. But while this stance is not unique to the existentialist position, its rationale is rooted in the notion of existence as a dynamic and transcendant process.

Fourth, the stress on choice, responsibility, decision, as of central concern: 'Intentionality is at the heart of the therapeutic process'[53]. While part of the therapeutic task is to understand the limits and restrictions on the patient's freedom, which hold him back from being fully and freely himself, this is by no means all. The therapist also supports the patient in discovering himself through experience and tries to help him make actual the blocked potentialities within him.

It is a doubtful whether existentialist writing is either widely known or read among social workers. Nevertheless, it has been thought to merit particular consideration here. This is largely because R.D. Laing, who draws for his inspiration in part on the work of Sartre, has made considerable impact on psychiatry in recent years, and it is likely that the philosophic and value stance from which Laing approaches psychiatry has permeated social work also to some degree. This stance is based upon an existential commitment, and contained within it is an ideological position which places high value on such concepts as growth and freedom.

> ...to an existential psychiatrist the purpose of therapeutic intervention is to support and re-establish a sense of self and personal authenticity. Not mastery of the objective environment; not effective functioning within social institutions; not freedom from the suffering caused by anxiety ... but personal awareness, depth of real feeling, and, above all, the conviction that one can use one's full powers, that one has the courage to be and use all one's essence. [54]

Such a position compels a radical critique not only of psychiatry, but of social work, which stresses precisely the aims played down in the above quotation — mastery of the objective environment, effective functioning within social institutions, freedom from the suffering caused by anxiety. From an existential stance, much social work (with its emphasis on problem treatment by an expert practitioner) must appear suspect, as a controlling rather than a liberating venture; a concealed attempt to persuade or coerce the erring or deviant individual (albeit gently) into the paths of conformity and socially adjustive behaviour. Thus the existentialist's model of man, from which his ideological commitment derives, is distinctive and fundamentally different from the kind of models that underlie psychoanalysis or behaviour modification, which are considered in a later chapter.

1.9   The Extension of Psychoanalytic Theories to Groups and Families

While psychoanalysis is essentially a theory of personality, an intrapsychic theory, an important dimension has been added in recent years with the extension of psychodynamic theories to the understanding of group and family behaviour.

Psychoanalytic work in the group field is associated both with the Institute of Group Analysis and the Tavistock Institute of Human Relations. The group-analytic approach associated with the work of Foulkes and carried on at the Institute of Group Analysis takes as its starting point classical psychoanalytical theories, but sees the group situation as introducing powerful and new parameters of its own. The Tavistock Institute has been influenced particularly by object-relations theories and the work of Bion[55] on the nature of the unconscious forces operating in groups. Social workers have had contact with both of these major British orientations; with the first through the training schemes run by the Institute of Group Analysis, and by the extension of its principles of work to such fields as family therapy; and with the second through the Leicester — Tavistock Conferences run since 1957, and other similar ventures designed as group relations training through direct experience of and participation in groups[56]. These conferences have stimulated the development of similar courses sponsored by such bodies as the Grubb Institute of Behavioural Studies and the British Association of Psychotherapy. While the Tavistock has been concerned with group relations (rather than clinical) training for those involved in groups as part of their ordinary business or professional life, the Institute of Group Analysis is primarily concerned with therapy; both, however, attempt to extend psychoanalytic understanding to interpersonal and group situations, representing a major development from classical psychoanalysis. For such developments, object-relations theories have provided a bridge.

It could be argued that in recent years the major thrust in social groupwork and group therapy has been nonpsychodynamic. A significant influence has been the burgeoning of the human potential movement, particularly in the development of encounter groups, under the inspiration of Carl Rogers, and of Gestalt therapy, associated preeminently with Fritz Perls at Esalen. Both are

24

concerned with facilitating growth and liberating blocked or unrecognised potential and creativity within the person; both are, however, remarkable for their explicit and conscious rejection of psychoanalysis. Perls refers to 'debunking all that Freudian crap', and Rogers makes clear in his *Autobiographical Note* his growing disillusion with psychoanalysis and its methods of work. On the face of it the whole human potential movement seems to represent a shift away from psychoanalysis and a rejection of its concepts as well as its techniques; nevertheless, the concept of the unconscious seems to creep back in various disguises. For example, there is much emphasis in Gestalt on getting in touch with repressed, dammed-up feeling, often of an early, primitive and unrecognised kind; the aim (the discovery of what is repressed) is similar to that of psychoanalytic therapy, though the means are different. In Gestalt, the emphasis is on releasing blocked feeling through nonverbal means; in psychoanalysis, language is the vehicle of insight.

A second field in which psychodynamic concepts are used in conjunction with other theoretical systems is family therapy, where the psychoanalytic understanding of the individual has been used alongside other types of approach concerned more with the 'here-and-now' and with the interaction and communication of people within the family system. Thus a psychoanalytic frame of reference may be combined, for the purpose of therapy, with an interactional perspective. Much of the work on which social work has drawn in developing family-focussed approaches in the last decade has been the result of psychoanalysts moving into these new psychotherapeutic fields in an endeavour to find methods of helping more effectively (and with better use of skilled professional resources) those experiencing difficulties in their interpersonal relationships. Much work in the marital and family field has been influenced by social science concepts and developments in such fields as group and intergroup relations. Ackerman, a pioneer of family therapy, observed:

> As we survey the field today a pervasive shift is occurring in attitudes towards the challenge of psychotherapy. The trends towards change can be identified. Psychodynamic science is making room for social science; social science is making room for psychodynamic science. As a broader science of man evolves, a new conception emerges of the responsibilities of the psychotherapeutic specialist.[57]

In Ackerman's view, psychotherapy is to be understood in terms of the relations of the person with his social group and the interpersonal supports extended to him; thus it becomes a psychosocial therapy. He has spelled out some of the changes to which such a conception leads: greater appreciation of the 'here-and-now' aspects of the patient's problems, in that 'a one-sided absorption in the conditionings of past experience is outmoded. The determinants of the past are examined in the context of contemporary problems and conflicts'[58]; a flexible approach to treatment accommodated to the unique nature of the patient's situation and problem; a less authoritarian stance on the part of the therapist. In sum, he writes:

25

A shift of emphasis is taking place away from the traditionally exclusive emphasis on intrapsychic conflict, rooted in the unconscious, to patterns of coping, defense, ego integration, and social interaction ... In effect, the therapist extends his sphere of interest and concern from the entrenched, intrapsychic mechanisms of personality to a systematic evaluation of the total functioning of personality within a range of social situations.[59]

Psychoanalysis was originally concerned with the intrapsychic, the inner world of man, and the way in which early experience influenced and structured later events. Increasingly, psychoanalysts working with families are combining their psychoanalytic with an interpersonal frame of reference, making use of communications and systems theories, as well as those concerned with small group phenomena. Work such as this has a great deal to contribute to some of the central problems encountered in social work, and is more in line with its developing social and behavioural science perspective and with its emphasis on social functioning than are the classical psychoanalytic approaches.

This extension of psychoanalytic interest has been accompanied, significantly, by a move towards a more modest conception of its scope, exemplified in the attempt to find a new language to express its central clinical concerns. A distinguished analyst, Roy Schafer, has described psychoanalysis succinctly as 'an interpretive discipline whose concern is to construct life histories of human beings', to establish meaning and significance where none had been before[60]. To express this enterprise he sees the need for a new language, a modest empirical theory of naming and interpreting the human activity which goes on in psychoanalysis, in contrast to the all-encompassing theoretical system implied by the classical language of psychoanalytic metapsychology.

In brief, the essence of the psychoanalytic contribution to social work lies less in its particular theories and concepts than in its unique and characteristic perspective on people and their problems; psychoanalysis looks for those hidden meanings and motives which throw light on behaviour, particularly the 'forgotten' but still active and dynamic events of the past. 'An alertness for the unconscious, the sexual, and the infantile', wrote Waelder, 'may be called the psychoanalytic point of view'[61]. What psychoanalysis has demonstrated above all else is the continued existence of the child within the adult, and the persistent effects of the events and emotions of years long past on adult behaviour in the present, and it is this point of view, rather than the intricacies of its theories, that is the concern of this book.

2
Social Work and the 'New Psychology'

Before exploring more fully the implications of psychoanalysis for contemporary social work, we shall return to some of the questions posed at the beginning; namely, how much impact has psychoanalysis had on British social work, and in what form and through what channels has its influence come to be felt? As we have seen, there has been little study of this important but neglected aspect of social work history, and, for this reason, an historical review is essential to set the later discussion in its social and historical context. This chapter will consider the growth of the psychoanalytic movement in Britain and its influence on social work in the 1920's.

2.1 The Growth of Psychoanalysis in Britain

Freud's early neurological work was reviewed in the English journals well before 1900 and his name was therefore familiar to specialist audiences long before his psychoanalytic work was developed. The journal *Brain* (which had already published an abstract of the 'Preliminary Communications' of Breuer and Freud) in 1896 carried an extended critical review of the *Studies in Hysteria*[1] within a few months of its publication in Leipzig the previous year. The reviewer, Dr. J. Michell Clark, a specialist in hysteria, accorded it a favourable reception as an 'original and valuable contribution to the theory of hysteria', commenting that 'the book is written in an interesting style, and bears the stamp of originality, and of much patient and painstaking observation'. Admittedly on some aspects of their method he maintained a cautious British reserve: 'Into the question of the advisability of penetrating so intimately into the most private thoughts and concerns of a patient I do not go; it would seem likely that the patient would, in many cases at least, strongly resent it'.

Interest in the early work on hysteria came also from psychologists interested in psychical research. The earliest reference to Freud's work in fact occurs in the *Proceedings of the Society for Psychical Research* for 1894, where F.W.H. Myers reviewed the 'Preliminary Account of the Psychical Mechanisms of Hysterical Phenomena', published in the *Neurologische Centralblatt* in January 1893. A similar account can be found in Myer's *Human Personality*, which is an attempt to apply scientific method to the question whether man has an immortal soul or personality which survives his bodily death. Here he made use of the *Studies* in discussing disintegrations of

27

personality such as occurred in hysteria.

The man who first brought Freud's work to a wider public, however, was the psychiatrist Bernard Hart. In 1908 he contributed a paper to the *Journal of Mental Science* entitled 'A Philosophy of Psychiatry' which reveals some of the new avenues opening up in psychiatry early in the century[2]. In particular he was concerned with the application of the new science of psychology to psychiatric problems; from the researches of Janet, for example, he had the impression 'that a powerful searchlight is being thrown on the dark places of insanity'. For many years, psychiatry had been tied to a view of mental disease as *brain* disease, to which the answers would ultimately be found in anatomy and physiology. Now a new objective psychology was being developed, using familiar scientific methodology, which promised a fresh approach to insanity. In the hands of men like Janet, Freud and Jung, psychotherapy, Hart maintained, was emerging as 'a potent field of therapeutics'.

In a paper in 1910 his aim was explicitly that of setting out the general principles of Freud's teaching, and of explaining its central concepts[3]. In his view the contributions of Freud were 'some of the most valuable and stimulating ever made to the progress of psychiatry'. A similarly enthusiastic account occurs in a paper[4] on 'Freud's Conception of Hysteria' published in the same year, and demonstrates how much interest Freud's work was at the time creating:

> The system of psychology founded by Professor Freud of Vienna has during the past few years aroused a widespread interest. His doctrines have met with every variety of reception, ranging from an enthusiastic acceptance to an uncompromising and complete rejection. Whatever the ultimate verdict of science may be, the problems involved are of such undoubted importance that all will be agreed as to the desirability of thorough investigation of Freud's theories and an accurate determination of their claim to scientific validity.[5]

The bibliography lists no fewer than 208 references dealing with psychoanalysis. Nearly all were published in America or on the Continent (the only British references being to Hart's own papers) but many of those published in America (for example in the *Journal of Abnormal Psychology*, first issued in 1906) were readily accessible to medical or psychologist readers. It was evident that a fairly characteristic pattern was already beginning to emerge. While America produced a number of doctors and psychologists wholly committed to a psychoanalytic approach who were themselves trained by Freud (A.A Brill, for example), the British response was more characteristically one of partial or qualified acceptance. 'Many critics' wrote Hart, and it was true also of himself, 'are prepared to accept certain of Freud's conclusions, but decline to identify themselves with his psychology as a whole' In his view the stage had now been reached when a searching and impartial evaluation of the subject was not only possible but essential, in order to separate the wheat from the chaff and determine which aspects of the theory should be rejected and which

28

retained. 'For there is a growing consensus of opinion that Freud's work bears everywhere the impression of an extraordinarily acute and original intelligence, that his theories are at any rate remarkably suggestive and stimulating, and that he points the way to many lines of research which have never been previously attacked'[7].

Hart is probably best known for his book *The Psychology of Insanity*, which was first published in 1912 and reached its fifth edition in 1957; as a readable introduction it has done much to popularise the work of Freud, in America as well as Britain[8]. In this book Hart attempted to present and discuss recent theories in abnormal psychology which offered promise for the treatment of the insane, and in the preface to the first edition he acknowledged his great debt to Freud: 'A very large number of the general principles enunciated in this book are due to the genius of Professor Freud of Vienna, probably the most original and fertile thinker who has yet entered the field of abnormal psychology'[9]. But he was cautious too:

Although, however, I cannot easily express the extent to which I am indebted to him, I am by no means prepared to embrace the whole of the vast body of doctrines which Freud and his followers have now laid down. Much of this is in my opinion unproven, and erected upon an unsubstantial foundation. On the other hand, many of Freud's fundamental principles are becoming more and more widely accepted, and the evidence in their favour is rapidly increasing.[10]

Another medical psychologist to take an early interest in Freud's work was Dr. W. Brown, later Wilde Reader in Mental Philosophy at the University of Oxford. In 1913 he was invited to address the Listerian Society at King's College Hospital on 'something connected with the science of psychology'[11]. He chose as his topic 'Freud's Theory of Dreams', as embodying most of the central conceptions of psychoanalysis. Though as his later work makes clear he was never committed wholly to a Freudian view, the informed interest of a distinguished psychologist did much to help psychoanalysis to be considered seriously in medical circles. *The Lancet*, for example, complimenting Brown on his paper, commented that 'whatever may be thought of Freud's teaching, and whatever its ultimate fate, it cannot be gainsaid that his enthusiasm for his theory has proved infectious and has already been remarkably stimulating to psychological research'[12]. And Dr. Eder, a distinguished analyst, expressed delight 'at having reasoned criticism from so distinguished a psychologist as Dr. Brown, and one so sympathetic to this work'[13].

Not all the references, however, were so laudatory as these, and indeed one of the characteristics of psychoanalysis has been the intensity of the controversies that it has aroused. One noted critic, expressing perhaps some wishful thinking, maintained that 'psychoanalysis is past its perihelion and is rapidly retreating into the dark and silent depths from which it emerged'. His own account of psychoanalysis was, he said, intended to provide a systematic exposition of that theory before it joined 'pounded toads and sour milk in the limbo of discarded remedies'[14]. *The Lancet* in 1916 carried a correspondence which was mainly critical; the most extreme view (and one which vividly illustrates the reaction of some medical practitioners to the sexual theories of psychoanalysis) was probably that of the correspondent who affirmed that from his own 'practical experience and knowledge of the effects of psycho-analysis upon those among whom the craft is practised, that in so far as it is a probing for hidden and forgotten sexual occurrences, it is repulsive and disreputable, ethically objectionable and deserving of the strongest condemnation'[15].

In 1913, an event took place that was to have great significance for the spread of psychoanalysis in Britain. This was the return from Canada of Dr. Ernest Jones, and the founding, on his initiative, of the London Society of Psychoanalysis, of which he was the president. To Jones must be ascribed much of the impetus which the psychoanalytic movement in Britain subsequently gained.

Ernest Jones was born in 1879 and trained in medicine at Cardiff and University College, London. In 1900 at the age of 21 he qualified as a doctor and took up various hospital appointments. His interest then was in neurology in which he intended to make his career. In 1905 he and Wilfred Trotter set up practice together in Harley Street; Trotter, wrote Jones, 'was my best friend and — apart from Freud — the man who has mattered most in my life'. They worked together at University College Hospital, and in 1910 Trotter married Jones' sister. It was Trotter who first introduced Jones to the work of Freud by calling his attention to Michell Clark's Review in *Brain* in 1903. This chimed in with Jones' developing interest in psychopathology and medical psychology; he was already familiar with the work of Janet and the concept of the unconscious mind. The first of Freud's works he read, the Dora case, made a deep impression on him: 'My German was not good enough to follow it closely, but I came away with a deep impression of there being a man in Vienna who actually listened with attention to every word his patients said to him'[16]. From Freud, he took the ideas of the unconscious mind, the techniques for exploring it, and the concepts of sexuality and repression; these, he related, contributed to his growing understanding of and interest in the relation between mental process and functional disorders.

The importance of Freud for Jones can best be explained in his own words. Already he was familiar with the three main figures in the world of medical psychology — Janet in France, Boris Sidis and Morton Prince in America. With Prince he was already in correspondence, as a result of a paper he had contributed to the *Journal of Abnormal Psychology*, which Prince edited. But in Freud Jones found for the first time a man whose interest in mental processes was scientific:

> Hitherto scientific interest had been confined to what Sherrington calls the world of energy, the 'material' world. Now at last it was being applied to the equally valid world of mind. For Freud, the most casual remarks of his

patients were really facts, data to be seriously examined and pondered over with the same intentness as that given by the geologist, the biologist, the chemist to the data provided in their respective fields of work. What a revolutionary difference from the attitude of previous physicians who would hear, without listening, their patients' remarks, discounting, forgetting, or even pooh-poohing them while their own thoughts were elsewhere, concerned perhaps with the patients' welfare but from a totally different angle.[17]

In order to further his knowledge of Freud's writing, and with typical thoroughness, Jones began learning German seriously. Still in line with his intention of specialising in neurology he attempted to acquaint himself with the treatment of insanity, and in 1907 he attended a postgraduate course in psychiatry at Kraepelin's Clinic in Munich. Earlier in the same year Jones had met Jung on the occasion of an International Congress of Psychiatry in Amsterdam (July 1907) at which the two men had struck up a warm friendship. Jung had described to Jones with enormous enthusiasm his first meeting with Freud and his admiration of his work[18]. On the way back to England, Jones visited Jung in Zurich and spent several days at Burgholzi Hospital, where Jung was in psychiatric practice.

In 1908 Jones spent six months on the continent and, with Jung, drew up plans for the first psychoanalytical congress which took place in April 1908 in Salzburg. This included papers by Freud, Jones, Jung, Abraham, Stekel, Ferenczi, Adler and Riklin, and it was the occasion of Jones' first meeting with Freud. Freud's own paper dealt with the analysis of an obsessional case (the Rat Man) and he was listened to 'from eight in the morning until nearly one o'clock by a rapt and attentive audience'[19]. After the Congress, Jones went to Vienna and had lengthy discussions with Freud and this was followed by a visit to Ferenczi in Budapest. But in September of that year his medical career was shadowed by his enforced resignation from the West End Hospital for Nervous Diseases and he left Britain to take up an appointment at a psychiatric clinic in Toronto. Not only had three difficult and disappointing years in London put paid to his hopes of a neurological career, but his heart sank at the prospect of sowing psychoanalytic ideas 'on the peculiarly arid soil provided by the medical profession of London'.

Although Jones' departure delayed the establishment of psychoanalysis as a psychiatric specialism, other practitioners were also familiar with Freud's ideas. In the same year as Jones returned to London and established the London Society of Psychoanalysis (1913), Dr. Jessie Murray opened the Medico-Psychological Clinic of London. This was for psychotherapeutic treatment, and for its inspiration drew in part on psychoanalytic ideas. The director was James Glover; both he and his brother Edward subsequently became analysts, and at that point (1923) the Clinic was wound up. Other medical psychologists such as Hugh Crichton-Miller were also beginning to use psychoanalytic concepts in the treatment of nervous disorders, and such developments proved fertile soil for the growth of psychodynamic ideas.

Among academic psychologists, Freud's work had created considerable interest, and was being read and critically appraised well before the First World War. McDougall was early interested in Freudian concepts, particularly as they linked with his interest in the emotions; he gave some of the earliest lectures on psychoanalysis while a lecturer at the University of Liverpool[20]. In 1914 William Brown published a paper on 'Freud's Theory of the Unconscious', which was followed by a paper by T.H. Pear on dreams in relation to psychoanalytic theory[21]. In the same year, a symposium on 'The Freudian Theory of Forgetting' was presented at a Joint Meeting of the British Psychological Society, the Aristotelian Society, and the Mind Association at Durham. Among the lay public also there is evidence that Freud's work was known. For example, Leonard Woolf reviewed Freud's *Psychopathology of Everyday Life* for the *New Weekly* in 1914, and records that he and Walter Lippman had discussions about Freud's ideas[22].

Already by the outbreak of the First World War, therefore, the roots of what became as the 'new psychology' had taken hold, though it continued to be the subject of violent controversy. 'Without any conspicuous publicity such as the famous Clark University Conference with which psychoanalysis came to America, without any signal event of this kind, psychoanalysis silently percolated into the ken of British psychologists, medical men and philosophers in the years immediately preceding the First World War.'[23] Nevertheless, it was after the war that it became popularised. Ernest Jones has recalled:

> There seemed to have been a psychological moment in every country when interest in the newness of psychoanalysis became acute. This naturally happened first in German-speaking countries, but it came about also in the United States before the war. I should date this 'moment' in England to be within the first five years after the end of the war, some ten years before it happened in France and Italy.[24]

The war stimulated the development of psychoanalysis in unexpected ways, both in medical and in popular directions. In the first place, treatment of an analytic psychological kind derived from psychoanalysis, which had proved successful in the treatment of the war neuroses in the later phases of the war, was increasingly applied to the treatment of nervous illness in peacetime. A form of psychotherapy came to be practised which although eclectic in form owed much to Freud's theories, and in particular relied less on suggestion than on an analytic approach to the illness which consisted in trying to uncover and understand its concealed causes. In the second place, the applications of analytic theory to nonmedical fields and their implications for such diverse fields as teaching, the ministry and the penal system were beginning to be explored.

The first of these directions is well illustrated by *Functional Nerve Disease: An Epitome of War Experience for the Practitioner*, published in 1920 under the editorship of Hugh Crichton-Miller. Its contributors included a number of distinguished physicians and psychiatrists with war experience. Its purpose was to present 'the functional neuroses of war to the medical practitioner in such a way that the lessons taught by the Great War might be fully understood'. This book is valuable not only for its major content, but also for the critical summary by the psychologist William McDougall it contained. He pointed out that the view of the book was not in fact Freudian, though certain Freudian concepts (notably repression, regression, unconscious mental conflicts) were fairly generally accepted. Further, Freudian terminology was sometimes used in a nontechnical sense (for example, 'transference' to mean the patient's confidence and goodwill towards his physician) which gave the book a spuriously Freudian flavour. Nevertheless, it revealed a large measure of agreement among the contributors on the central role played by unconscious mental processes in the causation of neurotic symptoms — the primary psychoanalytic idea taken over by British psychiatry.

Although critical of certain uses of the term 'unconscious', McDougall considered that it was impossible to deal with cases of neurosis 'without being brought to infer the reality of processes which resemble conscious mental processes in every way except that the patient can give no account of them'. In his view, the discovery of these principles could be counted among 'the most difficult achievements of modern science'[25]. While accepting this, however, and recognising the value of a psychotherapeutic method (which he calls mental exploration or mental readjustment) designed to explore these hidden processes, McDougall's attitude to psychoanalysis proper is made unequivocally clear. The term 'psychoanalysis' (which he himself preferred not to use) 'implies that these procedures are undertaken by a physician who accepts a mass of highly speculative doctrines emanating from Vienna; and, since the friends and followers of this school have an indisputable claim to this term, it is only fair and expedient to avoid the use of it when it is not intended to imply the acceptance of these esoteric doctrines'[26]. The approach represented by *Functional Nerve Disease* illustrates an attitude beginning to be common in British psychiatry — a qualified acceptance of some but by no means all of Freud's theories. Crichton-Miller, for example, while acknowledging a great debt to the work of Freud, also avoided the term 'psychoanalysis' in relation to his own clinical work, since he did not accept the theory in toto. Nevertheless, it was his view that 'no-one who has studied its conceptions can fail to realise that they introduce a fresh era into psychological thought'[27].

Those who were committed psychoanalysts were by and large preoccupied in the early years with establishing psychoanalysis as a reputable branch of medicine, and with the treatment of patients in private consulting rooms. Their writing was mainly technical, and their contact with the kinds of problem encountered in the outside world by social workers, teachers and general practitioners was minimal. Few ventured into the mental hospitals, and Glover has remarked on the very small part played by analysts in penal developments in those early years[28]. It was not until the late 1920's and 1930's that analysts began to play any significant role in the world of social affairs. In consequence, those who were primarily responsible for the spread of psychodynamic psychology into nonmedical fields were those whose orientation was eclectic, who like Crichton-Miller were influenced by and made use of Freudian concepts, who accepted the theory of unconscious mental processes as revolutionary, but who maintained a scepticism in respect of other aspects of Freud's theory. What became popular was not psychoanalysis so much as what Hearnshaw has called 'a watered-down depth psychology' culled from a variety of sources, and it was this with which social workers mainly came in contact.

Crichton-Miller himself made a notable contribution in exploring the relevance of psychodynamic theories to allied professions. In 1921 he gave a series of lectures at the Tavistock Clinic, subsequently published as *The New Psychology and the Teacher*, a fresh and vivid account of some of the contributions Freudian psychology could make to educational practice. He never advocated the view that teachers should become quasi-analysts, but held that the importance of the new psychology lay above all in the self-knowledge it could give, and the insight the teacher could gain into his own attitudes and prejudices; its value should lie primarily in the teacher's increased power, through self-insight, to allow the child freedom of growth.

In 1920 Dr. Crichton-Miller founded the Tavistock Clinic to provide psychotherapeutic treatment of a psychoanalytically oriented kind for civilian patients suffering from neurotic disorders. Throughout its history, the Tavistock has valued the contribution of social workers to the alleviation of psychological distress, and has made a significant impact on British social work, through its training programmes and its out-reach to the frontline helping professions. From the first, the clinic was psychodynamic in its orientation, as H.V. Dick's valuable account of its history shows:

> This origin of the Tavistock Clinic in psychodynamic thought is stressed from the outset of this book because it has imparted a lasting orientation to the Clinic's structure and staffing, despite departures from strict psychoanalysis, and because it has provided a special image of the Clinic both to its staff and to the British medical scene.
>
> The focus that is characteristic of the Tavistock is the emphasis on the, until then ignored or misinterpreted, sphere of the neuroses and personality disorders now illuminated by the 'New Psychology' originating in Vienna and Zurich. This distinctive 'mix' was in the four fold aim of *understanding and treatment*, the furthering of *research* into causation in the hope of finding rational means of *prevention* in mental hygiene, and on *teaching* the emerging concepts and skills to future specialists as well as to all those, medical and nonmedical, concerned with mental health and human relations.[29]

Thus 'the Clinic from the first had a curiously independent, indeed isolated, position somewhere between official psychiatry on the one hand and 'orthodox' psychoanalysis on the other'. This eclecticism, emphasising an appproach which stressed the importance of unconscious factors in the aetiology of neurotic disorders, but yet allowing flexibility and growth, undoubtedly made the Tavistock's contribution more acceptable to the general medical practitioner, though it did little to endear it to the psycho-analytic movement.

Psychoanalysis itself was still pursuing a storm-tossed course, the centre of bitter attacks, especially from the medical establishment. In 1925 a tragedy occurred which unleashed a torrent of correspondence in *The Times* and illustrated the controversy which psychoanalysis continued to arouse. This was the suicide of a young barrister, said to have been under psychoanalytic treat-ment; his physician claimed that the young man had indicated his intention of discontinuing treatment because of the sense of degradation given to him. 'This sense of degradation, as is well known', observed *The Times* 'is often experienced by persons who have submitted themselves to mental analysis'[30]. In a sharp attack, its leading article called for an investigation into psychoanalysis.

This weapon, whether truly forged or not, is capable of inflicting terrible injuries, a point made with urgency at the last annual meeting of the British Medical Association. There is no doubt that an inquiry by competent persons into the whole subject of psychological treatment is now overdue. The present position, which is giving rise to a great deal of anxiety, is one of the consequences of the neglect of psychology by the medical schools of this country.

Although it was subsequently shown that the young barrister was not in fact the patient of a trained analyst, the ensuing correspondence demonstrated the hostility to psychoanalysis and the contradictory attitudes towards it to be found both among the medical profession and the lay public. The National Council for Mental Hygiene set up a committee to investigate the status of psychoanalysis, but it produced no report. Following further representations at the BMA Conference in the summer of 1926, a BMA committee was set up which finally reported favourably and gave psychoanalysis a recognised status and a protected title in the field of medical specialties — an outcome due in no small measure to the support of Dr. Edward Glover.

The conflicts in which psychoanalysis was engaged during the inter-war years are primarily of interest to historians of the medical profession. But they also help to explain the very limited influence of psychoanalysis on British social work before the Second World War. In the face of the critical onslaughts of the doctors, and particularly the opposition of the organically based school of British psychiatry represented eminently by Dr. Mapother of the Maudsley (who was much involved in the training of social workers), British psycho-analysts entrenched themselves behind their professional barriers, and only a few brave spirits such as Grace Pailthorpe and Edward Glover ventured out into the broader world of social affairs. As Dicks reveals, the Tavistock Clinic was in the centre of this conflict; not only did it attract the opposition of Dr. Mapother, but also that of the psychoanalysts themselves, who disliked the Tavistock's dilution of Freudian theory, and the employment of psychodynamic approaches by those who were, for the most part, not trained as analysts[31]. In the midst of such conflicting and diverse approaches, it can occasion no surprise that social work, eager to absorb psychiatric and psychological knowledge, retired baffled as to which contributions could most profitably be explored.

2.2 Psychiatry, Psychoanalysis and Social Work in the Early 20th Century

In order to understand the initial resistance to (and later impact of) psychoanalysis in social work in Britain, it is necessary to examine what may be termed the professional ideologies of social workers — the dominant theories and beliefs that influenced their practice and to which the new psychology offered a tremendous challenge.

The beginnings of modern social work in the activities of the Charity Organisation Society have been traced by a number of authors, in particular Woodroofe and Owen. By both it is regarded as the central tradition in the evolution of casework, and its ideology is therefore deemed to have had a lasting and pervasive influence on social work thinking and practice. The work of the Society was grounded in a strongly individualistic theory which viewed the problem of poverty as rooted in the failure or incapacity of the individual. The solution to it lay in charity, in the voluntary assumption of responsibility by the better endowed for those less privileged than themselves. Charity was far more than philanthropic activity: it implied nothing less than a vision of a new Utopia, a society in which the relationship of members to one another was characterised by brotherly love and mutual responsibility, in which each member was independent, self-supporting, yet caring for his neighbours. 'Charity', wrote C.S. Loch, for many years Secretary to the Society, 'is love working through the individual and his social life'[32]. Charity was not to be exercised through large-scale schemes of state assistance, but through casework, through moral influence exercised within an authentic and personal relationship.

Such a view — of society as a community of independent men and women, working towards a common end and subordinating selfish desires to the common good — implied not only a moral but a political theory. It took for granted the class structure of Victorian society and its continuance, and was the antithesis of a socialist view that looks to the role of the state in equalising wealth and opportunity. The notions of class and citizenship, Tawney has observed, are incompatible, and, as the latter conception grew in strength and influence, so the former could no longer survive unquestioned.

After the turn of the century, the COS came increasingly under attack for its tenacious adherence to principles which were out of key with modern

36

conceptions of democracy, for its failure to take account of new evidence as to the structural causes of poverty, and for its dogmatic opposition to developing state schemes for social welfare — an opposition most marked perhaps in relation to school meals, which the Society viewed as a reprehensible erosion of parental responsibility. It was not surprising that the very word 'charity' 'stank in the nostrils of thoughtful working men and women'[33], and that the social-work tradition associated with it was tarred with the same brush. This may be one reason for the lack of vigorous development in social work practice or literature during the first half of the 20th century; after the rich harvest of social-work ideas put forward in the writings of Victorian social workers such as Helen Bosanquet and Octavia Hill, there is scarcely any literature at all until after the Second World War, and none comparable with that of Mary Richmond in the United States.

It is therefore very doubtful how far social casework in the COS tradition ever was central to the development of modern social work. Certainly its identity was maintained, and the COS regarded itself unequivocally as the leader in the field; equally certainly some key themes which it articulated (for example, the importance of personal individual care and the need for training) have persisted as commonly accepted principles of modern practice. But, during the first two decades of the 20th century, alternative conceptions of social work, more compatible with the social thinking of the time, were coming into being — less coherent, less clearly articulated than that of the COS, but nevertheless clearly distinguishable. The dominant conception was that of the social worker as social servant — a conception that differed greatly from that of the COS, and in some respects represented a reaction against it. Social service, by which charity was superseded, was seen as an expression of citizenship within an evolving context of social rights and equality of status. This represents a major shift in thinking, and it is this latter idea (and not that of charity) which dominated the development of social work and social work training in the first half of the 20th century.

At the end of the Victorian era, very different views as to the nature and causes of the ills which were the Society's raison d'etre were gaining strength — views which received support from the work of Booth and Rowntree at the end of the century; and the solutions to which their analyses were held to point ranged from Marxism to a limited collectivism. What they had in common, however, was a conviction that these evils were located in the structure of industrial society rather than in the character of individuals, and that they could only be solved by parliamentary intervention to bring about greater control of social and economic affairs and a more equitable distribution of the wealth of an advancing industrial society.

The philosophy of charity (and the view of social work grounded on it) which the COS *par excellence* embodied represented a waning influence, and even some of the Society's originally ardent supporters, such as Samuel Barnett, came to recognise the necessity of socialism, albeit of a limited, diluted and 'practicable' kind. The degree to which the idea of charity (and that form of social work associated with it) came to grate on those who hoped for a juster and more equal society in which rights and obligations were to be construed in terms of citizenship rather than of class, is apparent from many contemporary writings, particularly those of the Webbs, and the thoughtful and informed criticism of Barnett and Violet Markham. The new dynamic of philanthropy thus went, as the 20th century moved on, into forms of activity designed to increase individual liberty by societal and legislative change, though of a reforming rather than a radical kind.

At the personal level, then, the concept of charity gave way to that of social service. The personal work undertaken by the secretaries and visitors of the COS was essentially rooted, just as much as its social theory, in the class divisions of Victorian society; as the organised labour movement grew in strength and influence, so this tradition could not ultimately survive, though the burial did not finally take place until 1946 when the Charity Organization Society became the Family Welfare Association. The charitable tradition was based on the concept of duty, of the responsibilities of the wealthy and cultured towards those without these advantages; but however altruistically and unselfishly such an ideal was pursued, it was at root paternalistic and class bound. A conception of social work based on an almost feudal idea of class dependence inevitably grew anachronistic.

Until the 1880's the dominant tendency in social thought was towards individualism, of which Herbert Spencer was the most extreme exponent; it was not surprising that the social theories of the COS, conceived and born in the 1860's, should have been so strongly influenced by his views. After 1880 the influence of laissez faire (nonintervention as the pre-eminent duty of the state) was passing; Socialism, in both its reformist and its revolutionary forms, was shortly to flower; and T.H. Green was lecturing at Oxford on the interdependence of individual and community and the obligation of the state to ensure for each of its citizens the conditions of moral development. By that time, the inadequacy of a laissez faire view, implicit in the utilitarianism of Mill and Bentham, was increasingly evident as a basis for dealing with the large-scale problems consequent upon industrialisation. Lindsay remarked that the individualist creed of the earlier utilitarians which had set out to be a doctrine of reform and liberty came in the end to represent a philosophical justification of reaction and privilege: 'If democracy was to grapple with these new problems with any success, some way had to be found of reconciling a true individualism with the new functions which were being thrust upon the State'[34]. In the 1870's a new liberalism emerged, which owed much to the work of Green and Arnold Toynbee, and which had important implications for the development of social welfare. For social work, the thinking of the Oxford idealist philosophers — Green and Bosanquet — was of especial significance. From Oxford came a number of able young men who made their mark on the civil service, politics and social work; C.S. Loch was a pupil of Green and acknowledged a great debt to his teacher, not only in the development of his ideas, but even in so basic a matter as his choice of career; and the sermons of Samuel Barnett are eloquent testimony to the influence of the same teacher. Bosanquet himself, as is well known, left the academic world of Oxford to seek the practical expression of his philosophical ideas in the social work of the COS. 'To find in life new material for philosophy and to take back to life the wider views gained by philosophical insight — this I think may be said to have been his vocation', wrote Helen Bosanquet of her husband[35]. Although the work of Green has been held to point to political philosophies as divergent as those of Loch and the Webbs, it undoubtedly provided a justification for that more positive view of state intervention in the lives of citizens which was a necessary basis of the liberal reforms of the early 20th century.

The central problem tackled by Green was the reconciliation of freedom and control, of the liberty of the individual to pursue his own moral ends with the more active reforming role in which the State was beginning to engage. It was not in his view (any more than in that of Mill) the business of the state to compel morality; but the good life cannot exist without freedom. What *is* the business of the state, therefore, is to promote conditions favourable to freedom — and ultimately to the good life — by removing the obstacles and hindrances to freedom. To talk of the state as the realisation of freedom 'to an untaught and underfed denizen of a London yard with ginshops on the right hand and on the left' (wrote Green in a famous passage) is as much a mockery as to talk of it to an Athenian slave[36]. The function of government, then, is to promote and maintain conditions of life (good health, adequate income, and, above all, education) in which freedom and morality shall be possible for every citizen. Freedom itself is essentially a property of the individual and the activities of government thus have, in the final analysis, an individual reference.

Such a philosophy, as Barker has observed[37], could satisfy the new needs of social progress because it refused to worship a supposed individual liberty of the few at the expense of the freedom of the many. Green himself started from the standpoint of the ordinary citizen and was no remote academic philosopher; he was deeply engaged in social work and political life, as an Oxford City Councillor and on the School Board, and he believed passionately in the worth of the ordinary man; there was nothing elitist in his views. His conception of freedom and of the relation of politics to morality held immense appeal for those such as Samuel Barnett, who were deeply involved in the life of the East End, and daily in contact with the poor, the deprived and the ignorant, who could in no sense be regarded as 'free' in Green's sense of the word. 'Freedom', Green had said, 'is a positive power or capacity of doing or enjoying something worth doing or enjoying, and that too something that we can do or enjoy in common with others'[38]. The only genuine freeman in this sense, his disciple Samuel Barnett maintained, is the fully developed man and citizen, and all who come short of this are but freemen in the making: 'Citizens, if they are free, must not only have the right to self-government, they must also be fit for self-government'[39]. In the end the social need that Barnett saw as underlying all others and the most essential to freedom was that of education.

2.3 The Settlement Movement

The influence of Green is clearly to be discerned in the beliefs and aims of the Settlement Movement, that distinctive form of personal service associated with the universities in the later 19th century[40]. As originally conceived by Samuel Barnett, Toynbee Hall was the expression of a distinctive ideology. Although the Settlement Movement (like the COS) was a response to a particular set of social conditions (the crises of the last quarter of the 19th century) and represented only a limited and ephemeral approach to urban problems, to it were attracted some of the ablest men of their generation — men like C.R. Attlee, W.H. Beveridge, R.H. Tawney, E.F. Urwick, T. Hobhouse — whose contribution to academic life and to the development of British social policy has been immense, and whose ideas were, to some degree at least, shaped by this experience.

Among the major elements of this ideology were:

(i) a belief in 'settlement' as a way of overcoming the physical separation of the classes and of breaking down class barriers;

(ii) a belief in education (more particularly the cultural values enshrined in the older universities) as essential to individual freedom;

(iii) a belief in the need for the unity of the working classes and educated men in the cause of social reform; and

(iv) a belief that wise social progress could only be based on genuine first-hand experience of working-class life by those in a position to make, guide or influence policy.

The 'people's condition', exposed by the unemployment of the 1870's, lay heavy on the consciences and exercised the minds of economists, philosophers and reformers alike. 'The fact that the wealth of England meant only wealth *in* England and that the mass of the people live without knowledge, without hope, and often without health has come home to open minds and consciences'[41]. The new awareness of the conditions of people 'has made a strange stirring in the calm life of universities, and many men feel themselves driven by a new spirit, driven by a master idea' — the kernel of Barnett's message in his famous address at St. John's College, Oxford, in 1883, from which Toynbee Hall was born[42]. The explicit concern on which the movement centred was the class divisions of urban life, symbolised by their physical and geographical separation in London's two 'cities', the East and the West End. How, Barnett asked, could these barriers be overcome and rich and poor 'learn to consider one another and work for some common end'[43]? One solution was that of settlement; scattered encampments of the cultured and educated, taking up residence in the East End, and coming into a relationship of friendship with the working man. The settlement movement had something of the patronage from which the COS could never divest itself, but the settlers desired above all greater contact and mutual understanding; from this, in itself, mutual benefits were believed to accrue. In place of class differentiation, Barnett hoped to see a fuller recognition of citizenship hased on equality of rights and opportunity.

Above all, he believed in education. Toynbee Hall was a Whitechapel Oxford, from its graduate and undergraduate residents to its quad and its chapel; its annual reports list its enormous range of educational activities, from lectures on Greek literature to literary, philosophical and travel societies. Not only did Barnett value it for its own sake, but in education, ultimately, he saw the hope of social progress:

If sometimes I am asked what I desire for East London I think of all the goodness, the struggle, the suffering I have seen — the sorrows of the poor and the many fruitless remedies — and I say, 'more education', 'higher education'... People must raise themselves... People must have the education which will reveal to them the powers within themselves and within other men, their capacities for thinking and feeling, for admiration, hope and love. They must be made something more than the instruments of production, they must be made capable of enjoying the highest things.[44]

What perhaps has been less clearly recognised is the third element in its ideological commitment — the political aims of the settlement movement. Not only were the residents themselves thought likely to provide new resources of educated leadership in local government, but Barnett saw the hope of social progress in its political sense to lie in the alliance of the working class movement with the human values and the accumulated knowledge reposing in the universities. 'A Settlement in the original idea was not a mission, but a means by which university men and workmen might by natural intercourse get to understand one another, and cooperate in social reform'[45]. If he were a millionaire, he once remarked, he would try to bring about an alliance between the universities and the Labour Party, so that trained minds were available in the service of organised labour[46].

The fourth element which has been noted (the necessity of first-hand experience of working class life for the development of wise policies) finds its clearest expression in the words of Beveridge, author of the famous Report on *Social Insurance and Allied Services* of 1942. Beveridge spent two years at Toynbee Hall, and it was there that he undertook his earliest work on dock labour and unemployment. None disliked 'slumming and good works' more than he:

If anyone ever thought that colossal evils could be remedied by small doses of culture and charity and amiability (he wrote) I for one do not think so now. The real use I wish to make of Toynbee and kindred institutions is as centres for the development of authoritative opinion on the problems of city life[47].

A settlement, he wrote later, should not be a permanent residence, but a college to pass through, 'a school of postgraduate education in humanity'[48]. In a letter to his mother (1904) the significance of Toynbee Hall for him was again succinctly expressed:

> I came to the conclusion that such places represent simply a protest against taking things for granted. No man can really be a good citizen who goes through life in a watertight compartment of his own class... Toynbee Hall produces therefore a sort of general culture in social and political views; it doesn't necessarily lead all men to one particular view... One might not become a specialist in any one social subject; one would at least be in a position, having seen all sorts and conditions of men, to have reasonable views on all social proposals[49].

The Settlement movement was a distinctive response to the social conditions of the 1880's but one which, if it touched chords in the idealistic young men of the universities, received but a lukewarm response from other contemporaries. Octavia Hill thought settlements were wholly artificial, though she came to hold a more positive view under the influence of her friend Miss Sewell, Warden of the Womens University Settlement in Southwark. Nevertheless, the movement held powerful ideological appeal and attracted eminent support. Although it shared with the COS a belief in personal influence, its ideology was very different from that of the COS and looked to the newer liberalism where the COS looked to the old[50]. Barnett himself moved from his early strongly individualist views to a belief that social problems must be tackled not only by individual work, but at source, and thus he came to see something fundamentally wrong with the philanthropic commitment represented by the COS. More and more, he recognised that the problem of poverty required more than goodwill, more than benevolence, however wise and systematic: 'There is only one remedy for the poverty of the poor, and that is increase of their means, and this increase must be at the cost of the richer classes'[51]. Charity had to fail because in the end it depended on the 'wayward interest of subscribers or fitful attendance of members'; charity 'will be representative, if one may so put it, of the good will rather than of the justice of the community; it will aim to do kindly rather than justly'[52].

Towards 1914 Toynbee Hall changed markedly. Residents had always seen themselves as individually responsible for the work of the settlement rather than as committed to any explicit programme or ideology. By that time, the early belief in personal influence had begun to wane, and there was a growing interest in social investigation leading to social reform rather than in practical philanthropy — an interest which owed much to the lines of work pursued by Beveridge.

The significance of Toynbee Hall in this context, and the beliefs to which it gave practical expression, rests in the fact that very strong links can be traced with the social studies movement in the universities, and in particular with the London School of Economics. This therefore represented a strong influence on social work in the first two decades. At least six Toynbee residents after 1897 held positions in the Department of Social Science and Administration at

42

LSE[53]; these included R.H. Tawney, in 1913 as Director of the Ratan Tata Foundation for the study of poverty, and later as Reader and Professor of Economic History; C.R. Attlee (later Labour MP and Prime Minister) as a lecturer in the department; and E.F. Urwick, Head of the Department and later Professor of Social Philosophy. Two Directors of the LSE, William Beveridge and Alexander Carr-Saunders[54], were both former subwardens. Another significant link was provided by J. St.G. Heath, a former lecturer in Social Economics at Woodbrooke, Birmingham, who was warden in 1914 and became first Secretary of the Joint University Council for Social Studies.

2.4 The School of Sociology

In the 1890's the COS and the settlements had together taken a joint initiative in training, in the form of a series of lectures. These beginnings led to the formation of the School of Sociology in 1903, under the auspices of the COS. The choice of E.F. Urwick, a former subwarden of Toynbee Hall, as its principal was to prove of great significance. In an address to the Society in 1904 Urwick set out the aims of the School as he saw them. The old empirical methods of the past would no longer serve and social work could most safely be grounded, Urwick believed, in the infant science of sociology which 'finds its place waiting for it as the director of the new social interests and as the interpreter of the complex social life which now for the first time has become an almost universal object of thought'[55]. In this early statement is unequivocally spelt out a scientific commitment rooted in later 19th century positivism, which has remained a central feature of the professional ideology of social work. Further, the direction of this commitment was also becoming clear, and was towards the social sciences; this orientation remained characteristic of British social work education for the next 50 years, and was not seriously challenged until the mid-1950's, when it was to some degree displaced by psychodynamic psychology.

It 1912 an improbable but productive union took place between the School of Sociology and the London School of Economics and Political Science, a creation of the Webbs. Urwick became director of the new department of Social Science and Administration, but the change had important consequences. The School had a strong staff, including Sidney Webb, and of the two bodies was by far the more powerful. Henceforth the major work of the LSE was in economics, sociology, political science and kindred disciplines, and social work education enjoyed an anomalous and peripheral position on the fringe of its activities. But the traditions represented on the one hand by the COS and the School of Sociology, and on the other by the Webbs and the London School of Economics merged in the new 'social studies' movement, and the nature of the social work training carried on at the LSE was greatly influenced by its scholarly interests in the social sciences. The distinctive influence and ideology of the COS, Pinker has commented, 'lost its identity in

43

a larger department not notably sympathetic to a Spencerian view of social welfare'[56], and social work training as it developed there after 1912 was far more deeply concerned with social reconstruction than it was with individual regeneration.

Clement Attlee had a major teaching commitment on the course for the Diploma in Social Science, as did R.H. Tawney (author of *The Acquisitive Society*, *Equality*, and *Religion and the Rise of Capitalism* among many other works). Tawney, who was at the LSE for more than 30 years, and was not only revered as a scholar and teacher, but 'loved and respected'[57] as a man, must have had a strong influence on generations of students. He had had experience of social work with the Childrens' Country Holiday Fund and was sympathetic towards it, though more deeply interested in broader social questions. He is said to have 'thought more highly of (Richard Titmuss) than anyone else at the LSE at the time he left it'[58]; Titmuss was the first professor of Social Administration at the School, and it was in his department that the first generic social work course was established in 1954. Tawney's abiding concern was for the creation of a more just and equal society, and his commitment to democratic socialism must have represented a far more potent influence on social science students who attended his courses than the narrow concerns of the COS. The development of social work training in this country thus differs markedly and significantly from that in the United States and Canada; in Britain the initiative in training passed to the universities and was never separated from the broad study of the social sciences and of fundamental social questions. The social work agencies (of which the COS remained the most important), though they provided opportunities for practical training, had little influence on the nature and content of the courses themselves.

2.5 The Joint University Council

The aims and content of the social studies courses, and the work of the Joint University Council for Social Studies set up to coordinate them, provides some insight into contemporary views of the nature of social work. The social studies courses will be considered in some detail, for they too were the bearers of a distinctive, though less explicit, ideology. Not only did they embody the idea of social work as a profession for which specific training was required, but the content of the courses was based upon certain assumptions about the nature of social work. Four characteristics that can be detected were: first, a broad interest in social and political philosophy and thus in such concepts as rights, equality and freedom; second, a 'scientific' approach to the study and alleviation of social problems, via economics and sociology; third, a conception of social work as inseparable from the practical administration of the state institutions developed to promote social welfare in its broadest sense; and fourth, a total rejection of the moral and evangelistic outlook characteristic of so much Victorian social work.

By the First World War, courses of social study were already established in several universities, and the war itself gave an impetus for its further development in relation to certain fields of work, notably factory welfare[59]. The JUC's first report on *Social Study and Training at the Universities* (1918) gives a good picture of the situation at the close of the war. It refers to social study as 'a significant recent development in teaching within British universities', and indeed claimed it as 'a new movement'. But perhaps no writer captured the spirit of the social studies courses more vividly than Clement Attlee, then a lecturer in the Social Science Department at the London School of Economics:

> The Social Service movement of modern times is not confined to any one class, nor is it the preserve of a particular section of dull and respectable people. It has arisen out of a deep discontent with society as at present constituted, and among its prophets have been the greatest spirits of our time. It is not a movement concerned alone with the material, with housing and drains, clinics and feeding centres, gas and water, but is the expression of the desire for social justice, for freedom and beauty, and for the better apportionment of all the things that make up a good life. It is the constructive side of the criticisms passed by the reformer and revolutionary on the failure of our industrialised society to provide a fit environment where a good life shall be possible for all.[60]

In place of the individualism of the 19th century and its faith in a slow but assured evolutionary process towards a better society had come a turning toward community and social action, as an expression of the desire for equality of rights and opportunities in a democratic society. Within this context, social work was no longer associated with charity but was a form of social service, based on a sense of common citizenship in which 'we particularly emphasise the position of men and women as citizens... we are all united as members of the State'[61]. The social worker, said Attlee, 'is one who feels the claims of society upon him more than others, he brings to all his work this conception of his duty as a member of a civilised society to make his contribution to the well-being of his fellows'[62].

From the point of view of social workers in the field, the social studies courses, despite their evident strengths, had two main weaknesses: the lack of casework training, and the somewhat academic teaching in psychology, which contained little reference to those developments in the clinical field from which, in the 1920's, social workers were eager to learn. The omission of social casework teaching from the syllabus is due both to the environment in which the social studies courses took place, and to their view of the nature of social work training itself. From the start, the courses had to maintain a somewhat tenuous position in an academic environment not generally sympathetic to vocational training. It was never very clear (and perhaps this very ambiguity of objective was necessary to their continuance) whether the courses were aiming to provide a vocational training at all, or merely a general education in the

45

social sciences. Increasingly, the situation came to be clarified by practice, and those intending to take up social work as a career proceeded on completion of their social science course to one of the specialised trainings provided in almoning and, rather later, family casework and probation work.

There is no reference in the JUC's 1918 Report to the practical skills taught in American schools of social work at that time, and Miss Macadam of Liverpool University, commenting that such subjects as casework, family work, community organisation did not appear in the English syllabus at all, admitted in retrospect:

'Technique' in Britain is less developed than in the United States, largely because training here has been removed to the universities, whereas in the United States it remained in the hands of practical workers much longer. Nevertheless, though 'technique' may to British eyes appear to be overdone across the Atlantic, we must admit the possibility that we have gone too far in the other direction and sometimes neglected the science of practical administration.[63]

In Britain, the American conception of social work training had been explicitly rejected by the first secretary of the Joint University Council, J. St.G. Heath:

If we turn to the Report of the Commission of Education on 'Education for Social Work'... we find it stated that 'the object of the professional school is to teach methods, to put tools into the student's hands; the student as a result of his school work should be able to appreciate the value of technique in case work in any part of the field'... In the view of the writer the first and foremost aim of the Social Training course is *to give the student the right attitude towards and the right outlook upon* Social Work as a whole, while the understanding of case work and technical efficiency is only of secondary importance.[64]

Miss Clement Brown, subsequently tutor to the Mental Health Courses at LSE, makes some interesting comparisons between training in Britain and America in the 1920's which highlight these different approaches;

It was indeed a curious experience to travel from a British University Department of Social Study to the New York School of Social Work in the early twenties and to find so little in common between them ... to the British student there was both excitement in being able to discuss the 'Nature and Varieties of Human Behaviour', the principles and skills of casework service, in the sober atmosphere of the classroom, and also a sense of bewilderment and loss of perspective in the neglect of wider social issues which became so important to American Social Workers ten years later.[65]

2.6   The Beginning of Child Guidance

During the decade 1920—1930, the developments in psychology and

46

psychiatry described earlier had a discernible but remarkably limited impact on social work, expressed chiefly in demands for new forms of training. These came from a number of different directions — from Evelyn Fox and the Central Association for Mental Welfare, from the Institute of Hospital Almoners and from magistrates and educationalists concerned with the problem of juvenile delinquency. Some of these threads were drawn together in the formation of the Child Guidance Council in 1927, and contributed to two major innovations — the establishment of the London Child Guidance Clinic and the initiation of the Mental Health Course at the London School of Economics and Political Science in 1929. Apart from these two initiatives, however, the 'new psychology' had little widespread influence until after World War II.

Much of the initiative for the development of training in psychiatric work for social workers, and for the extension of teaching in this area on existing courses, came from Evelyn Fox, Secretary of the Central Association for Mental Welfare[66]. The CAMW was initially set up (as the Central Association for the Care of Mental Defectives) to assist with the implementation of the Mental Deficiency Act of 1913. It played a formative part in the development of services for the mentally handicapped, initiating, pioneering or sponsoring such schemes as training and occupation centres. High importance was attached by Evelyn Fox to training; in 1915, with the cooperation of the Birmingham Education Committee, the first course of training for special school teachers were held, and in London in 1924 a course of lectures on Mental Diseases for social workers was given at the Maudsley Hospital under Dr. Mapother's direction[67].

But short courses, however useful, were clearly insufficient, and in 1925 and 1926 negotiations were in progress with the Joint University Council and university social study departments in order to secure more adequate training in psychiatry and mental health[68]. The initiative for this came from CAMW and in November 1926 a meeting of the JUC and CAMW took place to discuss proposals put forward by the latter body. These were of two kinds. It was suggested in the first place that an elementary course in mental welfare should be included in the curriculum of all students preparing for a social science qualification, and, in the second place, that an advanced course was necessary for those who were intending to specialise in this field. In the event, no action resulted from these proposals, since by then the Commonwealth Fund had already expressed interest in setting up a mental health course, and the CAMW was one of the signatories to the letter of invitation sent to the Fund. Nevertheless, Evelyn Fox's comments on the need for the incorporation of psychiatric teaching as part of the training of all social workers were far-sighted (foreshadowing educational developments of 30 years later) and deserve to be on record:

The developments of recent years in the spheres of psychiatry, individual and social psychology have emphasised the need for some knowledge of

47

modern psychological methods in dealing with many of the social misfits in the community.

Every social worker, in whatever branch of his professon, is brought into contact with problems which demand a knowledge of the factors influencing the reaction of the individual to his environment, and of the general principles underlying this reaction in order that he may judge whether the reactions are normal or abnormal.

He may have to deal with the maladjusted and delinquent child and young person; the older delinquent and recidivist; the problem of responsibility involved in rescue and preventive cases; the mental sequelae of physical illness; the position of subnormal and unbalanced individuals; the disastrous effects of mental strain consequent upon bad home conditions, family disagreements, unsuitable employment, extreme poverty or financial uncertainty.

To do this successfully he must be given opportunity of acquiring modern information regarding the views of psychiatrists and psychologists on the special mental problems involved.

We are therefore strongly of the opinion that it is essential to provide such psychological training as part of the necessary equipment of every social worker.[69]

The need to incorporate more teaching in psychology and psychiatry and to prepare staff to work in psychiatric hospitals was also a matter of concern to the Institute of Hospital Almoners. From the beginning, the almoners had aimed at high professional standards, and to 'select, train, and arrange for the training of suitable candidates' was the primary function of the Institute of Almoners — training that aimed at 'high attainment, thoroughness and efficiency, and sound knowledge of the conditions of all classes'[70]. Of the candidates who presented themselves, only a proportion were accepted (58% in 1922) for, besides a good educational background, unusual qualities of character and personality were also regarded as necessary.

Training began in 1907 when the Hospital Almoners Council (later incorporated as the Institute of Almoners) was formed, and at that time the training period consisted of 12—18 months. By 1921 this had been extended to two years and was organised in two parts. Part I consisted of four months wholetime work in a COS office in London, followed by nine months' theoretical study in social subjects in the Department of Social Science and Administration at the London School of Economics. Part II consisted of 11 months at a hospital training centre, under the direction of an experienced almoner[71]. In 1926, a Joint Committee was set up by the JUC and the Institute, which suggested no major revision, but recommended that, in future, students under 20 should be required to qualify for a Certificate or Diploma in Social Studies as a preliminary to the more specialised almoners' training[72]; as a result, training became three years and the principle of a broadly based social science training preceding specialisation, to which the almoners subsequently firmly held, was thereby established.

48

In 1924 and 1925 it was evident that almoners were keenly interested in the developments in psychiatry and medical psychology, and were anxious to equip themselves for work in this field. This meant both an increase in the psychology teaching undertaken by all almoner students, and a specialist training to equip some almoners for work in mental and neurological hospitals. At a meeting of the Hospital Almoners Association in 1924, a discussion took place on the training of almoners for work with 'psychopathic' patients, but it was recognised that more knowledge of what was needed was required before any definite proposals could be made[73]. In January of the following year a resolution was passed calling the attention of the Council of the Institute of Almoners to this matter[74]. The Institute responded to this request. Psychiatrists whom they consulted considered a course of elementary psychology desirable, but some difficulty was anticipated in finding suitable teachers. For that reason, it was not considered feasible to include psychology in the general course for the time being[75]. Ambitious plans for a three-month course of training in psychology for trained almoners were whittled down, in the actual event, to two lectures on psychology. The matter, however, was still under active consideration. At the end of 1925 Miss Cummins of the Institute of Almoners attended a meeting organised by the Central Association for Mental Welfare to consider the advisability of some organised means of training social workers in mental welfare; as a result a committee was formed to explore the whole question. The Institute thereupon addressed themselves to their own plans with renewed energy and a special meeting was held to discuss the provision of training for almoners in neurological and psychiatric work, to which were invited Dr.Crichton-Miller of the Tavistock Clinic, Miss Doris Robinson, social worker at the Clinic, Dr. Mapother of the Maudsley Hospital, who was already engaged in providing training for voluntary workers with the CAMW, and Dr. Shrubsall of the LCC, who was familiar with the American Child Guidance movement.

The Institute was firmly of the view that any specialised psychiatric training should follow a general training in hospital social work (and therefore must have viewed CAMW's vigorous planning with great misgivings) but they were perplexed as to what precisely this specialised training should be. The idea of a three-month postgraduate course had been mooted but the psychiatric advisers agreed that, while useful, such a short course could not be considered adequate; Dr. Mapother considered that the ultimate aim should be a postgraduate course leading to a diploma. As a result of this meeting, the decision was taken, firstly, that some further teaching in normal psychology should be included for all almoner students, and, secondly, that the Institute itself should provide specialised training in mental and psychological work. Meantime, however, Mrs. Strachey's negotiations with the Commonwealth Fund regarding the establishment of a Child Guidance Clinic were already under way, and the Institute agreed to join with the CAMW and other societies in approaching London University with a view to the provision of a special course of psychological and psychiatric training for social work. These other plans, together with difficulty in reaching decisions as to the most helpful course of study in the face of a multiplicity of schools of psychological thought, made the Institute's own plans for a postgraduate course redundant and they were abandoned. Dr. Mapother's antagonism to the Tavistock Clinic has been referred to by Dicks[76], and it is not surprising that an expert advisory group containing both Dr. Mapother and Dr. Crichton-Miller, with their wholly incompatible approaches, should have intensified rather than dispelled the Institute's confusion[77].

By 1928 the University of London's plans had crystallised, and were to comprise both the inclusion of courses in psychology and psychiatry in the normal two-year certificate course, and the institution of a new advanced course of a year's duration for social workers wishing to specialise in mental welfare. The Institute of Almoners did, however, go ahead with its own plans for incorporating a psychiatric 'option' in the general course, and selected students were able to undertake a three-month period of practical work at the Maudsley Hospital under Dr. Mapother's direction, in place of a part of the normal hospital placement. In 1928 the Child Guidance Council had proposed a scheme of child guidance training, and a meeting was held to discuss the use of both this and the Maudsley scheme. Bernard Hart, who was adviser on the psychiatric training of almoners, was anxious that the opportunity of some training in child guidance should not be lost, and suggested that both schemes should be combined for the same group of students, since 'he felt that the training at the Maudsley was exceedingly valuable for almoner students... At the same time he felt that the Child Guidance Council stood for a new aspect of social work; and that it would be good thing for students to get even an inkling of the work and to see something of its point of view'[78]. In fact, no students wished to take advantage of the combined schemes, though some were selected for the Maudsley option. Almoners interested in specialising in psychiatric work were to be encouraged to take the Mental Health Course, and Miss Roxburgh and Miss Streitfield were among its first intake; in 1928 Kathleen Butler had been among the first group to train at the New York School of Social Work. By 1930 seven almoners altogether had trained in psychiatric social work. The Institute considered that

> while it would be a mistake to lay too much emphasis during the period of training on psychiatric work, it feels that an insight into its methods and point of view must be of value to all almoners in their everyday dealings with patients and others.[79]

The London School of Economics did not however adopt the Institute's view that a general almoner's training should precede a psychiatric specialisation, and the Mental Health Course led to the establishment of a separate Association of Psychiatric Social Workers (as had happened in the United States) and to a virtual separation of medical social work from that in psychiatric clinics and hospitals. This was despite the view of many psychiatrists that a knowledge of the mechanisms of human behaviour was essential to social work practice in any field[80].

Except for those few who took the specialised training (few of whom returned to medical social work) the promising discussions of the mid-1920's had very little outcome for the almoners themselves. As Miss Snelling has observed: 'The spirit had really gone out of the psychiatric movement for the almoners as a whole, who felt that it had passed them by, and by 1934 they were indifferent about openings for the students'[81]. Thus the developments in casework which might have resulted from increasing psychological understanding did not come about, and almoning training itself remained virtually unaffected until after the Second World War.

At about the same time, strong pressure was growing for the establishment of better facilities for the treatment of neurotic and delinquent children. In 1925 Mrs. St. Loe Strachey, wife of the Editor of the *New Statesman* and an experienced magistrate, visited the United States, and was impressed with the child guidance work she saw there[82]. She interested the Commonwealth Fund in the possibility of supporting similar ventures in Britain, and on her return contacted a number of bodies likely to be interested in such a venture. A preliminary meeting took place at her home on 24th March 1926, at which representatives of the Central Association for Mental Welfare, the Howard League, the National Council for Mental Hygiene, and the Magistrates Association were present[83]. An ad hoc committee was formed which invited the Commonwealth Fund to send an investigator to England in order to see whether it would be feasible to establish a child guidance clinic in this country. In June 1926, Mildred Scoville, the Fund's Executive Assistant, spent two weeks in this country, undertaking a programme of visits and discussions arranged by Evelyn Fox. Following this, a scheme was drawn up for the establishment of a demonstration clinic for training, service and research; this was intended to provide not only for delinquents but the dull, backward and neurotic child. A representative committee (the Child Guidance Council) which included the four original Associations, the Institute of Almoners, the COS and a number of doctors, psychologists and magistrates was formed early in 1927, with Evelyn Fox as Honorary Secretary until such time as a full-time appointment could be made[84].

This was not the first clinic of its kind. By the late 1920's, several hospitals were making provisions for the maladjusted or mentally disordered child, notably Guy's, University College, Great Ormond Street and the Maudsley. In Scotland, a clinic for mentally defective children had opened at the Royal Hospital for Sick Children in Edinburgh in 1904, and many of these children also presented conduct or behaviour problems. In 1925 James Drever had opened a clinic in Edinburgh for any child showing problems of educational or mental retardation, and a similar clinic was started in Glasgow in 1926. This had strong connections with schools, and in many cases children were referred for difficulties in school performance. In Scotland, child guidance remained within the orbit of the educational system, and such problems were defined as educational rather than medical — a difference from the English system. Two other important developments in London were the opening of the Tavistock Clinic's Children's Department in 1926 under Dr. W.A. Potts, and the start of a clinic explicitly modelled on the American pattern — the Jewish Health Organisation's Clinic at the Jews Free School in Stepney, under the direction of Dr. Noel Burke and Dr. Emanuel Miller. This was the first clinic to be patterned on American work, and a very full account of its philosophy, organisation and work is available[85].

The Commonwealth Fund's support of the Child Guidance Council was generous and virtually total. Some voluntary support was received, but no financial aid came from authority sources until 1935. Initially, the Fund undertook to support the Council until the autumn of 1928, though in fact its support was continued, on a decreasing basis, until 1944. It also sponsored three-month visits for ten selected people from different fields to the United States to enable them to gain some first-hand experience of the clinics and their operation. Amongst those who visited the United States in the autumn of 1927 under the Fund's auspices were Evelyn Fox, Dr. Letitia Fairfield, Divisional Medical Officer of the LCC, Miss T.M. Morton, Principal Organiser of Children's Care Work to the LCC, and Dr. Ralph Crowley, Senior Medical Officer of the Board of Education. Dr. F.C. Shrubsall, of the LCC's Health Department, had already been to America in the summer of 1926, through introductions arranged by Miss Scoville, and had written an account of his impressions, particularly of the clinic in Philadelphia[86].

On the training side also the Fund made a generous offer. It undertook to meet the expenses of five social workers to undertake a year's training at the New York School of Social Work in 1927, and again in 1928, and the first were Noel Hunnybun, then an assistant children's care organiser with the LCC, Catherine Craggs of the Central Association for Mental Welfare, Doris Robinson, social worker at the Tavistock Clinic, Kathleen Butler and Elizabeth Horder.

With the cautious approval of the LCC and the Board of Education, the Child Guidance Council went ahead with its plans for a new clinic, and this was opened in Canonbury Place in 1929. In the same year, a one-year mental health course was established at the London School of Economics and Political Science to provide training in psychiatric social work with adults and children.

The child guidance movement provided a new conception of social work practice based upon clinical models, and opened up fresh directions of professional development which were free from the charitable associations social work had never been able to escape. The expertise on which the social worker's claim to professionalism might be based was now psychiatry. Whereas social work in the older tradition was founded on a knowledge of charitable resources and social services (knowledge, potentially at least, available to every citizen), psychiatric social work had as its basis knowledge which was clearly specialist and exclusive. The overt justification for social work intervention was still a scientific one (as it had been for the COS) but derived from psychology and psychiatry rather than the social sciences; the scientific ideology therefore changed direction and was at the same time powerfully reinforced. In this new context the social worker's function was defined as one of treatment[87], and the treatment model is probably still the most dominant of all the professional models. To begin with (as the next chapter shows) the influence of psychoanalysis on child guidance was slight, but from the 1930's this became an increasingly significant feature of its professional ideology, and the child guidance movement was one of the major channels through which this influence in social work generally was mediated.

3
Psychoanalysis and Social Work in the Thirties

When the Mental Health Course began in 1929, it represented an important new direction in social work education. Sponsored by the Commonwealth Fund, the new one-year course was established at the London School of Economics and Political Science, and this mixed parentage no doubt shaped the orientation and professional 'culture' of the course. Certainly it contributed to a breadth of perspective, and to differences in emphasis from comparable American trainings. Although the child guidance movement was a major stimulus to its inception, the course was also designed to train workers for adult psychiatric work, and it was intended to prepare students for work both with psychiatrically ill and mentally subnormal patients and their families. Theoretical content was combined with fieldwork in both a child guidance clinic and a mental hospital (initially the Child Guidance Training Centre and the Maudsley Hospital) and the inclusion of both types of experience was a cherished feature of the course throughout its history, and a principle to which the Association of Psychiatric Social Workers always firmly adhered. Great emphasis was placed on the supervision the student received while undertaking this fieldwork, and to be appointed as a supervisor to the course (and to have one's name included in the Calendar of the School) was a mark of high professional esteem.

The content of the course and its changes over the years have been documented in detail by Timms[1]. The first course was strikingly eclectic in its theoretical content. As Miss Clement Brown, for many years Senior Tutor to the Course, later observed:

> The independent committee advising the School was evidently anxious to include the many able practitioners and lecturers who had eagerly supported the movement. Teachers of outstanding ability in psychiatry, psychology, child development, mental deficiency, were enthusiastically drawn in, with more concern for comprehensiveness than cohesion.[2]

In view of the myths that have grown up around it, it is of interest to examine the orientation of the course and its professional 'culture' in the early years. Despite Forder's comment that the course was based on an American pattern 'where social caseworkers had found in psychoanalysis not only a source of insight into human behaviour, but also a theory that seemed relevant to practice', there is nothing in the teaching to suggest a strong orientation towards psychoanalysis in the first decade — rather the reverse[3]. Initially the main course in which students were introduced to psychoanalytic theory was that of

Dr. Hadfield of the Tavistock Clinic who lectured on Mental Health in Early Childhood; though not himself an analyst, his knowledge of and sympathy with this approach is evident from his writings[4]. Later this course was joined with that on Mental Disorder in Childhood given by Dr. Moodie, who then taught the combined course under the title given above. This included references to the psychoanalytic account of the aetiology of the neuroses and to the theories of Freud, Adler and Jung, but the syllabus suggests that it was one among several theoretical approaches, rather than a dominant orientation. In fact Dr. Moodie was not an analyst and held considerable reservations about it, particularly as a form of treatment. One of the fears which early child guidance workers had to contend with among education committees and at the Ministry of Education was that they were 'psychoanalysing' their young patients. Such was public anxiety on this score that in order to win support psychoanalytic connections were played down within the child guidance movement, which was in any event, in the true tradition of British psychiatry, eclectic and somewhat atheoretical. Dr. Moodie was at some pains to make it clear that in child guidance 'the psychoanalytic method is never employed ...'[5].

For many years the main body of psychiatry teaching was undertaken by Dr. Aubrey Lewis, whose writings indicate an attitude towards psychoanalysis which may best be described as courteous but unconvinced[6]. Cyril Burt's main interest, as the syllabus indicates, was in individual differences, mental measurement and cognitive processes, and Dr. Tredgold (though psycho-analysis was not likely to enter into his teaching area of mental subnormality directly) was one of its harshest critics[7]. The attitudes of the tutors were also significant. Miss Clement Brown was Senior Tutor from 1930 to 1946, and was followed by Mrs. K. McDougall until the demise of the course when it merged with the Applied Social Studies course in 1970. Although both were interested in any aspects of psychology or psychiatry that might contribute usefully to psychiatric social work, neither was committed in a narrow or single-minded way to any particular school of psychological thought. It might indeed be doubted if the course could long have survived in the intellectually critical atmosphere of the London School of Economics if that had been the case.

Miss Clement Brown, who did much to establish the ethos of the course, was primarily interested in social psychology, and her interests were wide ranging. Her early background was a degree in philosophy and sociology, and she owed an intellectual debt to many of the outstanding scholars at the LSE during the 1930's — Hobhouse, Mannheim, Ginsberg, and especially R.H. Tawney. As her writings show, she was always concerned that social work training should not be conceived in any narrow or purely technical sense, but that the student should be educated to a broad interest in the social causation of problems and an alertness to the philosophical and ethical issues raised by social work practice. She has observed that the course was by no means as narrowly focussed as its title suggested, and that 'it was recognised from the outset... that these new departures were relevant to all personal social services. There was no desire to create a special expertise, protective of peculiar insight'[8]. The trend towards specialisation which took place later was not, she suggests, due to the influence of the Mental Health course but occurred 'when some psychiatric social workers became dissatisfied with the broadly based approach and the shortness of the training, and identified themselves more with psychoanalysis than with social treatment'[9].

The other major influences on mental health course students were the clinics and hospitals in which their fieldwork was undertaken. Child guidance, certainly in its early years, seems to have owed more to behavioural and environmental approaches than to psychoanalysis, and indeed to have been extremely pragmatic in its approach to childhood problems; the methods used, Dr. Moodie insisted, were 'comparatively simple', consisting of a combination of physical, psychiatric, psychological and social methods[10]. Psychiatric treatment 'merely takes the form of a frank discussion of actual conscious happenings and pointing out to the child where he might improve his outlook one way or another'[11]. The psychologist gave remedial teaching, and to the social worker 'falls the duty of discovering and arranging all necessary social activities, Scouts, Clubs and so on', and of discussing difficulties with the parents while conveying to them 'advice and instructions from the psychiatrist, which he himself could not afford the time to discuss'[12]. This was hardly a view of the social worker's function designed to encourage therapeutic ambitions! As far as the psychiatric treatment of the child himself was concerned, 'discussion, mainly on the lines of an ordinary commonsense conversation, is usually all that is required for a child worried by his own abnormal thoughts — but direct treatment of this kind is rare'[13]. In the great majority of cases, no such discussion was thought necessary or advisable. But by 1936 marked changes were becoming evident:

> Diagnosis is becoming more accurate and treatment more rapid. Emphasis has swung away from the manipulation of environmental factors to a more direct treatment of the child. Child guidance is, in short, becoming a more efficient therapeutic weapon as knowledge accumulates of the factors lying behind behaviour difficulties and the methods by which they can be alleviated.[14]

During the 1930's, several younger psychiatrists undertook analytic training, and among the Fellows at the London Child Guidance Clinic were several who were to become distinguished analysts — John Bowlby, William Paterson Brown, Michael Fordham. In the late 1930's, the psychoanalytic orientation that was to become characteristic of child guidance was thus beginning to take hold.

In the first decade of the Mental Health Course, then, students were introduced to psychoanalytic theories but only as one among many theoretical systems, and a psychoanalytic orientation was never characteristic of British psychiatric social work training, nor were its perspectives dominant in the way that they had become in the United States. The Mental Health Course itself was broadly conceived and eclectic with regard to its selection of theoretical perspectives. While psychoanalysis was not ignored it was, at least until the Second World War, a peripheral rather than a focal theoretical orientation. In the war years a much stronger psychoanalytic element was introduced. In 1941, Dr. Susan Isaacs took over the teaching on the Psychology of Childhood and Adolescence, and from 1946 Dr. W.H. Gillespie gave the course earlier undertaken by Dr. Moodie on Mental Health and Mental Disorder in Childhood and Adolescence; this was then given a more specifically psychoanalytic framework, and in the courses given by Dr. Isaacs and Dr. Gillespie respectively psychoanalytic theory was taught more systematically.

The mainstream of psychoanalytic influence undoubtedly came through the child guidance movement, which in the late 1930's was beginning to be influenced by the thinking and approach of younger psychiatrists trained as psychoanalysts. The strong influence of psychoanalysis on some psychiatric social workers has been attested by Miss Goldberg, then a psychiatric social worker in child guidance. Commenting on the social worker's failure to lead the way as the 'social science arm' of psychiatry, she observed:

> This is due to the fact that they were busy absorbing new discoveries about personality and techniques of treatment made in psychiatry, and especially in psychoanalysis. This new knowledge deepened the social workers' understanding of human behaviour and relationships, and helped to improve diagnostic and therapeutic skills. However, it led to a temporary neglect of an important former source of knowledge, the social sciences.[15]

The more extreme psychoanalytic viewpoint referred to by Miss Goldberg was not typical of social work or even of psychiatric social work, and represented the orientation of an elite and articulate group of workers who had found in psychoanalytic theory (and often in personal analysis[16]) both a new understanding and a new direction of commitment. The APSW always contained within it widely differing views, and even in the 1950's, the heyday of clinical specialisation, there were many (among them Miss Clement Brown, Miss Waldron and Miss Goldberg) who were alert to the dangers of a loss of social focus, and were concerned to integrate social approaches and perspectives into psychiatric social work.

Psychoanalysis, as we know from other sources, scarcely ventured into the psychiatric hospitals at all before 1939. Within British psychiatry as a whole, empirically founded physical methods predominated and it is likely that the psychoanalytic viewpoint was given little serious consideration. The psychoanalytic approach has been more directly related to problems of neurosis and the kind of behaviour disorders encountered in the child guidance clinic than to those chronic and severe problems confronted in the mental hospitals, and it is unlikely that many psychiatric social workers working in this field had much contact with analytically oriented psychiatrists either during their training or in their subsequent professional careers. This would especially be true outside London, where even now trained analysts are a rarity.

It is likely then that the influence of psychoanalysis on psychiatric social work generally in the 1930's has been grossly exaggerated, though the strength of its influence on individual workers is evident from Miss Goldberg's observations. The major impact of psychoanalysis on social work belongs rather to the period following the Second World War, when the psychoanalytic movement gained immeasurably in strength and momentum, and analysts themselves actively engaged in social questions and in research with important implications for social work.

If the influence of psychoanalysis was limited even in the field of psychiatric social work, in other areas of social work it was virtually nonexistent. Those trained on the Mental Health course were small in number and worked mainly in clinics and mental hospitals. As Miss Clement Brown pointed out, the content of the Mental Health course was considered relevant to social work in any field, 'and it was expected... that the new training would fertilise personal social services as a whole. Each year students came from and entered a variety of fields'[17]. But before the Second World War these numbers were small. In 1936, out of 86 members of the APSW employed in Britain, 55 were working in clinics or mental hospitals, 4 in teaching or organising work, and the remaining 27 in other forms of social work[18]. In 1937, this last group numbered 24. In 1941, when membership stood at 219, 135 members were in some form of psychiatric or mental health work, 18 engaged in work 'of national importance', and only 18 in 'general social work'.

A review of the literature of family casework and almoning reveals few traces of psychoanalytic influence before the Second World War, perhaps because psychiatric social workers (who might have been a channel of such influence) themselves were in the 1930's 'a struggling pioneer group'[19] uncertain of their professional status and prospects, dogged by wretched salaries, and only slowly winning the confidence of a sceptical medical profession. On the whole it would seem that those trained as psychiatric social workers exercised only a limited influence on the broader field of social work. Interaction and communication between the different fields was encouraged in local groups such as those set up by the British Federation of Social Workers, but until the advent of *Social Work* in 1939 there was no commonly read professional journal which might have assisted in spreading innovations and ideas. Social workers in the various fields retained a sense of identification with their respective branches and worked in relative ignorance of each other's function and approach. In Britain, therefore, psychiatric social workers did not attain to that professional dominance and leadership which can be discerned in the United States until after the Second World War, when they became much in demand as tutors, fieldwork teachers and consultants — a development that indicates an increased recognition on the part of other social workers that psychiatric social workers had something to offer them, and a heightened receptivity to a psychiatric approach.

It is true that the *Charity Organization Quarterly* had a number of references to psychoanalysis, and American social work books such as those of Jessie Taft were regularly reviewed. In particular, a lengthy article was concerned with the relevance of Jung for COS practice[20]. It is difficult to avoid the impression, however, that Jung's work held particular attraction because of the support his concept of individuation appeared to give to COS individualist political theories — a misuse to which Jung himself, surprisingly, does not appear to have taken exception — rather than for its psychological insights[21]. During the decade 1930—1940, there were only four articles that dealt with the application of psychodynamic psychology to casework practice[22]. In so far as the concerns of the *Quarterly* indicate the interests of social workers, therefore, it is quite clear that psychoanalysis was not among the most central of them.

In the 1930's, the attitudes of other social workers towards the psychiatrically trained were curiously mixed, and this also tended to maintain the barrier and sense of distance already created by their special training. Miss Hunnybun has vividly recalled the antagonisms which the early psychiatric social workers encountered on their return from New York[23], and the reasons for this were probably emotional rather than rational, compounded both of envy and hostility; the superior skill of the psychiatric social worker no doubt had basis in fact, but was greatly exaggerated by fantasy. This seems to have lead to a tendency to discount and denigrate what mental health training had to offer that was new, and to rest content with the methods and practices of the past. J.C. Pringle, General Secretary of the COS, for example, saw most of the major American developments as simply recalling what the pioneers of family casework in the COS of the later 19th century had already discovered[24].

In retrospect it seems that whatever the intentions of the founders of the Mental Health Course, while it did a great deal to raise the standards of training and skill of social workers in the psychiatric field, it did little to improve the quality of work generally and indeed created a barrier between psychiatric and other social workers. A great deal of the knowledge imparted on that course (whatever the hopes and intentions of the tutors) thus became identified as 'psychiatric', and its relevance to the problems encountered by the family caseworker or probation officer — or for that matter the settlement worker or youth leader, who equally dealt with human problems — was little appreciated. The Commonwealth Fund had, it is true, set out with the limited though important objective of demonstrating the results that could be obtained by highly qualified and well trained social workers, and in that it achieved results, as the warm endorsement of the Feversham Committee showed; but it failed to affect the broader development of social work in Britain in any significant way. Despite the development of clinical interests and therapeutic skills among some psychiatric social workers, social work retained its traditional association with poverty and material relief, and the role model of the worker was that of a coordinator and dispenser of resources. Family casework, wrote one author,

> seeks to assemble for the benefit of the family which has fallen on evil days
> the particular forms of help required — the outfit for the father who has

59

providentially found work, blankets, coals or boots which are lacking after a long spell of unemployment, spectacles to enable the grandfather to read his paper, convalescent change or rest for the mother, and a home help to take care of the children in her absence.[25]

Apart from the trail blazed by psychiatric social workers, it is difficult to point to any fresh departures or significant developments in social work in Britain up to the Second World War. A great deal of social work activity there had always been, but as a professional occupation it was weak and undeveloped. When the British Federation of Social Workers was formed in 1935 (marking a new phase in social work professionalisation) it was pointed out that in a great part of the country the trained social worker was 'not used, not known, not acceptable'[26]. The first five decades produced little development of either practice or theory and hardly any literature. As Miss Younghusband summed it up: 'Our School of Sociology died. We produced no Mary Richmond, no Charlotte Towle, no standard books, and practically no general literature on social work'[27]. Whether this is to be seen as a period of stagnation (as Miss Younghusband viewed it) or as a period of latency (as Miss Clement Brown prefers) the most noticeable feature of the first half of the 20th century is the withering of the promise of the later 19th , as far as the development of social work as a profession was concerned.

3.1 Psychoanalysis and American Social Work

In North America, by contrast, social work built strongly on the 19th century British foundations. Charity organisation was enthusiastically taken up, and Schools of Social Work established training for social work on a clear professional footing. A number of strong professional specialisms were emerging: The Family Service Association of America (1911), the American Association of Medical Social Workers (1918), the National Association of School Social Workers (1919), the Child Welfare League of America (1920), the American Association of Social Workers (1921) and the American Association of Psychiatric Social Workers (1926). All this was evidence of a vigorous growth which contrasts markedly with the small and struggling groups in Britain. There was also a counter-trend towards the definition of a common identity based on a common skill, that of casework. The issue of generic versus specific casework was faced in the Milford Conference of 1919 and resolved in favour of the generic view. It was asserted that 'the problems of social casework and the equipment of the social caseworker are fundamentally the same for all fields... generic social casework is the common field to which the specific forms of social casework are merely incidental'[28].

In 1917 Mary Richmond's *Social Diagnosis* provided the first major conceptual account of the social work process and remains a classic work; this was only the first of a rich professional literature in the 1920's and 1930's from which it is possible to chart the development of social work theory in the United

States with some certainty. *Social Diagnosis* is of importance in the present context from a number of points of view. First of all as the first theoretical account of casework it was a basic textbook for British as well as American social workers and therefore had wide influence in this country. Second, although Mary Richmond conceived of the client as essentially a part of his social environment and was predominantly concerned with environmental issues, she also stressed the need for greater psychological understanding and less economic and material bias in the approach adopted by the social worker. Mary Richmond herself, though she was acquainted with Jung's work and was a close associate of Adolf Meyer, the psychiatrist, made no use of specifically Freudian or psychodynamic concepts, and, for this reason, her work tends to be dismissed by more psychodynamically trained social workers as 'static', so that its significance in pointing towards a more psychological perspective has not always been fully appreciated.

Third, and of lasting significance, Mary Richmond conceived of the social worker's activity as being essentially scientific, consisting in the objective evaluation of data in order to reach a diagnosis, and ultimately a cure. The conceptual model she used, which still dominates casework perspectives in both Britain and the United States, is the medical model[29]. The social worker's activity is regarded as analogous in the social field to that of the physician in the medical; it consists of acquiring as much relevant data as will make clear the extent and causes of the problem in order that a diagnosis can be made and subsequently a rational treatment plan. This cycle of study, diagnosis and treatment is still the most usual way of conceptualising about the social worker's approach to a problem[30]. What is of even greater significance than this way of looking at the social worker's activity is the particular kind of perspective on the problem to which the model tends to lead. Implicit in it is the idea of the defective or diseased organism, to which some sort of therapeutic intervention can be applied.

In retrospect (wrote Carel Germain) it is easy to see that one of the unplanned outcomes of adopting the medical model to implement the scientific commitment was to direct attention to presumed individual defect, thus obscuring institutional or social inadequacies. The model tended, in use, to obliterate awareness and concern with social systems and social processes. Contrary to Mary Richmond's own involvement with environmental issues, yet inherent in the model, was a focus on individual processes which all but ignored the social context in which they are embedded. Although social casework, in the thirties and beyond, did attempt to overcome a one-sided approach by conceiving the unit of attention to be the person-situation, the model itself implied that the problem or need exists within the individual, who must be understood, treated, and, it is hoped, cured. Thus, try as we might, an inherent bias in the model kept us — over the long run and with exceptions — more concerned with the person than the situation.[31]

This model received powerful reinforcement from the strong development of psychiatric social work whose practitioners, working closely alongside medical personnel and influenced by medical ways of thought, found a clinical stance a natural one to adopt. It received further confirmation through the rapid assimilation of psychoanalytic ideas by American social workers in the 1920's and 1930's.

3.2 The Impact of Psychiatry on American Social Work

Psychiatry and the blossoming mental hygiene movement appear to have made a formidable impact on American social workers after the First World War. In 1918 the first training for psychiatric social workers was instituted at Smith College with the aid of Dr. E.E. Southard and the Psychopathic Department of Boston State Hospital. The aim, initially, was the modest one of training suitable women to assist the psychiatrist in getting case histories and in the social readjustment of psychiatric cases. 'It was clearly understood from the beginning', it was stated, 'that we were not to make psychiatrists and that we were not making half-doctors. These women were to be aides to experts. The first lesson that was taught all the members of the school was professional modesty'[32]. The understanding that psychiatry could give to the social worker in nonpsychiatric settings was stressed by Mary Jarrett; it was equally important to the charity organisation worker as it was to the psychiatric social worker, she held, and could illuminate all those 'irregularities and contradictions' of personality which made social work such a baffling and frustrating occupation; not only this, but mental hygiene principles could lead to the promotion of normal healthy development. Mary Jarrett therefore looked for the inclusion of psychiatric teaching in all professional social work education[33].

The National Conference of Social Work in 1919 reflected in a symposium the eager interest in what psychiatry had to offer:

> Atlantic City in 1919 was a landslide for mental hygiene; the Conference was swept off its feet. In every section, psychiatrists appeared on the program. The psychiatric social worker was present in person for the first time and violent indeed was the discussion which raged about her devoted head — what should be her training, what her personality, and what the limitations of her province? Should she remain forever different from other caseworkers or should every other caseworker be reborn in her likeness: that was the meeting which burst its bounds and had to be transferred to a church a block away. Dignified psychiatrists and social workers climbed out of windows in order to make sure of a good seat.[34]

The conference touched on two major issues. The first was the question of whether psychiatric social work was a specialty, or whether psychiatric knowledge was essential for all social workers in whatever setting. The second was the role of the psychiatric social worker, already chafing at the bit implied in the initial definition of her role as a psychiatric aide.

Jessie Taft, later a distinguished social work teacher, saw emerging nothing less than a wholly new concept of casework which had profound implications for all social work:

My conception of the new casework, which perhaps has always been the unconscious method of the born caseworker, but which owes its coming to consciousness largely to mental hygiene and psychiatry, is that of a social technique such as may be secured in any good training school combined with an understanding of human psychology which enables the social worker to deal with the personality of the patient in his social setting as intelligently and constructively as the psychiatrist deals with it in the hospital.[35]

This was not merely a new way of conceptualising an old function; it involved a new sphere of activity for the social worker. The psychiatric social worker, in particular, rejected the role of psychiatric auxiliary, and she now laid claim, on the basis of her psychological and social training, to a function different from but in no way inferior to that of the psychiatrist. For such a claim adequate psychological training was essential. This implied a first-hand working psychology, for in the last analysis the social worker is one who 'even as the psychiatrist, accepts responsibility for adjusting the mental and social life of other human beings'[36].

Although the thinking of psychiatrically trained workers such as Jessie Taft was no doubt remote from the body of actual social work practice at the time, the proceedings of the Atlantic City Conference clearly showed the hunger for new understanding and new ways of working which led to the collaboration with psychiatry. During the 1920's, psychiatric knowledge was being indiscriminately sought from any likely source; by 1930, however, this interest had become more specific, and the theoretical basis of the psychological knowledge needed by social workers was asserted by leading educationalists to be psychoanalytic. Also clearly underlined was the therapeutic role of the social worker. Virginia Robinson, author of a classic text, was in no doubt that if the caseworker's growing interest in psychology had led in the 1920's to an absorption with history-taking, the next phase was to be 'the worker's growing acceptance of responsibility for the treatment relationship between himself and the client in the dynamic new experience in which therapeutic change may take place'[37]. An important factor in developing skill in the use of relationship was not technique or method, but the worker's own understanding of himself and his attitude towards his client: 'It becomes increasingly clear that, in acceptance of himself and of the other, a development of self-consciousness in relationships, a constant process of analysis of himself and of the other in interaction, beyond what is required for the contacts of successful everyday living, is demanded of the worker, if this emphasis on relationships is to be safe and therapeutic'[38].

From Otto Rank, Virginia Robinson took the fundamental belief that psychological illness derives from inadequate relationships. The Rankian emphasis was on the therapeutic potential inherent in the analytic relationship itself rather than on this relationship as instrumental to the achievement of insight and self-understanding. Rankian therapy is therefore a 'relationship' rather than an 'insight' therapy, and the essence of social work, likewise, was to provide a warm and accepting human relationship, within the functional limitations of the role. Thus in the new articulation of the essence of the professional social work task, the theoretical disciplines to which it was most closely allied were psychology and psychiatry; in Britain, by contrast, social work was closer to the social sciences. Virginia Robinson's book marked the beginning of a new epoch; its therapeutic orientation is evident, yet it represents a reaction against the psychoanalytic caseworker, modelling himself on the techniques of the analyst, and decrying the specific disciplines of casework. A new conception of casework as having a function and a dignity of its own, limited and defined by the functions of the agency in which it is practised, was emerging in the work of both Robinson and Taft.

There were great differences between the functional (Rankian) school associated with Jessie Taft and Virginia Robinson at Pennsylvania, and the diagnostic (Freudian) school of Columbia, represented most notably by Gordon Hamilton, Annette Garrett, Florence Hollis and Lucille Austin. The former, as we have seen, stressed the casework relationship as a matrix for growth, within the limits of agency function; the diagnostic school was deeply influenced by psychoanalytic theory and particularly the psychology of the ego which was the focus of Anna Freud's *The Ego and the Mechanisms of Defence* (1936). The shift from id to ego psychology (with its focus on the relationship of the individual to the external world, and with his ways of coping with the demand of his inner instinctual drives on the one hand, and of the social world in which he moved on the other) brought back a more social focus, and was also much more easily adapted for use by caseworkers, whose work problems typically lay in the individual's interaction with his environment.

> The focus on the ego (commented Austin) was more readily useful to casework in its efforts to influence adaptive capacities than was the early emphasis on the 'unconscious'. This new theory also made for shifts in psychoanalytic techniques, placing greater weight on current reality adaptations as well as the analysis of childhood neuroses. Hence the two professions, casework and psychoanalysis, drew closer together in their common aims. Each profession reached its present formulation of methods of psychotherapy within the disciplines of its own practice but with extensions, by both, in areas of responsibility and treatment skills. The meeting ground, psychotherapy, is a more partial therapy than psychoanalysis and a more comprehensive therapy than our former 'intensive' casework.[39]

The heavy reliance of diagnostic casework on psychoanalytic theory, which even in its ego-psychological form remains a theory of personality rather than a dynamic theory of interaction between person and environment, ensured that the personal therapeutic orientation remained dominant, and there remained as characteristic of the diagnostic school an emphasis on psychoanalysis as the only fully effective method of altering personality structure; those methods that lay somewhere on the continuum between insight and supportive treatment (such as casework and psychoanalytically oriented therapy) were by implication less effective and less radical. Insight was a primary goal.

The functionalists, by contrast, laid greater stress on the growth potential inherent in the helping relationship, and were concerned to translate psychoanalytic theory into the special idiom of social work. They therefore emphasised the different and limited function of social work, and preferred to conceive of it as a helping rather than a treatment process. The functionalist/diagnostic controversy has not been of any great importance to British caseworkers and need only be touched on here; although J.C. Pringle, Secretary of the COS and Editor of the *Quarterly*, favoured the approach of Jessie Taft, on the whole the diagnostic approach appears to have been better known, by way of textbooks such as that of Florence Hollis, and through the personal influence of Charlotte Towle in the 1950's. This influence has brought with it an emphasis on the treatment interview, and on the development of insight as a major strategy of intervention.

By 1930, therefore, the reform orientation and the environmental focus of American social work had given way to a preoccupation with psychological problems, though Kadushin observes that 'the social component was not absent; it was merely muted'[40]. In addressing the Second International Conference on Social Work in Paris in 1932, Gordon Hamilton remarked on the more conscious use now being made of the worker-client relationship as a treatment procedure in itself, not merely as a means to other treatment:

> In this form of treatment, adapted at least in part from psychoanalytic method, the client attempts to reorganise himself against the 'screen' of the caseworker's personality. Didactic interpretation and directive elements are sparingly used and the client's will to organise himself must be present. Miss Robinson has expressed this idea quite clearly in a recent book and our whole technique of interviewing has been modified by recent contributions from psychiatry. The method here is one of therapy rather than education, of insights rather than new experience, an emphasis upon what the client has to offer, rather than upon what we have to offer. This direct, face-to-face therapy is indeed very old, but it is receiving special psychological emphasis.[41]

That social workers were not (and could not be) indifferent to the environmental distress of the early 1930's is amply evident from the discussion on the effects of unemployment. America was then in the fourth winter of its distress. 'Will industry' cried Joanna Colcord, 'ever be brought to assume proper responsibility for its own diasters, or must social work, public and private, be forced indefinitely to go on with the hopeless task of trying to mend at retail the lives which an outworn industrial system breaks at wholesale?'[42].

Nevertheless, social work was in a dilemma — a dilemma fundamentally derived from the individualist ethos of psychoanalytic psychology:

> Casework today (Gordon Hamilton admitted) is in some confusion whether to look outwards to broad avenues of social reform for help or inwards to an increase in man's powers of self-knowledge and self-direction. The best caseworker does both. The caseworker who is truly successful realises how little he does of himself, how much he must ally himself with forces that lie within the personality of his client and within society.[43]

Although the eagerness with which social work espoused psychoanalytic ways of thought is beyond dispute, it is evident that the 'psychiatric deluge' (as Woodroofe has described it) was by no means as total or as undiscriminating as it has been depicted, and that many social workers were keenly aware of the faults in the structure of industrial society whose repercussions they had to do what they could to mitigate. For this reason, the term 'deluge' with its implications of total immersion is quite misleading and the whole question of the precise extent and nature of the influence of psychoanalysis on American social work has recently been examined afresh[44]. It is, however, beyond dispute that the adoption of a medical model of casework intervention with its tendency to focus attention on treatment processes in relation to the individual made a social or a reform perspective more difficult to maintain; it is also beyond argument that a great deal of the *theory* development in social casework in the 1930's and 1940's (whatever may have been true of practice) was concerned with treatment techniques rather than these broader issues, involving a certain diminution of social perspective. We may therefore accept Meyer's authoritative observation that 'the development of casework method has drawn heavily on psychoanalytic theory and dynamic psychology; and their perspectives invade (this) training ...'[45].

The work of Freud opened up entirely new vistas for the whole field of psychiatry; above all, it was a shift away from the conception of man as a rational, conscious, purposeful being, and shed new light on areas of experience that had hitherto been little understood, if indeed considered worthy of study. The need for understanding of 'character' had been evident to social workers from the first, but until around the time of the First World War little had been available that would help in the problems they daily encountered. Neither the 19th century concern with metaphysics nor the newer experimental psychology had much that could help in the understanding of man.

Freud's work, although initially concerned with the psychopathology of hysteria, had soon become extended to psychological processes at work in everyday behaviour, a highly significant shift represented by *The Psychopathology of Everyday Life* and *The Interpretation of Dreams*. This brought it out of the consulting room and into the street; henceforth, psychoanalysis became part of the heritage of the ordinary man. What these works emphasised was the *purposiveness* of behaviour, viewed from the psychoanalyst's standpoint. Mistakes, parapraxes, slips of the tongue — all could be understood if their unconscious determinants were made clear. It is in its illumination of the unconscious factors in behaviour, and the new light it cast on that side of man's behaviour which is hidden even from himself, that the psychoanalyst's greatest contribution lay.

Thus psychoanalysis made some sense of those irrational, unpredictable aspects of behaviour which had constantly puzzled caseworkers and frustrated their well-meaning efforts.

> The concept of man as a rational being dominated the caseworker's early thinking on the (casework) relationship; therefore intellect was expected not only to govern thinking and doing, but also to fashion it. The caseworker accordingly relied heavily on imparting information and on appealing to reason in effecting change in behaviour. Psychological insight, however, brought a focus on the irrational self. It gave prominence to the point of view that feelings fashion thinking and prompt action. Therefore rational behaviour was contingent on a change in feeling.[46]

But psychoanalysis not only offered a new understanding of behaviour and a new perspective on man; it also suggested methods of working that might prove more effective in dealing with problems where the social worker all too often had to admit failure. At that stage of its development, psychoanalysis, with its new slant on deviant and criminal behaviour as well as neurotic illness, had achieved some significant successes in treatment. Its potentialities seemed boundless, and its limitations as a treatment method were as yet unexplored. The therapeutic fervour of its practitioners sometimes led to extravagant claims which the cold light of scientific assessment tended in later years to modify. And by 1940 this was reflected in social work, which was already looking along other avenues, and there was evidence of a renewed interest in social aspects and a lessening of concern with the intrapsychic.

3.3   Social Work in Britain and America: Contrasts

During the first half of the century, social work in Britain and America had thus taken very different courses. In the United States, the role of the social worker (certainly as reflected in Kasius' selection of articles of the 1940's) was perceived in predominantly clinical and therapeutic terms, and by far the most important body of theoretical knowledge taught was that of psychoanalysis. In Britain, social work was still environment rather than personality focussed and psychoanalysis, far from being a major theoretical component in social work education, had made little impact. These differences were strikingly brought out by Donnison in comparing social work training at the University of Manchester and Toronto in 1955[47]. Among the more important reasons for the varying degrees of assimilation of psychoanalytic theories were differences in the extent of social work professionalisation, in the status of psychoanalysis in the two countries, and, most important, in the social and cultural context within which social work was practised.

The relation of theoretical development in social work to its professional advance will be considered in later chapters; it is sufficient to observe at this point that the need to provide acceptable theoretical foundations for social work practice capable of supporting its professional aspirations provided a partial explanation of the new interest in psychoanalytic theory, and in both countries its assimilation has been associated with professionalisation. In North America strong professional associations were being formed after the First World War, and specifically vocational training for social work was being undertaken in a number of schools of social work, notably the New York School of Social Work, Smith College, and the University of Pennsylvania. For these schools, there was pressure to refine and develop a coherent body of theory on which training could be based — a pressure which had become more urgent since Flexner's address to the National Conference on Social Work in 1917, which called into question social work's professional claim, pointing out that it lacked the basic requirement of a specific skill applied to a specific function.

...Professions need to be limited and definite in scope (he said) in order that practitioners may themselves act; but the high degree of specialised competency required for action and conditional on limitation of area cannot possibly go with the width of scope characteristic of social work. A certain superficiality of attainment, a certain lack of practical ability, necessarily characterise such breadth of endeavour.

In Flexner's view, the social worker was to be seen not as a professional agent 'so much as the mediator invoking this or that professional agency... as controlling the keyboard that summons, cooperates with and coordinates various professional specialists'[48]. This, it has been argued, was taken seriously and quite uncritically:

The effect of Flexner's paper was profound and far-reaching. The challenge was accepted at its face value, and has set social workers to refining and perfecting their methods with a single-mindedness of purpose that has all but blinded them to the fact that method is only one test. Philosophy — what it is all about; why it is undertaken; what are its ultimate goals, and its relationships to other activities — is as essential to a profession as a method.[49]

This need of a theory coincided with the rise of a psychology which seemed to provide precisely what was lacking — a scientific basis for understanding and for effectively treating the problems with which the social worker was confronted. By some authors, the enthusiasm with which Freud was accepted is to be understood almost wholly in terms of its search for a professional basis, for, as Kadushin has argued,

the emphasis on a treatment methodology as against a reform orientation

68

made professionalisation possible. We lacked then, and lack today, any adequate scientific base that would make possible a social action approach. Psychoanalytic psychology, in offering a scientific base for the professionalisation of methods of helping, encouraged the possibility of professionalisation, which in turn strengthened this orientation.[50]

In Britain, professional development had been weak up to the Second World War but accelerated rapidly thereafter; it was not however until the mid-1950's that psychoanalytic psychology came to be a major component in professional training.

At that time, not only were other theories of personality lacking which might have offered an alternative basis, but psychoanalysis was already beginning to enjoy high prestige within American society. This is still the case; Sargent[51] has claimed that it is difficult to obtain any high academic or teaching post in psychiatry in the United States without having undergone a didactic analysis — a situation which he claims prevails in no other country in the world, except Israel. The status conferred by its close association with psychoanalysts was therefore a further consequence of the adoption of a psychoanalytic perspective in American social work, whereas in Britain psychoanalysts tended to occupy a more peripheral position within psychiatry.

Most important of all, the social and political climate was very different in the two countries in the inter-war years. American society, following the reformist trend of the pre-1914 period, had entered a phase in which the dominant political climate was one of conservatism. Success and achievement were highly valued, while failure was a mark of personal inadequacy. In this individualist ethos, and when the problems of the social order were given less prominence, psychoanalytic ideas with their emphasis on the individual easily took root. The Levines have commented that this emphasis is clearly to be seen in the thinking behind the Commonwealth Fund's delinquency programme in the 1920's[52]. The problem of helping children, they maintain, 'was approached with a limited appreciation of the broader social forces which had brought the problem of delinquency to the forefront of concern earlier', and this individual emphasis was manifest in the almost purely clinical focus of child guidance in the 1930's and 1940's. In consequence, the child guidance clinic became oriented entirely toward intramural, intrapsychic therapies, and away from the broader goals of social reform, or even institutional change — an orientation which, in the Levines' view, necessitates now a radical reorientation towards closer engagement with the community, and to a change in the role model of the mental health professional from that of physician and healer to that of educator, reformer and social planner.

There may also have been a wish to escape some of the broader social problems during the 1920's; social reform seemed potentially dangerous, with the spectre of communism hovering darkly on its fringe. At the same time, society itself was unstable, trying to incorporate and synthesise immigrant cultures, yet remaining unaware of or unsure how to tackle the new problems of urban immigration and poverty. Thus, argues Cohen, 'in this atmosphere of reaction, escape and insecurity, social work turned inward. With social reform out of fashion or politically dangerous, social work turned to working more intensively with the individual and to sharpening its technical skill'[53]. The focus on the individual was not new, but in the 1920's, he maintains, it intensified, almost eclipsing the other traditional concern of the social worker — the broader perspective of the social and cultural situation of which the individual was part. Whether or not there was an unconscious attempt to escape the sheer magnitude of the structural problems of American society, represented most urgently by the depression of the 1930's, social workers were certainly conscious of their inability to affect any radical change. Though they were daily reminded of the effects of unemployment, chronic ill health, disability and poverty, as a profession they were impotent to alter them in any fundamental way; thus a certain pessimism may also have contributed to the channelling of professional interest to more hopeful areas where constructive change could perhaps be achieved; namely, in the person rather than his situation.

In Britain the political and social climate was very different. The individualist ethos of the Victorian era had given way to a determination to tackle the structural ills of society — if not by means of radical change, at least by introducing new institutions such as national insurance and pensions, and by reforming those aspects of the old most in need of change. After the First World War, the dominant theme was reconstruction and the slow, piecemeal, but inexorable process of bringing about new public services on the lines suggested by the *Minority Report of the Royal Commission on the Poor Laws* of 1909. An individualist emphasis held little appeal, particularly in relation to these problems of poverty to which social work was still strongly geared. The most hopeful avenues of social progress were seen less in terms of individual treatment than in the development of better education services, better housing, better health, and protection against the major economic contingencies of working life. Through such measures, it was hoped that individual problems would largely be obviated.

Psychoanalytic theories had made some incursion in Britain, as we have seen, and there were memorable developments in forensic psychiatry. Even the Home Office, not likely to be swayed by transitory enthusiasms, was assessing the implications of the new psychology for the treatment of delinquency and expressing guarded optimism[54]. In relation to poverty, however, the individualist approach of the psychoanalyst would have appeared largely irrelevant. Indeed, what already came in for trenchant criticism was social work's failure to modify its traditional individualism sufficiently to take account of changing social conditions and of a suprapersonal factor in poverty. Of the COS, Miss Macadam wrote in 1934:

It is impossible not to deplore the stubbornness with which some at least of its leaders and spokesmen have persistently deprecated, if not actually opposed, one legislative social reform after another. From an excess of loyalty to the past, the COS... tends to cling blindly to interpretations of social principles designed to fit an entirely different world. Unwillingness to admit that methods of meticulous and elaborate casework carried out by volunteers, which may have been suited to a period when widespread unemployment was rare and short-lived, are wholly unsuited to meet the chief needs of a time when unemployment is on a vast scale and is mainly due to the breakdown of society and not of the individual sufferer. The attitude of the workers is no longer that of submissiveness to their 'betters'; they are keenly conscious and resentful of their helplessness in the face of economic forces; and the idea that charity comes to the aid of those who, whether by fault or misfortune, have failed to make good excites bitter mockery.[55]

To the family caseworker struggling with the acute problems of 1930's, such as those described by Dorothy Keeling in *The Crowded Stairs*, the clinical approach becoming dominant in the United States could have made little sense; the typical problems encountered by such workers were squalor, low income, bad housing, ill health. The dominant trend therefore was that represented by the setting up of the Beveridge Committee in 1942 — to find broad solutions to those problems represented by the giants of want, disease, ignorance, squalor and idleness, by the establishment of new social institutions available to the citizen as of right and without distinction of class, means or desert.

By 1940, therefore, social work in the two countries was facing very different issues. American social work education had been far more strongly influenced by Freud, but inherent in his theories were dangers which have perhaps become clearer with hindsight. With its focus on intrapsychic factors, it concentrated attention on the individual and it could too easily lead to causative explanations of social problems in purely individual terms. Cohen has remarked that this 'was especially true on the American scene, where the deeply rooted concept of individual moral inadequacy as the basic factor in most problems of poverty, dependency and disease could easily be supplanted by an overemphasis on personal (psychological) inadequacy without sufficient regard for the social realities which the individual had to face in a highly industrial and competitive society'[56].

In Britain, the emphasis on the establishment of social services as the right of every citizen, and a desire to avoid at all costs the implication that the receipt of those services implied any moral failure, meant that individual needs were if anything underemphasised, and a far greater understanding of basic emotional development was needed by social workers generally. Marjorie Cosens commented in 1943:

In this country we have not experienced the swing of casework to a too close identification with psychoanalytical techniques. Instead we need to take over far more than we are yet taking from the understanding of behaviour that the analyst has made available. We need also to study... the dynamic force of the relationships that are formed between us and our clients, as shown in our interviews, so that we may understand the 'shifts' of feeling that take place (the break-up of tensions and their re-creation in a new form) through which movement is made possible.

So far from being a psychiatric deluge, in Britain it might more aptly have been described as a drought.

4
The Growth of Psychoanalytic Influence

During and after the Second World War one of the influences that came to make a significant contribution to social work was psychoanalysis. The most usual explanation of the assimilation of psychoanalytic ideas has been in terms of professionalisation. Thus Parker observes that 'social work became immersed in what Professor Miller has termed 'the psychiatric world view'. This close link with psychiatric theory was the key to professional development in social work...'[1]. In relation to the British scene, however, this explanation would appear to be correct but insufficient. It does not take account of the extent to which psychoanalysis was, after the Second World War, stimulating work in directions closely relevant to social work practice, nor does it account for the growing influence of these ideas on established professions such as teaching and medicine. Relevance appears to be an important factor here. In the psychological field, for example, psychoanalytic ideas have gained much more extensive acceptance in the fields of personality, therapy and abnormal psychology, than they have in such areas as perception and thinking[2]. This has more, obviously, to do with relevance than professional aspirations. Psychoanalysis has a high proportion of ideas which are 'ecumenic' rather than 'parochial' and thus tend to be assimilated by contiguous professions[3].

Further, the professionalisation hypothesis tends to underplay the extent to which areas of knowledge other than psychodynamic psychology were also considered important for social work professionalism and as essential to such a claim. Thus Heraud stresses the contribution of psychoanalysis and claims that 'casework has become increasingly centred on the personality of the individual, and has been influenced by theories of personality derived in particular from various types of psychoanalytic theory'[4]. Through this, he maintains, 'social workers have sought a recognised technique and status and have been able to identify with a practice which is derived clinically and which has direct therapeutic claims'[5]. Although he makes reference en passant to sociology and to other schools of psychology, he clearly regards psychoanalytic theory as the fundamental element and the core of training, and this is stressed throughout the book[6]. Not only is it extremely doubtful whether psychoanalytic techniques (dream analysis, free association, transference interpretation) have ever been employed to more than an inconsiderable extent in social work (if indeed at all) but more importantly, the knowledge regarded as requisite for practice has always been viewed in much broader terms. The United Nations *Third International Survey of Training for Social Work* (1958) covers a very extensive range of content: under the heading of 'The Study of

Man' it has reference to physical growth and functioning as well as psychological development and human behaviour; and under the heading of 'The Study of Society', reference is made to government, law and the courts, political theory or social philosophy, economics, sociology, aspects of social psychology and anthropology[7]. Although psychodynamic psychology was the newer element in the patterns of training which emerged after the war and as such received a special emphasis, social work education, certainly in Britain, has always been far more broadly based, though the degree to which this has been true has sometimes been disregarded by its critics.

The extension of psychoanalytic influence, then, cannot be wholly accounted for in terms of professionalism; it was also related to developments in British psychoanalysis of obvious relevance and significance for social work practice. The most important were the contribution of psychoanalysts to knowledge of child development, and their greater engagement in the social arena in problems of delinquency, marriage and the family. Not only were these developments of importance in themselves, but they led to greater interpersonal contacts between psychoanalysts and social workers, which have contributed to the use, by social workers, of certain psychoanalytic concepts. Some of the more important of these developments through which psychoanalytic ideas have been diffused will now be reviewed.

4.1 Child Development

In the late 1920's and early 1930's, important work was developing in the field of child psychology, which had many very practical implications in the social work field, particularly for those concerned with child care. In Switzerland, Piaget was engaged on direct observation of the social and intellectual development of children demonstrated in play, and his *Language and Thought of the Child* (1923) was the first of a series of works which yielded new theories and hypotheses as to the development of children's thought processes. In America, after the First World War and reflecting the widespread interest in child welfare, a number of large-scale studies of child development were carried out (among them those of Gesell at Yale) which led to the identification of growth sequences and the specification of norms of infant development.

Psychoanalysis had long been interested in the development of the infant, though Freud's own theories of emotional development were the result of adult analyses rather than of direct work with children. In the late 1920's and 1930's, psychoanalytic work with children was developing, in which analytic hypotheses could be directly tested. Anna Freud's *Introduction to the Techniques of Child Analysis* was published in 1928, and in England Susan Isaacs published in 1933 her study of aggressiveness in children[8]. In the war years, psychoanalytic interest in child development received great stimulus from the arrival in Britain of Anna Freud and Melanie Klein, both of whom were distinguished psychoanalysts who had been engaged for some years in developing analytic techniques using childrens' play. The experience and skill of Anna Freud, together with that of other refugees from Europe who had been trained in education and psychology, found a new direction in attempting to mitigate some of the disastrous effects of family disruption in wartime London, and in finding ways of providing for small groups of vulnerable children a stable and caring environment which could avert threatened damage to their physical and psychological growth. During the blitz, the Childrens' Rest Centre was begun in Hampstead and became known as the Hampstead Nurseries. This consisted of three separate houses: a residential nursery for babies and young children; a day nursery, for children from the nursery together with some outsiders; and a country house in Essex for evacuated children aged 3−6 years. The aim was to safeguard the care and education of children by meeting their needs for personal attachment, for emotional stability, and for permanency of educational influence. The primary aims were therefore to provide care for such children, particularly those who had through force of circumtances to be separated from their mothers, and to repair the psychological damage they might already have sustained. But the Nursery also provided a unique opportunity for observing the essential emotional needs of children and their reactions to the experiences they underwent, and for testing out different ways of attempting to meet their need for attachment and mothering. It was hoped that the Nursery could develop models of care which could be used by others concerned in the care of children; its work also included therefore a teaching element. The activities of the Nursery and some of the rich fruits of its research were made available both in the more technical literature and in easily available and nontechnical books by Dorothy Burlingham and Anna Freud[9]. Work of this kind not only had immediate relevance to the problems of wartime but also had relevance for the care of children in peace, and the subsequent work of Anna Freud at the Hampstead Clinic has continued to add greatly to our knowledge of child development.

4.2 The Work of Bowlby

Although numerically speaking the child guidance movement in Britain remained small, and its work was gravely interrupted by the closing of clinics and the departure of personnel on war service, the experience being built up, not only in Britain but in the United States and Europe, led to an increased understanding of the etiology of some forms of mental disorder which was of crucial significance for the social services and for the training of social workers.

Child guidance workers, and those in the child care field, were making discoveries about the development of personality and particularly of personality disorder, which were being supported and confirmed by the results of systematic research. As Bowlby pointed out in 1950, the striking feature of this research was the way in which certain central findings consistently emerged from studies undertaken by different parts of the world[10]. Most of this work was reported in the professional literature, and although some of it was familiar to those social workers associated with the mental health field, there can be no doubt that, in Britain, the implications of these discoveries for social work training (and even more important, practice) were little appreciated until the 1950's. Indeed, one of the major tasks, even now, is the dissemination and assimilation of a far greater understanding of this work in such a way that it can affect to a greater extent the practical day-to-day operations carried out by institutions and individuals engaged in the care of children and families.

The central concept which emerged from this body of work was that of 'maternal deprivation'. Baldly stated, this was that maternal care was essential to the development of mental health; or, as expressed in Bowlby's classic statement, 'what is believed to be essential for mental health is that the infant and young child should experience a warm, intimate, and continuous relationship with his mother (or permanent mother-substitute) in which both find satisfaction and enjoyment'[11]. Throughout the 1940's, evidence was accumulating as to the dramatic adverse affects experienced by children subject to institutionalisation or to separation experiences under certain conditions; of these some of the most distressing (and it would seem often irreversible) effects were to be seen among children in institutions; particularly, marked retardation in physical, mental and emotional development, and sometimes severe depression or psychosis[12]. Children in the age range 6 – 12 months were particularly studied by Spitz and Wolf[13], who found a clinical picture of 'anaclitic' depression — with sadness, withdrawal and apathy reminiscent of depressed patients in adult mental hospitals — to be a typical picture, particularly among children who had received previous good mothering which was suddenly withdrawn without the provision of an adequate substitute. Some of these tragic effects have been documented not only descriptively but visually, for example, in Appell's classic film *Monique*.

Although it was among institutionalised children that some of the most extreme and dramatic damage was to be found, studies of children subject to other types of separation experience have also been made, those for example in foster homes, or hospitalised for short or long periods. During the war, it was also possible to study by direct observation the reaction of children subject to sudden separation, as was done by Burlingham and Freud in a residential war nursery[14], by Susan Isaacs in the Cambridge evacuation study[15], and by Britton and Winnicott[16]. These studies demonstrated how limited was our understanding of child development, and how little this knowledge might affect the way in which administrative arrangements in child care were carried out. Burlingham and Freud found that the effects of bombing paled by comparison with emotional distress caused to the children by loss of the mother.

War had many lessons for social workers. Perhaps for the first time, it showed how vital was a knowledge of child development to the work of *all* social workers, not merely those working in clinical or psychiatric settings. The observations of those psychologists working in nurseries revealed only too clearly that the work of the psychiatrist or psychologist was not concerned with remote clinical situations; it had immediate relevance to the kind of situation involving loss and separation with which any social worker might be faced in providing care for children. In a very direct way, the work of the child development specialist was brought into immediate contact with the agencies endeavouring to care for distressed children and families; these studies highlighted in an unmistakable way the crucial importance of understanding and meeting the emotional needs of children, and of endeavouring to structure inevitable separation experiences so that the child was helped and supported through them. These studies were readily available to the general public yet they also demonstrated that to the trained eye much that was taken for granted or overlooked by the ordinary observer might take on a new significance.

Although some of these studies originated in the disasters and upheaval of wartime, the experiences with which they dealt were equally those of peace, and their implications had to be assimilated by those agencies concerned with child care. This was not easy. Above all, separation studies showed that good intentions were not the best guarantee of success, and that the very conditions under which children were being cared for by those concerned for their welfare might in fact be doing actual harm; in certain situations not only could emotional and physical development be stunted, but damage to the personality sustained which was irrecoverable, and this not as a result of malevolence or lack of care, but of lack of awareness. Not surprisingly the studies of the effects of separation have aroused much resistance, not least in professional circles; they meant a radical and painful reappraisal of work founded on a genuine desire to help, and a willingness to scrutinise established practices in a self-critical way.

In 1950 the United Nations Social Commission decided to undertake an investigation into the needs of homeless children, and the World Health Organisation offered to contribute a study of the mental health aspects. This was undertaken by Dr. John Bowlby, Director of the Department of Children and Parents at the Tavistock Clinic, and his report was published under the title of *Maternal Care and Mental Health*. A shorter version appeared in paperback[17] which was reprinted a number of times. As Bowlby has since remarked[18], the publication was timely; the study was widely read and had a very considerable impact on child care; it also aroused no little controversy which in itself stimulated further research and led to considerable modification and refinement of his earlier thesis.

The comprehensive survey of existing clinical and social studies carried out by Bowlby established beyond dispute the validity of his central hypothesis, though work carried out since has considerably refined that original statement and suggested other variables not then taken into account which are also significant[19]. The interim conclusions were stated concisely as follows: there is abundant evidence that deprivation can have adverse effects on the development of children (a) during the period of separation, (b) during the period immediately after restoration to maternal care, and (c) permanently. Further, severe deprivation can lead to impairment of the capacity for forming sustained relationships — the so-called psychopathic or 'affectionless' personality. Already some evidence was at that time available as to the periods of apparent vulnerability, and the kinds of conditions associated with extreme damage of this kind, and a great deal of further work has now been carried out into the development of attachment behaviour[20], which has yielded further knowledge in these areas. Thus the notion of critical or sensitive periods in development during which certain behavioural characteristics are acquired has formed one important area of study, and work is continuing in trying to specify much more precisely and exactly the relationship between the various kinds and timing of early experience, and different modes of adult behaviour[21].

A further disturbing feature was that in some cases damage appeared to be irreversible, particularly where no libidinal ties had ever been developed[22], and subsequent work in animal studies has shown that the effects of deprivation in monkeys may lead to impairment of the capacity for mothering[23], thus creating a circular process whereby the deprived parent grows up to produce a generation of equally deprived infants. There is also evidence of certain critical points in development; if appropriate stimulation does not occur, some developmental failure may result.

Studies such as those referred to have not only demonstrated the effects of loss in broad terms, but also shown some of the ways in which the fact of loss may be dealt with by the small child; what are in fact defences against pain may easily be interpreted by the untrained observer as healthy reactions. For example, the child who is withdrawn or listless may be thought to have made a good adjustment, whereas the child who protests vigorously (and naturally) by crying, screaming or otherwise making his distressed state known may be seen as less adjusted; similarly, a manic defence (well illustrated by the film *Kate*[24]) may be taken at its face value as indicating that the child is happy and that all is psychologically well.

The films made in recent years by the Tavistock Child-Development Unit[25] provide careful documentation of the responses of children of normal background and development to sudden separation. They suggest that the characteristic phases through which the child passes are those of protest, despair and detachment, the last of which (often interpreted as 'settling down') is a sign of severe disturbance and should be cause for grave concern. These remarkable films, and the painstaking observations connected with them, are continuing to yield evidence which is vitally important to child care, whether in hospital or community settings. And by moving into experimental settings, particularly in relation to foster care, the Robertsons are now being able to demonstrate not only pathogenic responses, but ways in which the risk of damage through unavoidable separation can be minimised. Thus current research is increasingly moving from an examination of the pathological consequences towards

78

the testing of ways in which the ill-effects can be minimised, thus avoiding the pessimism inherent in the earlier studies, and suggesting constructive lines on which child care practice can be based.

There is now a vast body of research findings available whose importance for social work practice can hardly be overestimated: many of them owe their origin to psychoanalytic observations. It is not necessary here to do more than indicate the scope and nature of this research, in order to understand something of the impact that Bowlby's work made on social workers in the 1950's. Indeed some of these implications, particularly as regards training, were brought out very forcibly by Bowlby himself. His findings suggested that any child received into public care was to some degree at risk; and although deference was paid to the idea of preserving the family unit, in practice children could be removed from the natural family without every effort having first been made to see whether the family could be enabled to cope more effectively with its difficulties, and without sufficient recognition of the importance to the child of the basic security which even an inadequate family might provide more effectively than a substitute. Much greater attention ought therefore to be paid to the socio-economic support of vulnerable families, such as those where a child was illegitimate. This was in line with the thinking expressed in Home Office· Circulars in the 1950's[26] which stressed the importance of the family unit.

Also needed, in his view, was much greater knowledge of mental health principles and psychoanalytic understanding — for example, of unconscious hostility and of ambivalence — among social workers called upon to help in family problems. Dr. Bowlby stressed the need for recognition of psychiatric and emotional problems, and the development of greater skill in working therapeutically with parents whose own emotional difficulties might be a major cause of failure. Indeed one cause of a certain fatalism and sense of impotence in tackling family problems might be this very lack of understanding. 'There is', he commented,

> a woeful scarcity of social workers skilled in the ability to diagnose the presence of psychiatric factors and to deal with them effectively. From what has been said hitherto, it is evident that unless a social worker has a good understanding of unconscious motivation she will be powerless to deal with many an unmarried mother, many a home which is in danger of breaking up, and many a case of conflict between parent and child.[27]

He noted as an impressive feature of the past decade the extent to which a psychoanalytic approach to casework had developed in American schools of social work, and the psychiatric consultation which many casework agencies there were seeking.

4.3 The Advanced Course in Social Casework: The Tavistock Clinic

Developments in psychological research based on psychodynamic theories had pointed up some of the deficiencies in social work training. An important development took place when the Advanced Course for caseworkers was begun in the Department of Children and Parents at the Tavistock Clinic in 1950. A number of factors, explicit and less explicit, probably contributed to the decision to inaugurate the course. Dr. Bowlby's own research had made him only too well aware of the potential for constructive or damaging work with children and families inherent in the social worker's function, and he had clearly indicated in *Maternal Care and Mental Health* his own views on the need for much greater psychological understanding and training on the part of such workers. Even the Mental Health course did not in his view afford casework placements of a length sufficient to allow long-term intensive work through which an opportunity to gain insight into personality dynamics might be afforded[28]. Secondly, the Advanced Course was designed to give caseworkers in nonpsychiatric settings an opportunity to gain systematic teaching in psychodynamic psychology, and especially to increase their understanding of the effects of early experience in shaping the adult personality. Through carefully supervised practice it was hoped to develop greater sensitivity to the unconscious factors affecting the casework relationship and greater skill in its use.

The theoretical components included seminars on psychoanalytic theory, on child development and personality growth (both given by psychoanalysts), infant and nursery observation, and psychological testing. The casework seminar, in the words of Noel Hunnybun,

> is concerned with the dynamics of seeking, accepting and giving help and of the worker client relationship. This includes discussion of reality and fantasy elements in the relationship and in particular the study of transference both in its positive and negative aspects, together with the various ways in which its manifestations can be dealt with in casework situations. Special attention is given to the causes and expressions of anxiety and resistance, and emphasis is placed on the value of helping the client to express or to admit his mixed feelings towards other figures in his earlier life. Attention is also paid to the worker's attitudes and feeling towards the client, which may at times include over-protective attitudes or over-identification, together with ways in which these difficulties can be met. In the summer term attention is focussed on relating what has been learned to casework in other settings, with special consideration of the needs, problems, limitations and opportunities which they provide.[29]

Those selected for the course were expected already to have undergone professional training and to have some years experience, and the training itself, though specifically psychodynamic and to that extent specialised and circumscribed in its compass, has to be seen within this broader context. It was hoped that the course would provide a number of field work supervisors and social work teachers; although it has always catered only for a very small number (a maximum of six a year) of whom a number go on to work in clinical settings, analysis of posts currently held by former students indicates that most hold senior posts in local government, in teaching and in field work supervision[30]; through them it may be supposed that the Tavistock's psychodynamic influence is more broadly diffused.

4.4 The Family Welfare Association and the Family Discussion Bureau: New Forms of Service and a New Ideology

A new link between psychoanalysis and social work had already been forged by the setting up of the Family Discussion Bureau in 1948.

The war years saw signs of change and movement. War led to all kinds of new social work tasks in a variety of areas — with evacuees, refugees, in hospitals, hostels for difficult children and rest centres — but family casework in particular rose to new challenges with alacrity. Foremost among these was the development of Citizens' Advice Bureaux, a novel and valuable development still in operation today. In the early years of the war, the COS set up a Reconstruction Committee, concerned with postwar planning, and in 1940 this Committee, together with the Institute of Sociology, organised a Conference in Oxford. This was primarily to consider postwar reconstruction, but it was also noted that as the public services offered new opportunities to social workers, so a new theory of social work was required. 'The theories now taught in the schools of social service have come over from the 19th century and seem no longer to fit', observed *Social Work*[31]. There was a vague indeterminate seeking for 'some new thing'. The necessity for quick decision by the individual social worker which wartime conditions demanded had called into question the traditional COS methods — careful and painstaking enquiry, committee decision — and had led to some rethinking as to what was the essence of good casework as opposed to methods which were merely hallowed by time and tradition[32]. But even more important, as the state took over a greater measure of responsibility for meeting financial need, what was to be the role, after the war, of a Society whose basic raison d'etre (whatever its claim) lay in the sphere of financial relief?

The ideology on which its work was based was still that of the 19th century; of the duties of one's station in meeting the needs of the poor. Social work was still viewed as an essentially voluntary activity which 'lost something of its sweetness' (in Octavia Hill's phrase) by being salaried; and many of the COS leaders, notably perhaps J.C. Pringle, had maintained Loch's attitude of scepticism towards the public service. As its role for the future became increasingly uncertain, the COS, if it was to survive, had to redefine its functions in relation to the statutory services, and even more essential, had to find an aim which was capable of inspiring and retaining the loyalty of its staff, attracting the necessary funds, and rendering it acceptable to the public which it served.

That great changes had already come about in its thinking is clearly evident from the welcome it gave to the Beveridge Report, and the vigorous way in which it set about redefining its own role and planning for the future. In 1946 it severed some of its links with the past by establishing a new constitution and changing its name to the Family Welfare Association, thus formalising the change in function which had long since taken place and giving recognition to family casework as its primary activity.

The Association's search for a rather more solid footing than that provided by a 19th-century ideology of philanthropic commitment had been reflected in a paper by Dr. A.T.M. Wilson of the Tavistock Institute of Human Relations in 1947[33]. This dealt with 'The Development of a Scientific Basis in Family Casework'; its significance lies not only in what Dr. Wilson had to say, but in its clear indication of the fact that it was to a 'scientific' foundation, and in particular that of a psychoanalytic nature, that the Association was now looking as the basis and legitimation of its work.

In Dr. Wilson's view, the opportunities presented by family casework represented an appropriate and urgent field for the development of scientific method, especially that psychological science which could only develop through 'action research' and as part of a therapeutic enterprise. He envisaged for the social worker with family problems a role comparable to that of the psychiatrist in relation to psychological illness, and he considered that a need had arisen for 'a fully professional nucleus... of social workers, with a technical status raised to the necessary high level by the results of scientific work beginning as practical therapeutic research, transmitted in training, and developed in day-to-day practice'. Although Dr. Wilson anticipated resistance to what he had to say, there can be no doubt that he 'spoke to their condition'. The vision of family casework he held up bridged the past and the future; it embraced a scientific approach which Loch would have approved and it was individualist, though in a psychological rather than a moral sense. At the same time it looked to a high level of training and skill in the professional worker which might again put the Association in the forefront rather than the rearguard of social work, and provide a solid basis for expertise in family casework.

The FWA was already involved in matrimonial work, and the great interest in matrimonial conciliation after the war reflected in the setting up of the Denning Committee gave a further impetus to this aspect. The Report of this *Departmental Committee on Grants for Marriage Guidance*, with its recommendation of grant aid for the National Guidance Council, the Catholic Marriage Advisory Council and the FWA, opened up fresh opportunities, and the FWA sought the help of the Tavistock Institute in preparing workers to develop greater skills in marital work, where in general they felt their competence to be poorly developed. The new interest was in part due to the belief that a greater part was played by psychological problems than by material need in the causation of family stress and 'the growing realisation of the complexity and of the immense mass of problems of human relationship which remain even in a society which has made some attempt to provide

82

statutory assistance towards a minimum level of satisfaction of material needs'[34]. It was based also on the assumption that the quality of the marital relationship was a main factor not only in the development of social behaviour in children, but in the maintenance of the family as a unit.

In developing this experimental work the FWA worked with the Tavistock Institute of Human Relations, the Tavistock Clinic and the Peckham Health Centre. The core of the training consisted of supervised casework carried out by a carefully selected group of workers, together with seminars and case conferences. Characteristic of the thoroughness with which the project was approached was the decision to spend some time in exploration of community attitudes to marriage before therapeutic work was even attempted.

Subsequently the Family Discussion Bureau became a unit of the Tavistock Institute, and has since been incorporated in it. Its work is widely, indeed internationally, known through its publications, and it may be said that the Bureau has made one of the very few (perhaps the only) original contributions by British social workers to the development of a theory of marital interaction and therapeutic intervention. Now known as the Institute of Marital Studies, it offers training of various kinds for experienced caseworkers wishing to improve their skills in working with family problems and offers one of the very few advanced trainings in practical skills in this country. Its theories and the model of intervention developed by the Institute have therefore been influential[35]. Its work is unequivocally psychodynamic in basis, and most of its caseworkers regard a personal analysis as desirable for increasing sensitivity to and understanding of unconscious processes at work in the personality; a number are also qualified as analysts or psychotherapists, and the casework consultant who was associated with the development of the Institute since the beginning is herself a member of the British Psychoanalytical Society[36]. While the model of intervention used within the Institute is only to a limited degree applied in less specialised social work settings, nonetheless the advance in knowledge, the high level of skill, and the sophistication and originality of the theoretical accounts developed there have given it both prestige and influence among social workers generally.

4.5 Child Care Training

University courses were also incorporating much of the newer work on child development, and in 1947 new trainings in child care to prepare staff for work in the new local authority Childrens Departments, set up in 1948, were started at the London School of Economics, and Birmingham and Liverpool Universities. In the light of greater psychological knowledge, the deficiencies in the quality of care provided by public authorities for children in their care showed up all too clearly. It is difficult now to appreciate the lack of individual care, or the extent of ignorance as to the developmental and emotional needs of children which then existed among those who held this responsibility; but that this was so is evident from the Report of the Curtis Committee in 1946. This Departmental Committee[37] was set up in 1945 following the death of a child in public care in circumstances that were a cause for grave concern. It had the following terms of reference: 'To inquire into the methods of care provided for children deprived of a normal home life and to consider what further measures should be taken to ensure that these children are brought up under conditions best calculated to compensate them for the lack of parental care...'. The Committee devoted much of its time to observing personally various aspects of care, through visiting different institutions all over the country; in the course of their enquiries no less than 400 establishments were visited. The Report itself was forthright and disquieting. Not only was the administrative responsibility for the care of such children fragmented and its machinery cumbersome and ineffective, but the quality of care, particularly of those children in workhouses and large institutions, was revealed as insensitive and unimaginative. The Committee was especially aware of the way in which the child's emotional needs might be ignored, not through ill-will, but through lack of perception, knowledge and sensitivity. Much of this was due to lack of staff of the right calibre and with the right training.

In addition to the administrative changes proposed (which resulted in the Children Act of 1948 and the appointment of Childrens Officers in each county borough charged with the responsibility for the care of children deprived of a normal home life) some of the Committee's most important recommendations related to training. So urgent was this thought to be that an Interim Report[38] dealing with the training of housemothers and calling for the setting up of a Central Training Council in Child Care and the establishment of courses for both field and residential staff, was published in March 1946. In its final Report (September 1946) the Committee dealt more fully with the question of training for field staff, and recommended the institution of one-year courses of training for boarding-out visitors covering child development, family life, social conditions, social services and their organisation, and incorporating practical work.

The Central Training Council in Child Care was appointed in 1947 and began work almost at once, with the result that courses on these lines were started in the autumn of 1947. By the time the Children Act came into force in July 1948, the first intake of students was ready for appointment in the new service. The courses varied in their orientation, but each had as tutor a psychiatric social worker with experience of evacuation, and that at the London School of Economics recruited Miss Clare Britton (later Mrs. D.W. Winnicott), who had had extensive experience in working with disturbed children in wartime hostels. Its students attended lectures given at the Institute of Education by Dr. D.W. Winnicott, a paediatrician and psychoanalyst with whom Miss Britton had worked closely during the war. Dr. Winnicott's influence on social work has been extensive, not only through those students whom he personally taught, but in his wider contacts with the social work field and through his many publications. Miss Britton herself was later to undergo

84

training as a psychoanalyst and subsequently became director of Child Care Training with the Central Training Council of the Home Office. In that capacity she did much to develop training not only among fieldworkers, but among residential staff, and has been especially concerned to relate the psychoanalytic point of view not only to social work practice, but to the much broader caring and administrative tasks of the social services[39].

4.6 Crime and Delinquency

One of Bowlby's major early interests had been in the delinquent child, and it was this which led him to explore further the relation between emotional deprivation in early life and later delinquency[40]. Work in this field has increasingly attracted psychoanalytic interest, and this has constituted an important channel of this influence on social work, particularly following the Second World War. Some of the earlier developments have already been described in the section dealing with child guidance, and while it cannot be claimed that psychoanalysis has itself inaugurated the movement towards such reforms as the establishment of juvenile courts and the probation system, the humanising of the prison regime, or the introduction of psychological assessment and treatment, it has lent powerful theoretical support to progressive ideas and has contributed to the tremendous changes in attitudes towards crime which can be discerned in the present century[41].

As a result of the work of Dr. Grace Pailthorpe, who carried out a series of studies of female prisoners, mainly in Holloway Prison, during the late 1920's, the Institute for the Study and Treatment of Delinquency and its offspring, the Psychopathic Clinic, were founded in 1932[42]. Those most involved were Dr. M.S. Eder, Dr. J.A. Hadfield, Dr. E.T. Jensen, and Dr. Edward Glover. Its chief aim was the provision of facilities for the examination (and in some cases, treatment) of cases of antisocial conduct, especially among young people; to this end a panel of doctors willing to give their services was formed. Initially, premises at the West End Hospital were used, but the Clinic later acquired its own premises and in 1937 became the Portman Clinic. In 1938 this became a practical training centre for the University of London's Diploma in Social Studies and courses were also offered for probation officers on 'Introductory Psychology' and 'The Nature and Variety of Human Behaviour'. Clinic staff also conducted seminars for social workers and others designed to discuss problems which arose in their day-to-day work and to add to their psychological understanding.

One of the original aims of the ISTD was to apply a number of scientific disciplines to the elucidation of both individual and social problems. Its clinical work was always based on the idea of the multidisciplinary team, and it had intended to coordinate existing scientific work on delinquency from a number of fields. Interest in criminological subjects was growing internationally, and in 1938 an International Association was founded as the result of the first Congress of Criminology held in Rome.

In Britain, too, interest in the application of psychological methods of treatment was growing after the Second World War and was reflected in a number of publications, particularly those of Friedlander[43], Glover[44] and Schmideberg[45]. In 1950 the Institute undertook the publication of a journal, the *British Journal of Delinquency*, with an editorial board composed of Edward Glover, Hermann Mannheim and Emanuel Miller. Although it was hoped to cover an enormous range of fields, including medical psychology, psychiatry, psychoanalysis, organic medicine, educational psychology, sociology, economics, anthropology, psychobiology and statistics, as well as to include contributions from social work and prison personnel, a large number of the contributions have always been of a psychoanalytic nature. The ISTD has thus been an important channel for the spread of psychoanalytic ideas. In the field of delinquency, psychoanalysts have worked closely alongside and on equal terms with other disciplines, and have joined with them in programmes of study, research and treatment. The Journal has also been an important medium for the communication of psychoanalytic ideas, being readily accessible to a wide public such as magistrates, social workers and prison officials, by whom the more technical and professional psychoanalytic journals would not have been read. This has undoubtedly been an extremely significant influence on that area of social work practice most concerned with problems of delinquency, namely the probation service.

By 1950, then, very considerable changes were taking place in social work thinking and a psychodynamic perspective was beginning to be incorporated, not only as a result of American influence, but through British developments which led to new forms of psychodynamically based training. These affected only small numbers, however, and of more extensive influence on the main-stream of professional social work was a new type of 'generic' training begun at the London School of Economics in 1954.

5
The Development of Professionalism

After the Second World War, social work in Britain expanded with dramatic rapidity; the establishment of the welfare state opened up fresh opportunities and the possibility of exciting roles in the administration of the new social services, particularly in the National Health Service and the local authority children's service. Arising out of the need for trained staff came the establishment of patterns of social work education leading to the articulation of a new professional identity, and the growth of a professional culture and orientation which in significant ways differed sharply from that which determined older social work perspectives. The central features of this accelerated professionalisation were the emergence of social casework as the core social work skill, and the redefinition of casework itself in terms of particular interpersonal and human relations skills.

One of the significant (though by no means the only) influence contributing to this new culture was psychoanalysis; during this period psychoanalytic theories and concepts for the first time came to be incorporated systematically in the training of social workers and this has greatly affected not only the content of training and the knowledge base considered necessary for effective practice, but the models of intervention and, more subtly, the perspective or frame of reference within which the social worker approaches his field of work.

There were two main factors relating to the development of new ideas in social work in the decade after the Second World War. The first was the rapid development of psychoanalysis in Britain, considered in the previous chapter. Two aspects of this development had particular significance for social work; in the first place, the work of psychoanalysts in child development research had obvious relevance for social work with children and with families; and in the second place, the engagement of psychoanalysts in the broader social field — in delinquency, in general psychiatry, and with a variety of social problems — led to new ventures in the training of social workers. The second major factor was the intensified impetus towards professionalism in social work associated with the development of a professional identity which transcended national boundaries and which owed much to the influence of American concepts and methods (transmitted through international conferences, seminars, exchange of personnel and professional literature).

Much sociological work on the professions has been concerned with attempting to answer the question 'Is X a profession?' by trying to discover how far it matches up to a professional ideal type, in terms of such criteria as a systematised body of knowledge, professional authority and technical competence of an exclusive kind, community sanction, means of professional control, and so on[1]. As Millerson[2] has pointed out, the 'check-list' approach tends to assume that professionalism is a static phenomenon rather than a dynamic process. The more interesting questions are those posed by Hughes: 'What are the circumstances in which the people in an occupation attempt to turn it into a profession, and themselves into professional people? What are the steps by which they attempt to bring about identification with the valued model?' In other words, the process by which an occupational group aspires to and sets out to achieve a desired status (and the consequences of this) is an area which is now of primary concern to sociologists interested in professionalism.

This process can be seen very clearly in the development of British social work, particularly since the inception of the British Federation of Social Workers in 1935, and at an accelerated rate after the Second World War when all the social work associations (which referred to themselves as 'professional associations') became deeply preoccupied with questions of training, standards, registration and professional organisation. Along with this went the need to establish acceptable theoretical foundations for social work *practice*, as distinct from social administration on which professional expertise had hitherto been based.

British social workers therefore looked to American social work which had gone much further both in achieving a recognised professional status and in developing theory for practice, and adopted (with modifications) many of the features and concepts of American practice. A distinctive feature of professionalisation has been the emergence of a professional ideology, and it is this ideology, rather than the process of professionalisation itself, with which I shall be concerned.

The term ideology has been viewed with some caution in recent years and there has been an attempt both to reach greater precision in its use and to divest it of the pejorative connotations of distortion and selectivity it has often carried. Earlier work was largely concerned with political ideologies, such as Marxism or the Nazi movement. Thus Shils[3] would distinguish ideology as one form of comprehensive pattern of cognitive and moral belief from outlooks, creeds, systems and movements of thought, and programmes, which are other types of pattern. Ideologies, he says, are characterised by their explicitness of formulation over a wide range of the objects with which they deal — for their adherents there is an authoritative and explicit promulgation; by their relatively high degree of systematisation or integration around a few pre-eminent values, such as salvation or ethnic purity; by their resistance to change; and by the complete subservience they demand of their adherents. In his view, the term ideology should be reserved for broad systems of belief with characteristics of this kind. More recently, however, the study of ideologies has moved from the political to the professional arena, and there have been a number of studies of professional groups in which the concept of ideology has provided useful insights into the behaviour of professional practitioners. A classic study was that of Bendix, who examined ideologies of management

88

serving to justify the exercise of authority in industrial enterprises, thus providing the rationale for employer-employee relations and for the subordination of large numbers of employees in the factory system[4]. Such a study, as he points out, implies 'a neglect of persons and private beliefs'; rather it will focus on those shared understandings through which ideas and action are related to each other. The mental health field has afforded particularly fruitful ground for the study of professional ideologies[5], and Halmos has provided a perceptive ideological study of 'the counsellors', a group of related occupations which includes social work, and which he regards as having fundamental beliefs and values in common.

The function of ideology is broadly, in Apter's words, that it 'links particular actions and mundane practices with a wider set of meanings and, by doing so, lends a more honorable and dignified complexion to social conduct'[6]. It may be seen as performing two main functions: in relation to a social group it fosters cohesion by binding individuals together on the basis of common beliefs and assumptions; in relation to the individual, it links his ordinary activities with this 'wider set of meanings' giving them both direction and significance. Most important, ideology serves to legitimise power and its exercise, and hence the particular importance of the study of ideologies within the context of professionalism.

A useful formulation is that of Geertz, who regards ideologies as 'systems of interacting symbols, as patterns of interworking meanings', the function of which is 'to render otherwise incomprehensible social situations meaningful, to so construe them as to make it possible to act purposefully within them'[7]. They are 'maps of problematic reality'. In an excellent paper[8], Marx has taken up this formulation and suggested that it can be used to conceptualise the nature and function of ideologies in professional fields:

> Specifically, the ideologies which are associated with professional subcultures represent consensually validated belief systems about problematic or incomprehensible aspects of the reality upon which practitioners must act. These ideologies serve as guidelines and rationales for purposeful professional action by providing shared meanings and interpretations of incompletely understood professional situations.

He goes on to suggest some specific attributes that make professional arenas 'strategic contexts for contemporary ideologies'. Professional activities are subject to two sets of conditions: on the one hand there is an expectation that they will be guided by a systematic body of knowledge; at the same time (and this is often overlooked) there are few areas of professional activity where action can be wholly and exclusively determined by reference to such knowledge:

> It is precisely this confluence of a normative expectation that practitioners' behaviour will be based on and guided by the extant body of systematic abstract knowledge within a field and, at the same time, an awareness that this knowledge is inadequate for understanding, predicting and controlling

89

the subject matter of professional concern, that sets the stage for the rise of competing ideological belief systems in professional arenas.[9]

Thus the significance of ideologies, he suggests, will be inversely related to the extent to which the phenomena with which practitioners must deal have been completely and definitively understood. On this basis, he goes on to delineate some characteristics of professional fields in which ideologies are likely to be particularly significant as determinants of professional action. These are:

1. Fields that are relatively new or recent and have undergone rapid growth in size, scope, social demand or significance. These conditions maximise social pressures for professional action while at the same time the practitioner is unfamiliar with, and uncertain about, the phenomena toward which action is demanded. The same conditions minimise the likelihood that the profession's intellectual resources are adequate for dealing with these phenomena.

2. Fields in which the application of empirically validated knowledge to concrete social problems depends upon personal, subjective-intuitive, 'particularistic' attributes of the practitioner. Where extra-scientific considerations inhere in the application of scientific knowledge to social affairs and where practitioners must rely, to an important extent, on the idiosyncratic 'art' of professional practice, the stage is set for divergent interpretations and, hence, competing ideologies.

3. Fields in which moral and ethical considerations surround both the subject matter and the ends of professional action. These considerations are usually phrased in terms of professional issues over social values — rather than in explicitly philosophical terms.[10]

These conditions apply to a high degree in the field of social work no less than in that of psychiatry and mental health (with which Marx's account is particularly concerned) and on this basis we would expect that ideas and beliefs of an ideological nature would play a significant part in the determination of the professional behaviour of the social worker. For the purposes of this study, Marx's formulation of professional ideologies provides, with only slight modification, a useful conceptual basis:

> The ideologies held by mental health professionals, then, are shared belief systems which guide and justify purposeful therapeutic actions in the absence of complete, 'scientific' knowledge about the nature, prevention, and, most importantly, treatment of mental illness. Thus, these ideologies represent a response, which is supported by the consensual validation of other professional practitioners, to the strains associated with professional responsibility for treating mental illness on the basis of incomplete and provisional information.[11]

It must be observed that a study of ideologies is a study of those beliefs, values and assumptions (explicit or implicit) that underlie professional activities; it is concerned with manifest aims, rather than an analysis of latent functions. Because it is concerned with beliefs, some of the analysis must seem naive to the sceptical eye of a sociologist approaching the same phenomena from a different standpoint; discussion of ideology is less concerned with what an institution is *actually* about than with what its adherents *believe* it is about, and the justifications they provide for their professional activities.

Related questions have to do with the *processes* by which innovation occurs and new ideas are accepted, affecting attitudes or actions. Work illuminating these processes comes from a variety of sources, including cultural anthropology, medicine, the study of farming practices and rural sociology, and work on mass communications, political influence and public opinion[12]. Further work relevant to this area has been done by social psychologists such as Katz and Lazarsfeld who have particularly studied the interpersonal aspects of influence and the conditions under which it occurs[13]. In considering the adoption of new ideological positions, therefore, and the influence of new ideas, we are able to make use of such accepted organising concepts as centres of spread, channels of spread and receptivity factors. Centres of spread are those centres (not necessarily themselves the source but often highly innovative and receptive to new ideas) from which fresh ideas flow outwards; for example, the Tavistock Clinic has been such a centre in relation to the spread of psychoanalytic ideas in Britain. Channels of spread are those avenues through which ideas are diffused; the media, educational activities, professional journals and the like. Particular attention is given in this and the previous chapter to the channels through which psychoanalytic ideas entered social work during and after the Second World War. In relation to professional ideologies, courses of education and training are particularly important since it is largely these that determine dominant professional ideologies and it is through them that professional cultures are established and transmitted to new generations of professional workers. Receptivity factors are those which contribute to a readiness to accept, or to resist, new ideas.

Particularly relevant to the adoption of new ideologies is Dibble's study of the conditions under which an occupational ideology is disseminated beyond its occupation of origin[14]. Likely to be important, he suggests, are the degree to which ideas are relevant to the accepting group, the status of the transmitting occupation, and the range of contacts which it has. First, then, is the question of relevance. An occupational group will tend to assimilate ideas that it finds relevant and useful in solving work problems. Thus it will take over those aspects of the ideology of another occupational group which are 'ecumenic' rather than 'parochial' or occupation-specific. For example, psychoanalysis has a high proportion of ideas which are ecumenic and relevant to the task of other occupational groups such as teachers and social workers. Second, ideas tend to have downward rather than upward mobility, and the prestige of the source is likely to be important in determining the extent to which its ideas are accepted beyond its own occupational boundaries. This prestige has undoubtedly been attached to psychiatry, and in the United States to psychoanalysis in particular. For social work, the incorporation of psychiatric ideologies can therefore be seen as status-enhancing and this has been one factor contributing to their ready acceptance. We would expect such ideologies to be particularly assimilated by those social work practitioners working in locales where psychiatry is the dominant (and most prestigious) profession — for example, in clinics and hospitals — and the greater assimilation of psychoanalytic ideas by social workers in child guidance than by those in, say, family casework, in the 1930's bears this out. Third, the work of Katz[15] (who has especially studied the role of intimate interpersonal relations in communicating information) points to the conclusion that, while information may be communicated through formal channels, few people adopt an innovation on the basis of awareness alone, and more personal sources are likely to be important as a condition of acceptance. It will be shown that such interpersonal contacts were in fact very important in bringing about the acceptance of new ideas in social work after the Second World War, and in determining which ideas and orientations were adopted.

5.1 The Carnegie Report

By the end of the 1940's there was apparent a growing sense of dissatisfaction with existing social work training, both among those teaching on such courses and among social workers themselves. There was a sense of ferment which was manifested in the intensified training activities of the various associations, and in a sharpened awareness of the need for change without any sure sense of the direction which that change should take.

Perhaps no single individual made a more significant contribution to shaping the course of development of the 1950's than Eileen Younghusband. At the end of 1944, the Carnegie United Kingdom Trust was considering which activities should engage its attention during the postwar period; one suggestion was the need for the systematic provision of facilities for the training of social workers. The Trust therefore invited Miss Younghusband to undertake a survey; the work for this was undertaken in 1945, although the Report itself was not published until 1947[16].

This was an enormous task. The field was ill-defined and the term 'social work' itself referred not to a single clearly definable function but to a wide range of discrete and specialised roles within a very broad statutory field, as well as to a variety of voluntary activities. As Miss Younghusband commented: 'The net result is to demonstrate the hopeless and unprofitable task of determining the frontiers of social work. Indeed, it becomes very clear that even the main territory is as yet occupied only by scattered encampments of trained social workers and that the untrained, semitrained and otherwise trained probably form the bulk of the population'[17]. The picture as regards training was a dismal one. Many of the deficiencies pointed up in the Report (poor standards of practical training, inadequate selection, lack of systematic teaching of principles and methods of social work) arose fundamentally from

92

the ambiguity implicit in the social science courses from the very early days but never squarely faced; as to whether the universities, through these courses, were or were not setting out to provide a professional training for social workers. If they were, the courses were manifestly inadequate; if they were not, then there was an urgent need for the institution of new forms of professional training beyond that provided by the various social work associations. This uncertainty was reflected in the organisation and content of the courses. No British syllabus mentioned personal suitability as a criterion for admission, though in practice many required candidates to attend for interview, and only five of the courses at that time offered any teaching in the principles and methods of social work. While practical work was an integral part of all courses, it was given a low priority on most. 'Much of it', Miss Younghusband observed, 'is quite clearly useful experience, but it is equally clearly not training'[18]. There was little attempt to develop adequate fieldwork teaching, or to integrate this aspect of the course with the theoretical content. Critical as they were, Miss Younghusband felt that the comments she had voiced summed up and reflected the view of social workers themselves towards their training:

> It is one of the most hopeful signs for many years that there is at the present time in the professional bodies a general wave of self-criticism, a tendency to stand back and look objectively at methods and a desire to seek guidance from their own best members and from outsiders in thinking out what they are trying to achieve and how.[19]

In her view, the present position was only satisfactorily to be resolved by a clear acceptance of the principle that the social science courses were providing a pre-professional training, so that an integrated third year could be devised in conjunction with the professional bodies which would (if the theory and practice of casework and groupwork had been begun in the second year) contain specialisms related to the student's chosen field of work. Only if this were accepted could both theoretical and practical aspects be fully related to the professional job the student would eventually undertake. In reaching this conclusion, Miss Younghusband was clearly influenced by American social work trainings, which pointed up the difference in educational objectives and emphasis. Although she was at pains to point out that the organisation of the American training was not necessarily directly applicable to the British scene, she herself drew her definition of social work and many of her concepts of social work education from American sources. She included, for comparative purposes, the syllabuses of two of the leading American schools of social work.

In addition to the institution of a third-year professional course, Miss Younghusband also made proposals for an entirely new departure. This was for the establishment of a school of social work as a separate school of a university analogous to the Institute of Education of the University of London[20]. This body could expect to make a major contribution to the development of theory and practice by engaging in systematic research and by undertaking the professional training of a small number of well qualified students. Although the Carnegie UK Trust gave detailed consideration to this proposal, financial stringency prevented its realisation. It is interesting however that in 1965, 20 years later, the first University School of Social Work, solely concerned with research and training in social work, was set up at the University of Leicester, and subsequently the National Institute for Social Work Training provided a partial realisation of the kind of institution Miss Younghusband had wanted to see.

The Carnegie Report had therefore indicated the major deficiencies in social work training and made recommendations for future lines of development, of which the most important were: the clarification of the status of social science courses in regard to professional training; the acceptance by universities of new responsibilities in the provision of vocational training in the field of social work; and the establishment of a school of social work.

5.2 International Contacts

The developments in social work going forward in Britain were part of a movement that was taking place all over Europe, in which the emergence of a supranational social work identity can be traced. After the Second World War, international contacts were growing, and these did a great deal to stimulate British thinking and to strengthen the influence of American concepts and patterns of training.

The first International Conference of Social Work had been held in Paris in 1928, the second in Frankfurt in 1932, the third in London in 1936. These had led to fruitful interchanges and there had always been a considerable amount of traffic across the Atlantic, by magistrates, university teachers, almoners and other social workers, so that many personal and individual contacts had been made — some of them developing into lasting friendships. After the Second World War, however, these became more formalised. In Britain the British National Committee of the International Conference of Social Work was revived in 1946, and sent a delegation to the fourth International Conference at Atlantic City in 1948. In the same year, the first British National Conference on Social Work was held, at which the importance of participating fully in international affairs was stressed. The fifth International Conference· was held in Paris in 1952. The International Committee of Schools of Social Work had been founded in 1929 with a membership of Schools providing full-time courses of training for professional social work through a general social training; its conferences have usually been held in conjunction with the International Conferences of Social Work, and have been concerned with common issues relating to social work education. These conferences affected British social work in a number of ways; they generated individual contacts, stimulated thinking, and promoted a common social work identity transcending national boundaries.

At the end of the 1940's the United Nations began to play an extremely active role in the social welfare field, particularly through its European seminars. The Social Welfare Seminar in Paris in 1949 was attended by a number of British delegates, among them Roger Wilson and Geraldine Aves, who both took part in the section concerned with social work training. The Social Welfare Seminars were broad in scope and covered social work only as one aspect of social administration; of greater influence on social work thinking were those designed specifically to develop the teaching and supervision of casework.

In 1950 Marguerite Pohek, who had been in England with the American Forces from 1943 and later with UNRRA and from 1947 had been Social Welfare Advisor to the Austrian Government, was attached to the European Office of the United Nations. There she made contacts all over Europe and built up a European Exchange Programme; social workers from all over Europe had the opportunity to study at the International Social Work Seminars which she directed. It was particularly in the realm of casework that Marguerite Pohek had a major influence on European social work development. She organised and directed casework seminars at Vienna in 1950, at Woudschoten, Pays-Bas, in 1951, in Finland in 1952, in Italy in 1953, and in Leicester in 1954, when papers were given by two British social workers, May Irving and Clare Britton (later Winnicott). These seminars undoubtedly had a formidable impact and necessitated fundamental rethinking as to the objectives and content of social work education courses — not merely in Britain but all over Europe[21]. They attracted distinguished teachers, mostly from Canada and the United States, and introduced what were to many European social workers new concepts and teaching methods; for example, supervision and the use of case records in the teaching of casework. The Seminar on the Teaching and Supervision of Casework held in Finland in 1952 has been the subject of a particularly vivid account by Jean Snelling; not only does this give an admirable picture of the content and nature of the teaching, but it also shows the personal impact that it made upon her. 'To attend it', she wrote, 'was a profound professional experience'[22].

The importance of these seminars for developments in British social-work education during the 1950's can hardly be overstressed. As a result of them major shifts in thinking took place in two areas: firstly, casework emerged as the central skill; secondly, the concept of casework was radically redefined. In addition new teaching methods and concepts of social work education were introduced which were incorporated in the patterns of learning that were developed in the mid-1950's.

5.3 The Emergence of Casework as the Central Skill

At the end of the Second World War, the term 'social work' was in general use, though its boundaries were fluid and it referred to a very heterogeneous collection of occupations and activities. In Miss Younghusband's 1947 Report the term 'casework' does not occur[23]. She envisaged professional training as catering for the needs of a broad range of workers, including personnel managers and youth leaders, and her suggested syllabus for the courses to be provided at the proposed school of social work included the principles and practice of social work. But by 1950 the term 'casework' was in general use, and a well known book published in 1950 by a group of distinguished social workers dealt only with social casework[24]. In 1954, the first generic course was a course in casework, not in social work. This was a highly significant shift, which calls for explanation.

In the first place, the American model presented at the United Nations Seminars was that of casework; this was the focus of the teaching and the expertise of the distinguished teachers who took part. The American pattern of training separated casework from groupwork and community organisation, and of all the forms of social work casework method was the most highly developed and casework theory and techniques the most systematised. This was therefore a natural model to adopt, particularly in the aftermath of war when there was a demand for those with the skills to deal with individual problems; here was a pattern of training and a body of theory which was easily adapted for use in European schools.

This is not, however, a wholly satisfactory explanation. Despite the prestige and influence of American caseworkers at the time, leading British social workers (particularly Miss Younghusband) had been at pains to stress the need to adapt American patterns in a way that was appropriate to British traditions, and to marry the best of both. But there is no evidence that the possibility of developing a generic social work course with specialisations in group and community work was ever discussed as a realistic possibility, and it is likely that the narrowing of focus to casework alone is most convincingly to be explained in terms of professionalisation. The very diffuseness and heterogeneity of British social work had hindered its achievement of professional status; and the concentration on providing a high level of training and skill for a 'core' group of case workers was most likely to substantiate professional claims. Some of the consequences of this will be discussed below.

5.4   The Redefinition of the Concept of Casework

The term 'casework' was of course by no means new, and had long been in use by the COS to refer to its work with individual cases, as opposed to dealing with categories of persons. In this sense the term is still commonly used. Between 1945 and 1955, however, the term came to be used in the social work field in a somewhat more special sense and to acquire a number of new connotations. It was used in at least three senses.

Sometimes it was used simply to differentiate a *focus*; that is, work with individuals and families as distinct from groupwork, community organisation,

96

research, administration and other methodological components of social work. In this sense, the term 'social work' is used to indicate a broad field of practice, and 'casework' a segment of it.

More commonly, however, it came to be used to describe a *distinctive orientation or approach to human problems*, rather than a method or even a range of techniques. The two essential features of modern casework as they emerged in the 1950's were its psychosocial focus and its emphasis on the use of the professional relationship. First, as a psychosocial form of treatment, it aimed at maintaining a concern for both the emotional and social well-being of the client, for his interpersonal as well as his economic and physical needs. In Gordon Hamilton's words:

> Casework is characterised by the objective to administer practical services and offer counselling in such a way as to arouse and conserve the psychological energies of the client — actively to involve him in the use of the service toward the solution of his dilemma... Reorientation and reconstruction are achieved through a combination of psychological understanding and social services in an integrated participating experience with the client.[25]

Second, it involved the recognition of the constructive possibilities inherent in the development of a warm, supportive, positive, yet disciplined and professional relationship. As Barbara Shenfield put it in 1953:

> It is an essentially enabling relationship, one in which the caseworker must use her disciplined, trained professional self with a readiness to accept and respect the right of the clients to hold their own opinions. American social workers think of casework at its best as a profoundly democratic process.[26]

This relationship was seen as characterised by certain accepted values and principles — it reflected a nonjudgemental approach in which the client's right to determine his own actions was to be respected. It was perhaps particularly this latter feature which made American concepts of casework so particularly attractive to the British social worker, reared in a tradition with strongly paternalist overtones. The capacity of good American caseworkers to listen in an attentive, noncritical and nondirective way was something which caught the imagination of British social workers and offered them a new perspective on their work.

The term also came to be used by some authors in a less inclusive (and less useful) way to indicate a particular *method*; that is, only the *counselling or psychotherapeutic component in casework practice*, excluding both non-psychological methods and environmental aspects of work. This is implicit in such phrases as 'skilled casework help of a psychotherapeutic kind' and 'a social casework method of therapy', or the use of the term 'intensive casework' to mean 'regular interviewing and social work with selected clients who are incapacitated by reason of their own personality difficulties, or because of acute problems of personal relationships within their own family or social groupings, and who cannot get psychotherapy, medical or psychoanalytic...'[27]. This more narrow use of the term still persists and we find psychotherapists referring to their casework and advertisements for clinical psychologists offering opportunities for casework; in both cases the term is clearly used as a synonym for psychotherapy, perhaps to avoid the interprofessional conflicts the use of that term might provoke. Not surprisingly, such a usage leads to unsatisfactory and misleading attempts to differentiate between psychotherapy and social casework in terms of depth rather than of function. More serious from the social worker's point of view is the loss of that psychosocial perspective on human distresses and events which was a distinctive and essential characteristic of casework in the thinking of the best American teachers. Not only does this definition lead to an overemphasis on clinical skills and a devaluation of other methods (for example, environmental focussed work and work with collaterals) as 'not really casework', but it involves the abandonment of that conception of social work as both personal and situational in focus towards which American social work was struggling in the 1940's. The persistence of this more narrow usage has led to widespread misconceptions as to what casework is all about, both within and outside the social work profession, to such as extent that it is now almost impossible to use the word even among professional colleagues with any assurance of mutual understanding. That a recent study of social work (that of Toren) simply equates casework with therapeutic counselling, without either acknowledgement or discussion of the broader connotations the term has traditionally had, serves to compound this confusion still further.

In view of the importance laid on the worker-client relationship and on the need for understanding the affective elements in this, and in view also of the fairly widespread suspicion of American casework as being 'psychoanalytical' it is worth examining the orientation of these European seminars. American casework, as we have seen, was deeply influenced by psychoanalytic psychology, particularly in the 1930's, but by 1950 there was already a renewed emphasis on the social aspects of social work; it was looking not only to psychiatry but to sociology for theoretical approaches which could be used in conceptualising about casework activities (for example, concepts such as role and function). Casework was being defined as a psychosocial process in which these twin foci were invariably present, and in which individual behaviour could be seen only as the result of a highly complex interplay between 'internal' and 'external' factors, including social and cultural influences. Although psychodynamic knowledge was seen as essential to casework practice (and the diagnostic school of which Gordon Hamilton was an illustrious exponent derived its central theoretical perspective from psychoanalytic ego psychology) the extreme individualism which was a consequence of the earlier biological psychoanalytic viewpoint had already been considerably modified. This of course was true also of psychoanalysis itself. In the hands of the Neo-Freudians such as Fromm and Horney, and through the influence of cultural anthropologists, new social perspectives were being incorporated in psychoanalytic

98

thinking, and efforts were being made to integrate psychological and social concepts[28].

Casework that sets out to be psychotherapeutic and to treat personality directly Gordon Hamilton saw as part of an 'awkward, naive and fumbling' early adaptation of psychiatric knowledge. Caseworkers, she wrote, discovered at once

> that it was not within their province to treat psychoses or psychoneuroses any more than to treat diseases such as tuberculosis. In treating even the mildest forms of neuroses they burned their fingers so badly as to warn them against operating directly in the fields of instinctual development and the unconscious.[29]

While there is a borderline between psychotherapy and casework, their objectives are different, and for the caseworker a social perspective must always be present. Although Hamilton saw a place for counselling or therapeutic interviewing within the total range of casework activity, it was marginal rather than central and played only a small part in casework practice; in the first edition of *The Theory and Practice of Social Casework* (1946) she devoted only four pages to this aspect. In the second edition, published in 1951, she gave it rather more consideration (19 pages out of 317) but stressed that it should only be undertaken on the basis of advanced and rigorous training, and even then with caution. To Hamilton, whose influence on British social work was so marked both through her books and her teaching on European seminars, casework was never a diluted form of therapy, but had a distinctive function of its own. Her view is quite unequivocal:

> In the view of the writer, caseworkers do not practice psychiatry nor psychotherapy in mild versions or diluted forms. They simply do not practice it at all, except in so far as relieving inner pressures through social techniques means an understanding of frustration, anxiety, guilt and other tensions of the personality.[30]

Therapeutic interviewing with the goal of insight into unconscious feelings was therefore strongly discouraged; more usually the caseworker would use methods such as explanation, clarification and the identification of patterns of current behaviour at a conscious level. Even this was only one element in casework practice, which also included ways of intervening to bring about some change in a social situation. That this was the orientation of the European seminars is borne out by Miss Snelling's observation that 'it was emphasised continually that a very able worker with a very good relationship might be able to help a client to see how he was behaving, but that it would be most unwise to try to let him see why he behaved thus'[31]. Nevertheless, central to the concept of casework as it emerged after the war was a dynamic relationship between worker and client which of itself could contribute towards change and growth and which underlay the use of any techniques or helping measures which might be employed.

The changing conception of the social worker's role, which derived from this concept of casework, can be illustrated from the writings of Eileen Younghusband. In her first report, Miss Younghusband had been concerned to depict the social worker as one concerned with individual and social needs rather than in the light of the traditional concern with poverty. This requires certain qualities of personality, as well as the particular knowledge and skills needed to advise and help the individual and to utilise the social services on his behalf.

> The basic equipment of the social worker resolves itself into (i) an understanding of man in society, including some study of ethics, (ii) a thorough knowledge of the social services and local and central government, and of social economics. To this must be added a good grasp of social-work principles and some competence to practice in a given field.[32]

The view of the social worker implicit in this is essentially that of a resource mobiliser.

By 1950, the conception of the social worker as one who uses her own personality to bring about some change was being stressed. This, as Miss Younghusband observed, was struggling with the older idea of the social worker as someone who manipulates the environment, who makes arrangements, who 'confers tangible goods upon grateful but otherwise passive recipients of her plans and good advice'[33]. The new conception, she suggested, had implications for practical work training and supervision, since the art of developing practice skills was thus seen to involve not only the acquiring of knowledge, but understanding of human motivation and the social worker's own personality. Miss Younghusband had clearly been much influenced in her discussion of this by Gordon Hamilton's *Social Work as Human Relations* (1949), in which the need for the development of self-awareness on the part of the student was stressed.

The First Report had made trenchant criticism of psychology teaching on the social science courses; in some departments it was optional; in others, students could emerge

> without that better understanding of their fellow human beings which should be the aim of such courses. There is fairly widespread dissatisfaction with the teaching of psychology; academic psychology and abnormal psychology are felt to be either useless or dangerous, yet courses which throw light on the behaviour of normal people both individually and in their family and community relationships, are sadly lacking.[34]

But although the need for the inclusion of teaching of developmental psychology in a manner relevant to the interests and learning needs of the student was stressed in Miss Younghusband's first report, there was no specific mention of dynamic psychology. By 1950, however, this approach was clearly central to her conception of an educational programme for social workers.

100

It was inevitable that the advances in psychology should sooner or later shatter the old secure framework of every profession involving close personal relationships. Each chapter in this book shows the new leaven at work throughout the range of social casework, sometimes welcomed, sometimes only partly understood, sometimes feared. The result is that the social worker can no longer rest satisfied with her knowledge of the social services and her manipulation of entities like relief funds, prams, pawn tickets, ambulance services, hostels and so forth, trusting to the light of nature for her understanding of the persons for whose benefit these services exist. It is now demanded of her that she shall seek to understand the person in need, not only at that particular moment in time, but in all the major experiences and relationships which have gone into making him the person he is, with conflicts of whose origin he may be unaware, with problems whose solution may lie less in external circumstances than in his own attitudes, with tensions, faulty relationships, inabilities to face reality, hardened into forces which he cannot alter unaided. Instead of seeing his situation through her own eyes and producing a ready-made solution, the social worker must be able to see him and his needs and relationships as these appear to the person in need himself.[35]

To the more traditional functions carried out by social workers — which included determining eligibility for financial assistance, administering personal services within public welfare programmes, interpreting legal enactments, and enabling the client to obtain necessary services — there had been added

in recent years and to a limited extent, to render a service to individuals which is concerned not only with environmental changes but also with helping the person to achieve some release from his personal problems and from the pressure of his family and social relationships.[36]

This represented, as she acknowledged, a potentially explosive factor; for, if the function of the social worker were more than manipulating the environment, then new forms of training were required, for new wine was fermenting in old bottles. The 'new wine' was the advances in psychological knowledge derived from psychiatry and dynamic psychology, on which developments in casework in the United States and Canada had been based. What Miss Younghusband now envisaged was far more than the 'third-year course' of 1945 grafted on to the existing though modified two-year programme; it was nothing less than a wholly new conception of training, marked by the close integration of theory and practice, in which the teaching throughout would be informed by an understanding of dynamic psychology. It was on this conception that Miss Younghusband's proposals for training hinged:

It is obvious that if the social worker's function is primarily to manipulate the environment, then the present practical training in which she learns how the social services operate and how things are done is reasonably

101

adequate. But if her function is also to improve personal adjustment, including the relationship between one person and another, regarding the use of services as only part of her total aim, then the situation is very much less satisfactory. In the second instance the aim of practical training would be both to teach the student what she needs to know (and it will be a great deal) about the operation of the social services, and also to help her towards a growing understanding of the variety of human motivation and experience, and to a clearer and more disciplined understanding of her own personality in relation to its impact upon this mass of hopes and fears, struggles and failures, desires and frustrations.[37]

The practical working out of these ideas came about with the inception of the first 'generic' course at the London School of Economics in 1954, of which Miss Younghusband was appointed tutor in charge.

5.5   Social Work as Human Relations

The growth of American influence described in the previous chapter posed very difficult issues for British universities in relation to the nature and aims of social work courses — issues that were both philosophical and diplomatic in nature. There was a fear that social work education might become too technical and narrowly based and lose that breadth of social and philosophical perspective which was the strength of the social science courses. Miss Clement Brown[38], in a thoughtful article on 'Training for Social Work' in 1945, had clearly brought out the different emphases on either side of the Atlantic. 'Social service', she stressed, 'essentially requires perspective in terms of social philosophy and of historical and scientific judgement'. It required intellectual discipline as well as self-understanding, and in her view there was ground for thinking that some American writers, in overemphasising the need for self-knowledge, had tended 'seriously to underrate the importance of knowledge and intellectual discipline'. In a later paper she again referred to what she regarded as the American preoccupation with emotional conflict which dominated much of their thought and practice. 'Along with this concern there goes an astonishing belief that both these conflicts and the practical problems which may or may not be associated with them will yield to personal therapy, though this can sometimes be offered only by those with comparatively little specialised training'[39]. American training, she suggested, was still preoccupied with techniques or processes rather than goals:

While the British student is struggling to think more clearly about such issues as freedom and how this may be affected by social planning, the American is considering the ways in which professional discipline may keep him from imposing personal prejudices on his clients. Such mental discipline as the students here may gain by an attempt to grapple with larger social issues, the American may achieve by his slow motion study of diagnosis and treatment of the problems of individuals, families and groups.[40]

Miss Black, of Sheffield University, had visited the United States in the early 1930's and again in 1948 and had noted that in some respects American and British trainings were drawing closer; in particular, she observed in the United States a greater awareness of the implications and theoretical foundations of social policy as related to practice. Nevertheless, in the New York School of Social Work the aim of training was clearly defined as the development of the student's ability to make use of the whole self in helping troubled people. If this definition were accepted, were British schools doing anything to bring about this process ?

> Are we in this country thinking of education for social work and of our responsibility to students in these terms at all? And if we disclaim an interest in what has sometimes been described as a 'clinical' approach to teaching in this field what is our objective, seen in terms not only of the students' development and of the work they hope to do but of the relation between them?[41]

Questions such as these continued to disturb the Joint University Council. In 1950, at a special meeting to discuss a survey of British social work education carried out by Professor Silcock, Mrs. Rodgers of Manchester University pointed out the confusion it revealed as to what constituted professional training, and what the objectives of the social science courses really were. As a result, it was finally accepted that these courses did not constitute a professional training[42]. The question of the status of the social science courses and the decision as to what the future pattern of training for social work should be was therefore the dominant question of the 1940's. In 1950 this was resolved, and thinking was turning to definite plans for a new type of course on generic lines.

Two major stumbling blocks, however, impeded this development, despite the high degree of agreement between the universities and the field that a new type of training was required. These were the shortage of adequately trained field work teachers and the lack of a systematised and critically developed body of social work theory on the basis of which fieldwork development could go forward. The latter point emerges very clearly from the draft syllabus drawn up by the Practical Training Committee of the JUC[43]. Although the 'core' of the syllabus was to be the theory and practice of social casework, the content of such teaching was unsophisticated by comparison with American syllabi. Although there is some mention of different kinds of worker-client relationship, the use of the professional relationship was not mentioned, and the impression is gained that the drafters were more than a little at sea as to what a course in the principles and practice of social work should in fact comprise.

In 1953 the Carnegie United Kingdom Trust made a preliminary offer to the London School of Economics to provide a generic course of training on condition that the professional bodies agreed to recognise it. Further consultation therefore became necessary to win their support. Naturally enough, some of the Associations, though fully recognising the desirability of such a scheme, had some anxiety as to whether standards could be maintained; the almoners, for instance, thought that a year was far too short[44].

In 1953 the JUC sent a memorandum on 'The Need for a Common Training for all Caseworkers' to the various professional bodies[45]. This showed considerable development of its thinking since the draft outline of two years before. It stressed the *qualitative* changes which were becoming needed in training, due in particular to the growing understanding in the previous two decades of factors affecting human behaviour which had led to new techniques in casework. The aim, it maintained, was now no longer to plan for the client, but to assist him to reach his own decisions and to accept responsibility for his own actions. This kind of work demanded a greater emphasis on applied psychology and a better understanding of the worker's own part in the process. Professional training, the document stated, should provide this knowledge, but the unity of professional purpose was being destroyed by the development of specialist trainings with different ideals and philosophies — in effect, different ideologies. 'If this purpose is to be recreated, it is essential that workers in every field should share a common education and look to the universities for their basic teaching in the theory and practice of social casework'[46].

The Central Training Council in Child Care, the Probation Advisory and Training Board and the Institute of Almoners all agreed to support a generically based course; this support included an agreement that students trained on this course should be recognised as qualified to work in the setting they had particularly studied during the course, and also that they should be able to transfer from one setting to another with, in some cases, a short orientation course. For all the bodies concerned there was much work to be done; fieldwork supervisors had to be appointed, and questions relating to the specialist teaching required for eventual practice in the different settings worked out. The question of selection of candidates raised important issues of principle for the 'recognising' bodies, and the university was careful to ensure their participation in selection procedure. For the first course, the students mainly comprised those already accepted by the training bodies grant aided by central government, and recommended by them; there were also some 'uncommitted' students, and two officers of the National Assistance Board.

The question of the inclusion of a psychiatric social work stream raised difficult questions, which are not especially relevant here; the first JUC Memorandum had made no mention of psychiatric social workers, and the Institute of Almoners felt strongly that they should be asked to participate. The APSW, however, while it considered that the generic course might be a preliminary to the Mental Health Course, did not see it as replacing it. There were practical difficulties also in the very size of the LSE Mental Health Course; its annual intake was approximately 40 students, whereas the generic course was to be limited to 21 — 24 students. The two courses were therefore run side by side until 1970.

Since the concepts incorporated in generic training have been a significant channel of psychodynamic influence, and had very considerable impact on subsequent professional training, the objectives and nature of the Carnegie course will be discussed in some detail.

5.6 Generic Training for Casework and its Effects

When the first generic course was established in 1954, concepts of social work had already been very considerably modified, largely as a result of American influence; before it took place both Miss Younghusband, the tutor in charge, and Miss Lewis, who was to lecture on casework, spent a period in the United States in order to incorporate the best American thinking and practice into the design of the course. Charlotte Towle was invited to spend a year as consultant under the Fulbright Scheme to assist in launching it.

The course incorporated a number of features, some of which were already part of psychiatric social work training and some which were new. An important place was given to the teaching of human growth and development on a psychodynamic basis[47], and this body of theory and frame of reference also permeated the casework lectures, which rested on 'an understanding of human behaviour, motives and social relationships'[48]. Other aspects of the syllabus were concerned with health and disease and (to balance the individual focus) social influences on behaviour. Social administration, law and court procedure were the other elements. Theory and practice were to be closely integrated, and an important feature was the significance placed on the level of fieldwork teaching; for this a number of experienced practitioners, several of whom had taken the Tavistock Advanced Course, were recruited; the development of a high standard of supervision was facilitated by the seminars for supervisors given by Miss Towle. Fieldwork was to be used 'not simply for purposes of observation but primarily to bring about changes in the behaviour and circumstances of those who come for assistance with problems of environmental pressure, personal conflict or relationships. The knowledge to be used in such situations is not applied haphazard or piecemeal but through an orderly process of diagnosing the situation and pursuing appropriate methods of treatment through the consciously directed relationship which constitutes casework'[49]. The features of the course that made most impact on one of its early students were the close integration of theory and practice, the intensive nature of the casework supervision, and the psychodynamic approach to human problems. That this dynamic approach was carried into the supervision process is evident from his comments:

> The student learned to recognise and respect his client's defences; to assess the meaning the casework relationship had for the client; to avoid being

105

unconsciously manipulated by the latter into behaviour that merely reinforced earlier unfortunate experiences: to become more aware of his own
reactions and irrationalities; to observe the complex interplay of attitudes;
and to evaluate any movement that had occurred.[50]

Students were encouraged to understand underlying reasons for behaviour,
and the influence of the past on behaviour in the present, and in their casework
practice 'to assist their clients to become less ruled by their unconscious fears
and needs, more free to act rationally'[51]. For this student, people began to
make sense in a way that they had not done before, and the understanding of
human personality that he had acquired led also to an increase of self-
knowledge. Thus the emphasis was on the analysis of human behaviour and of
the casework relationship in psychodynamic terms. The recognition that
professional education not only involves the acquisition of knowledge but
effects change in the learner is a central theme of Towle's book and this was
explicitly recognised in the organisation of the course. 'In professional education, we have the common obligation to impart certain essential knowledge
and to conduct our educational processes so that they are a means to
personality growth'[52].

Miss Towle's influence in shaping the content and philosophy of the course
was very marked, and her particular approach to personality development
(which formed the basis not only of her approach to casework teaching but to
the total educational process) has been extensively treated in *The Learner in
Education for the Professions*. Her standpoint is drawn essentially from ego
psychology, as is apparent from Chapters 3 and 4 where she relies particularly
on the work of French and Alexander. The course in personality development
at her own School of Social Science Administration in Chicago was 'essentially
a study of the development of the ego, its function in the integration of the
personality, and its capacities for adaptation and defence'[53]. Nevertheless,
Miss Towle was greatly concerned that the social component should be
adequately recognised and that social work should not be conceived as a form
of psychotherapy. Over the years, she pointed out, deepened social intelligence
had led social work 'to reappraise its heritage and to renew its identity as a
contributor to the application of social science in practice', a reappraisal that
she warmly endorsed[54]. In a further paper which may now be described as
seminal for the development of British social work in the 1950's and 1960's,
she had addressed herself to the question of social work's function and identity
and stressed that it was focussed on 'the relationship of man to his environment for the purpose of effecting a constructive interrelationship'; it was
concerned therefore with individuals within their social situation, and had
three functions: of helping the individual to deal with stresses, of removing
stresses, and of preventing their occurrence. In her view 'the social worker is
committed first and foremost to environment as treatment, and to the meeting
of reality need'[55]. In view of this clear and unambiguous statement from a
distinguished social work teacher as long ago as 1955, it is the more remark-

able that casework should still be so frequently and narrowly equated with psychotherapy or psychological counselling.

The sequence on human growth and development — an innovation as far as British social work training was concerned — was taught by Dr. G. Stewart Prince, whose paper to the UN Regional Seminar in 1957 illustrates his approach[56]. It was concerned with 'the origins, processes and conditions of personality development' toward both emotional maturity and social adaptation; basically psychobiological, such a course should in Dr. Prince's view be concerned with the whole man, and take into consideration intellectual, social and spiritual as well as physical aspects of development. Although classical psychoanalytic theory provided the backbone of the course, attention was paid to the different schools of thought, and consideration given to experimental confirmation of psychoanalytic theories and concepts; this was intended to encourage a critical approach by the student. Aspects Dr. Prince noted as important for inclusion in such a course were: personality theory; the dynamics of the mother-child relationship; the influence of the family and society on individual development; the impact of abnormal environmental experience on development — emotional deprivation, illness, handicap, bereavement; normal and anomalous psychosexual development — courtship, marriage, problems of parenthood; the concept of maturity; problems of middle and old age. In addition to this there was a course of lectures on clinical psychiatry which focussed on the relationship between psychiatrist and social worker.

> Experience suggests (wrote Dr. Prince) that this content, together with the student's concurrent experience in other classroom teaching, in fieldwork and in supervision, provides for him a powerful and self-illuminating experience of growing and developing which is good preparation for an independent career in social work.[57]

The Carnegie course also included a strong emphasis on organisational and administrative factors relating to social work. In 1954 Professor Titmuss had stressed the need to relate casework practice to the specific administrative setting in which the caseworker operated:

> Essentially we are concerned here with a person in a situation; the worker with his equipment of skill and knowledge in a specific administrative setting in which unspecified needs present themselves; the worker, the client and the setting are basic components of action and need to be viewed as a whole. To study the worker in isolation... and to focus attention solely on the personal relationship between worker and client (as social workers tend to do) is to miss out a vital element in a total process of action. Pieces of action are seen but not the whole performance.[58]

His central theme was that 'the effectiveness of the social worker and the effectiveness of a service cannot in practice be divorced if there is any meaning to the principles of casework'[59]. The syllabus suggest that Professor Titmuss' view was taken very seriously; in addition to 'settings' courses (designed to identify elements specific to different practice contexts) teaching in social administration from the start gave attention to organisational factors — to organisational goals, policy formulation and change, problems of priority and the allocation of scarce resources, professional/administrative conflicts[60].

The Carnegie course formed the model for later generic courses and has profoundly affected professional education for social work in Britain. Despite the sporadic developments referred to earlier, it was only with the development of these courses that the teaching of human behaviour in psychodynamic terms became recognised as an essential and fundamental part of professional training and was taught in systematic fashion by staff with clinical experience and, often, psychoanalytic training. It was therefore only from the 1950's that psychodynamic perspectives became incorporated into social work to any appreciable extent; from that time, and particularly in the late 1950's and early 1960's, psychodynamic concepts came to make an increasing and more widely diffused impact on British social work. Elizabeth Irvine, then Senior Tutor at the Tavistock Clinic and subsequently Reader in Social Work in the University of York, who has done much to relate the psychoanalytic point of view to social casework, commented in 1956 that British casework was experiencing a renaissance. 'It is no longer', she wrote (perhaps prematurely) 'the validity and relevance of psychoanalytic theory which is in question, but the extent to which it can be assimilated, and the ways in which it can be applied by the general body of social caseworkers'[61].

Such attempts to apply psychoanalytic understanding to casework problems can be seen in a number of fields during the 1950's. Perhaps the classic example is of the so-called 'problem family', which had seemed so intractable to the best efforts of social workers and administrators. In the 1950's, attention became increasingly focussed less on the social concomitants of the problem (poor housing, irregularity of employment, poverty, etc.) than on personality aspects which were seen by some authors as the major etiological factors. So Dr. Ratcliffe, in an address to the Institute for the Study and Treatment of Delinquency in 1957, maintained that if 'the problem family's real difficulty is a primary failure of human relationships, then the only way in which we can hope to modify the situation is by providing these people with some form of satisfactory relationship therapy. In other words we must provide for them, in a therapeutic setting, the experience of a relationship which they can come to rely upon, to trust and to use as the foundation for their future relationships with other people' — a task which he saw as lying within the province of the caseworker[62]. The spread of these newer conceptions of casework are reflected very closely in the professional literature, particularly in *The Almoner* and *Probation*.

Prior to 1952, there were few articles in *The Almoner* that dealt with casework, and none specifically on psychological aspects of the work. In 1952, a letter commented on the lack of psychological training afforded to almoners, with the consequence that almoners 'often limit themselves to the environmental factors in medico-social problems and ignore the less obvious, but by no means less important, psychological elements'. The writers went on to say: 'we do not feel adequately equipped for work which requires deep insight into the emotional problems of our patients, and only too often those who realise the importance of psychological factors in medico-social work, and who attempt to act on this realisation, are accused of entering the field of psychiatric social work'[63].

The next few years showed an increasing interest in casework and in the ways it could be taught — notably that method of teaching undertaken by the experienced practitioner in the field and known as supervision. Although supervision had long been part of the training of psychiatric social workers, it was used in other agencies more as a means of administrative control than as a teaching method. But as social casework came to be seen as a process of offering help through a relationship, so supervision came to have a different connotation, and to be viewed as a way of helping the student or new worker to acquire practical skills through the relationship established with the supervisor. The focus of supervision reflected the supervisor's view of what casework was, and by some supervisors it was seen primarily or wholly as a way of illuminating the psychodynamic forces at work in the casework relationship. Supervision or fieldwork teaching thus represents an extremely important means whereby the values and orientations of the profession are handed on to those entering it, and ensures the transmission of a common culture.

Experienced social workers were from 1950 onwards learning the new techniques. In 1956 Miss Rees[64], Director of Training for the Institute of Almoners, attended the UN Seminar on the Training and Supervision of Social Casework in Holland, and in 1952 Miss Snelling reported on that held in Finland[65]. In 1955 several almoners attended the course on student supervision arranged by the Association of Social Workers. The same year, an extensive correspondence on supervision took place[66] which illustrated both the interest that new ideas of casework were creating, and the anxiety they aroused for almoners well established in other ways of working and suspicious of American techniques. In 1956 came the first article specifically on a psychoanalytic topic: Mrs. Irvine's *Some Implications of Freudian Theory for Casework*[67]. In welcoming her article, the editor stressed three ways in which a knowledge of psychoanalysis was helpful to the medical social worker: the unconscious significance of illness, the ways in which anxiety might be marked by defence mechanisms, and an understanding of the worker/client relationship[68]. The medical social worker was especially concerned with the deeper understanding to be gained from the work of Freud and others of the unconscious significance, illness, disability, accident and death might have — for example, the unconscious meaning to the patient or his family of severe or chronic illness with its prospect of continuing dependency. Also of importance was an understanding of the feelings that might underlie defensive reactions such as hostility or restlessness. Lastly, psychoanalysis could help the worker to understand the mixed and less conscious feelings the patient might have about the hospital and about the worker himself.

Nevertheless, the new approach was much misunderstood and continued to cause confusion and uncertainty. Miss Butrym, lecturer in medical social work at LSE, in an 'Open Letter'[69] in 1961, clearly touched on matters of deep concern to many medial social workers. Much of the confusion was due to the misconceptions and mystique that had come to surround the whole idea of casework; in her view it was not possible to work with individuals who were sick or whose next of kin were ill and *not* practice casework. The growing prestige of casework together with uncertainty as to what it really was had added to

> the volume of misery and feelings of failure of those who do not regard themselves as practising casework because they do not know what casework is, and therefore equate it with an ability to speak a highly sophisticated idiom of psychological language or some other irrelevant criterion.

1961 was evidently a year of confusion and heart-searching for almoners, reflected in the correspondence following Miss Butrym's letter, as a result of which the foundations of professional practice were greatly clarified and a more balanced view of the medical social worker's function began to emerge.

Probation before 1950 had few articles or references indicating psycho-dynamic interests. There were some on psychiatric topics, but none by psycho-analysts[70]. In the 1950's, however, new themes began to emerge which indicated a considerable change in the conception of the probation officer's role, and a new interest in developing casework skills of a more psycho-therapeutic kind. In 1952, a UN Seminar on Probation Work took place at Church House, Westminster, at which the conception of probation as treatment was presented:

> The modern conception of probation involves personal assistance to the offender as a skilled process in which use can be made of the knowledge accumulated by the social and psychological sciences. These social and psychological skills are based on the essential principle that a personal relationship must exist or be created between the person treated and the person giving treatment, and that such a personal relationship must be deliberately and constructively used for the redirection of the attitudes and behaviour of the person treated.[71]

The Home Office was encouraging a number of experienced officers to take either the Mental Health or the Tavistock Advanced Course, and in 1954—1955 it organised a study group of nine probation officers with a psychoanalyst and psychiatric social worker, an account of which was given in *Probation* under the light-hearted title of *How Deep is Your Casework?*[72]. In 1956 a number of probation officers attended a conference on 'Self-Awareness in the Caseworker', organised by the Association of General and Family Case-workers; and in the same year, Miss Corner, in her address from the Chair to the NAPO Annual Conference, maintained: 'We may now, I think, as a service be said to be well launched on the exploration of the possibilities of casework through the skilled use of the personal relationship between individual case-worker and client...'[73]. For the future, she suggested, attention should be given to the development of other helping methods such as groupwork.

Meanwhile, efforts were already being made to introduce a kind of supervision designed to enhance the development of these professional skills, and a statement on this was discussed and accepted at the same annual conference. An article on *Casework Supervision in the Probation Service*, incorporating this statement and emphasising the need for senior officers to have the opportunity of learning about supervision in this newer sense, maintained that casework now 'is characterised by its recognition of emotional factors in the aetiology of delinquency and by the stress it lays on the use of the worker-client relationship as a therapeutic tool'[74]. Such statements do not of course necessarily indicate consensus, and there was some critical correspondence in *Probation* questioning the appropriateness of viewing delinquency as maladjustment[75]. Nevertheless, a senior probation officer clearly expressed a widely held view when she claimed that she had found no client 'whose conduct does not come, in part at least, from his own personal internal problems'.

As casework became defined as a treatment process using as its major means of intervention psychological help through verbal discussion within a personal relationship between caseworker and client, so the question of whether or not casework was to be equated with psychotherapy (and if it was not, precisely where and how it differed) became a burning issue. At a conference of the Association of Psychiatric Social Workers at Leicester in 1956 this was the main theme[76]. Dr. Sutherland, Director of the Tavistock Clinic, particularly emphasised the likeness between psychotherapy and casework (in that both used a knowledge of unconscious dynamics and of transference) and advocated a greater acquisition of therapeutic skill on the part of the social worker, and a greater fluidity of role between social worker and psychotherapist as that occurred. For although he considered social work to be more restricted in that it was concerned with the individual's difficulties in a social relationship, and not with a radical restructuring of the inner world, he clearly saw the central skills in casework as psychotherapeutic.

Other lecturers, however, though laying stress on psychodynamic understanding as an essential component in social work, saw the distinctive and different element in casework as lying in its social focus and (by implication) viewed therapy as only one of a range of possible role transactions between caseworker and client. This issue has remained an open one, and the case for psychotherapy is being strongly argued at present by the Group for the Advancement of Psychotherapy in Social Work. Nevertheless, there has been increasing recognition, on the one hand, that if a broad definition of psychotherapy is adopted (i.e. treatment of distress by psychological means) then social workers do undertake psychotherapy, though only a few would claim it to be their primary function; and on the other hand, it has become equally clear that the treatment model is only one of a number of possible models of social work practice, though it is probably still the dominant one.

111

.Some of the consequences for social work of the greater incorporation of psychodynamic psychology will be considered in detail in later chapters. The introduction of generic courses themselves however had other important results which it is relevant to consider here. Undoubtedly they raised standards of practice and introduced social workers in training to a body of psychological theory which was of great relevance to their practical concerns, and which had not before been taught in any very systematic way as part of social work training, with the exception of the Mental Health, and, more recently, child care courses. But they also had other less desirable results; they led to the development of a narrow range of interests and skills, and they greatly restricted the conception of the social worker's role.

First, by narrowing the focus to that of casework, the new directions in training tended to produce highly trained workers with a limited range of interests and skills. This is reflected in early examination papers of the first generic course. Those questions dealing with 'method' up to 1960 were wholly concerned with casework on a one-to-one basis, and reflected no interest in group, community, residential or even family-focussed social work. Further, other forms of social work did not share in these developments in training and professional organisation. The advances in casework training, unaccompanied by equivalent developments in training for other forms of social work, thus tended to create a gulf between caseworkers and social workers using other methods — for example in the residential and community work fields. Professional social work came to be equated with casework. This sharpening of professional focus and the emergence of a new professional elite not only made for difficulties in relationships with other workers, but it also meant that social workers have failed until recently to develop interests and skills in the use of non-casework methods of intervention, or an adequate conceptual basis for them. The striking development of the late 1960's was the expansion of the social worker's conception of his role and the experimentation with a very much wider range of interventive methods concerned not only with individuals, but with families, groups and institutions.

A second and equally significant consequence of the emphasis on casework was its tendency to concentrate attention on the development of skills and techniques in working directly with the individual client, and the consequent narrow conception of social work to which this led. Professional interest centred on the development of 'casework skills', and although the provision of advanced training was always envisaged as a next stage, social workers during the next two decades received little encouragement to prepare themselves for other types of professional role where they could make a positive contribution to the prevention and alleviation of social distress, for example in social service administration and planning. As a consequence, when local authority Social Services Departments were set up in 1970, social workers with administrative and management experience who could take senior positions and help to shape the development of the new departments were in very short supply. This is not to be explained only by the fact that professional training was itself relatively

112

new; it also reflects a conception of social work as being concerned with 'a direct person-to-person approach to the client and his... problems'. Thus roles related to broader developmental tasks — planning, resource provision, consultancy, policy development, administration, social work education — have not been regarded as vital aspects of social work activity, for which training and preparation is as necessary as for direct treatment roles, and which have their place in the broader concerns and objectives of the social work profession.

In retrospect, comparative developments in social work education in the 1950's in Britain and the United States show an extraordinary reversal of pattern. Up to the Second World War, the strength of American social work education had been in its development of clinical and technical skills and in the processes of supervision and consultation designed to enhance these. It was in this area that British social workers felt they had most to learn. Social work in this country had shown much less development of skilled professional practice, but, on the other hand, for many years British social workers had enjoyed an education in the social sciences which gave them a broad perspective and a sensitivity to policy issues which had been lacking on American courses. Around 1950 these patterns were sharply reversed. British social work, with its strong urge towards the achievement of a recognised professional competence, concentrated its efforts almost exclusively on the development of training for casework and direct treatment roles with individuals, at the very moment at which the Hollis—Taylor report on *Social Work Education in the United States* was challenging American social work to lose its parochialism and overemphasis on casework and to broaden its range of professional roles in order to make a more effective contribution to the planning and organisation of preventive as distinct from ambulance services. The report maintained that the profession had an opportunity to render services that greatly transcended the function of carrying out certain skilled processes:

> The great range of organisational and administrative problems connected with the rendering of service; the major questions of policy and the appropriateness of existing institutions and methods of meeting social needs; the vast field of prevention; the analysis of the nature and causes of social needs; the adaptation of American social work knowledge and skill to the needs and circumstances of other countries — all of these present a challenging opportunity to social workers if they have the vision, the courage, and the preparation to grasp and grapple with them.[77]

In Britain this broader conception of social work has still not gained acceptance, and it is still conceived primarily in terms of direct client contact. Training reflects this view, and the preparation of social workers for the wider roles they are already assuming remains secondary.

We have considered in some detail the professionalisation of social work and the emergence of a new ideology as exemplified in the Carnegie Course at the

London School of Economics and Political Science in 1954; this was of particular significance since it embodied new ideas drawn from a number of sources and made an important contribution to the creation and dissemination of a new professional culture. The core element was the emergence of a new concept of casework strongly influenced by psychodynamic ideas. Psychoanalytic theories and concepts for the first time were strongly assimilated into the professional culture of social work, and the professional literature, particularly that concerned with fieldwork supervision, reflects this influence. The developments in training of which the Carnegie Course was the spearhead led to the emergence of a new professional elite, the caseworkers, and it also contributed, for a time at least, to a certain narrowing of professional focus.

5.7 The Demise of 'Carnegie Man'

If the professional ideology represented by the Carnegie course had a heyday, it was certainly brief; by the mid-1960's new emphases were evident in the social work literature, and we find Eileen Younghusband spearheading not a Freudian revolution but a group to develop training for community work. What this symbolises is a broadening of the conception of social work, and in particular a renewed emphasis on its social and situational aspects.

The 'person-in-situation' has long been identified as the central unit of attention (the 'critical base' as Janchill puts it[78]) around which social work has organised its activities, its knowledge and its forms of service. For a number of reasons, however, the person dimension has been held in sharper focus — reasons which have to do in part with the accessibility and relevance of psychoanalytic personality theory and the lack of an equivalent theoretical base for effective social and community action. The social and behavioural sciences are now making a far greater contribution to theories of change, and thus to the emergence of new professional perspectives. A distinctive feature of social work since the late 1960's has been the growing interest in methods of intervention which derive from a view of social problems as primarily structural rather than personal in origin, so that intervention can be most fruitfully directed to the situation rather than the person. From being a somewhat peripheral and low status area of professional activity, efforts directed at the achievement of social and situational change have now moved into the forefront of social work thinking; indeed, it has been suggested that by starting with the individual rather than the community, social work made a serious error[79]. Wasserman has observed:

> Through the years, environmental theory and practice have come to be downgraded as an inferior kind of social work, something below the craft and skill level of a true professional. In some large agencies today, what is referred to as 'environmental work' (the provision of concrete goods and services, liaison work, brokering, advocacy) is designated as part of the

realm of the para-professional. The professional person who is adept in these areas is perceived by his colleagues as possessing unimportant skills. High status, prestige, respectability and glamor are extended to those who are most proficient in the psychotherapeutic arts. In casework circles, the expert clinician and not the expert advocate or resource-finder is the esteemed role model.[80]

There are signs that this is changing, and a major influence contributing to this change stems from the greater application of sociology to social work education. The syllabus for the first Applied Social Studies Course at the London School of Economics (which provided the model for subsequent one-year postgraduate courses) included no sociology, though there was a strong element of social administration. There were obvious reasons for this in that students had already undergone a basic preparation in the social sciences in their previous degree course and indeed this was a condition of admission. In the early 1960's, however, as a consequence of the *Report of the Working Party on Social Workers in the Local Authority Health and Welfare Services* (the Younghusband Report), new two-year courses of training were introduced outside the universities. They were designed for those without previous higher education, and incorporated a broad basis in the social sciences as well as professional subjects such as casework.

This development coincided with a great expansion in British sociology. Between 1962 and 1964, the number of chairs in sociology increased from three to twenty, evidence of the growing size and influence of sociology departments within academic institutions. In many colleges of further education it became a major teaching area. Sociology departments not only provided teaching on basic sociological theories and concepts for social work students, but also turned their attention to the sociological analysis of social work as an institution. The indications are that sociology is now a growing influence on social work courses, and is affecting both the nature of the training and the outlook and perspective of social workers. Sociological interest has directed attention to the structural origins of social problems and pointed to levels of intervention other than that of personal help; it offers explanations of human behaviour in interactional or sociocultural rather than in intrapsychic terms (for example the rich literature on deviance); and, lastly, it provides ground for a different stance towards the problems encountered in professional practice which is markedly affecting the ideology of social work and contributing to the development of different practice models.

Although it would not be appropriate here to embark on a discussion of recent directions in sociological theory[81], it is significant that similar tendencies can be discerned in both psychology and sociology which may have the effect of reducing the distance social workers have felt between the two and bringing about some rapprochement between them. There has been a marked reaction among some sociologists to positivist social science which attempts to emulate the natural sciences and consists in the collection and analysis of

115

'objective' data, and a move towards a more phenomenological stance. The phenomenologist attempts to set aside metaphysical presuppositions and to identify and describe the world of phenomena as it is subjectively experienced. This includes the subjective meanings which such phenomena have for the one who experiences them. This parallels the kind of development discussed under the heading of existential psychiatry in Chapter 1, and in it can be discerned a swing away from the dominant 19th century idea that 'scientific knowledge is the paradigm of all (valid) knowledge'[82] and that in science is to be found the solution to all major human ills — a belief which has dominated social work education from its beginnings.

In so far as phenomenology is coming to influence social work (for example, through the widely read work of Goffman) it marks a major ideological shift. The task of phenomenology is to 'observe, describe and analyse the structures, properties, dimensions and interrelationships of phenomena as they are naively apprehended'[83], and is distinct therefore from both learning theory and psychoanalysis, both of which are concerned with explanation by reference to origins. Phenomenology is concerned with experience and with meanings, not with causes; indeed, it attempts to eschew the search for causal explanations. 'Basic to (phenomenological) investigation is always the attempt to establish the 'what' of experience[84], to reconstruct the phenomenal world of the other, whether that other be the deviant, the sick person, or the client. It is thus closely akin to a *verstehende* psychology (such as psychoanalysis) which seeks an intuitive understanding of meanings and personal constructs.

A second major influence on the broadening conception of social work has been the development of social administration. As a discipline, social administration originated with the social study courses designed for the preparation of workers in the fields of social work and social services; after the Second World War, with the great development of social services which then took place, it emerged as a clearly defined area of study and research concerned with issues of social policy and the administration of central and local social services. This expansion can be seen in the rapid mushrooming of chairs in this discipline: as Parker notes[85], that of Professor Titmuss at the LSE in 1950 was the first with that specific title; his own at Bristol in 1969 was the 25th. The focus of social administration as 'the study of collective action for social welfare' has led to a great deal of work in the social problem area, some of the most important in the poverty field. The work of Townsend and Abel-Smith[86] in 1965 demonstrated that poverty as measured by the basic national assistance scale was far more widespread than had been popularly believed; basic problems of this kind, it was evident, had not been 'cured' by the Welfare State, and still contributed to or even created many of the problems with which social workers had to deal. Similar research with important policy implications has been carried out in a number of fields, notably education, and has led to a growing interest in the effects of such factors as social class and the urban environment on educational attainment, and to the development of new initiatives such as those concerned with positive discrimination. The

116

conclusions drawn from a growing body of research have led to new attempts to level up the grosser inequalities of opportunity and resource distribution, successfully or not. This has posed a sharp challenge to the psychological determinism current in social work in the mid-1950's and early 1960's, and the dominant question with which social work is now faced is: what part should be played by the social worker in a society characterised by inequality of resources, opportunity and power — an inequality which the major social institutions appear to reinforce? Is there a valid and morally convincing role for the social worker, or is he, by personalising problems, in effect 'privatising' public ills and thereby implicitly contributing to the maintenance of the very problems he is professionally committed to alleviating? The last few years have seen a number of publications which have attempted to grapple with these issues and to articulate a radical stance for social work practice[87].

A third major development, accelerated by the establishment of Social Service Departments in 1970, has been the diversification of the occupational roles in which social workers are employed. These include management, consultancy, policy-making and research; they involve social workers at a variety of organisational levels in the identification of need and the development of imaginative and flexible social service provision. Yet despite this great variety of tasks — in particular those concerned with policy and service development — the social worker is still viewed primarily as one who works directly with clients, and social work education reflects this. Training has lagged behind organisational growth, and as yet little training exists to prepare social workers for management or planning roles; on the whole these are regarded as moving out of social work, rather than into a different but important area of professional practice. This again clearly reflects the influence of clinical models and seems to be true internationally. Kendall has observed:

> A double commitment to what we now call 'macro' and 'micro' tasks in society has led to the introduction of community work, social policy, social planning, administration, and social action as functions for which schools of social work must take responsibility. Relatively few schools around the world are ready or equipped to prepare social workers for all these roles, but most schools at least recognise that such preparation is a future obligation.
>
> In no country with which I am familiar does social work as a profession regard itself as concerned only with remedial tasks and the palliative and rescue work of society. Preventive and developmental activities, such as urban development, family planning, land reform, housing programs, rural rehabilitation, are increasingly seen by social workers as areas of professional responsibility in concert with other professions.[88]

Not only has there been diversification of role, but the social work task was itself defined by the Seebohm Committee in a broader way. The Committee hoped to see social workers abandoning narrowly defined specialisations in favour of undertaking a wider range of work appropriate to a community-based, family-oriented Social Sevices Department. In keeping with this hope, it assumed the development of a common training that would equip the social workers of the future to work not only with individuals, but also with groups and communities — areas of skill in which contemporary training was less developed.

In summary, recent years have seen a broadening conception of the social work role, in which direct casework with individuals or families is only one of a number of possible modes and levels of intervention. This has been reflected in the development of the unitary approach — an attempt to provide a conceptual basis for social work drawn from systems theory — which undoubtedly represents an attempt to find novel ways of conceptualising this diversification of social work roles and methods.

This, however, is to anticipate later discussion, and first the psychoanalytic theme will be picked up and its implications for social work examined in greater detail.

6
Social Work and Freudian Man

I turn now to the impact of psychoanalysis on British social work, and attempt to identify some of the characteristic emphases to which it has led, and some of its consequences for social work theory and practice. The most profound effects of psychoanalysis on social work are to be seen less in techniques than in the changes in value system to which psychoanalysis has contributed in the last two decades — changes in which social workers have participated and which have profoundly altered their outlook and orientation towards the problems they professionally encounter.

Psychoanalysis can be seen as a scientific revolution, introducing a new paradigm within which human behaviour can be studied[1]. The psychology of Freud has brought about a novel conception of man — 'psychological man' as Rieff[2] has described him — which not only transformed the study of psychology, but has become part of the cultural outlook of the West. Where 19th century psychology saw man as a rational, willing being, in command of his own destiny, Freud stressed his irrationality, and the effects on action of motives and drives which were unknown to the actor and therefore beyond the control of his will. The theory of the unconscious made sense of otherwise bizarre, inexplicable behaviour such as was found in mental disturbance, particularly hysteria. It made possible a new approach to mental disorder and a new form of treatment — psychotherapy — through psychological means. Freud may be said to have opened up 'a new dimension of honesty'[3]; he was impatient with all illusion and self-deception.

But the implications of Freud's discoveries went far beyond the treatment of neuroses. The essential mechanisms at work in neurosis were no different from those involved in normal behaviour; for example, those manifested in dreams and parapraxes. In Freud's view the difference between the normal and the neurotic was only a matter of degree; thus it blurred the boundaries of normal and abnormal, and mental health and illness could no longer be seen as separate, distinct and unitary states. Implicit in this was 'an injunction to tolerance'[4]; it led to a compassionate approach based on the recognition of a common involvement in neurotic suffering, at least to some degree. It offered therefore a new way of approaching human distress; behaviour once viewed as sin, wilfulness, depravity or moral weakness could be seen as the result of sickness or of psychological damage.

The psychoanalyst holds that the unconscious is universal and consists largely of impulses or fantasies of an unsocialised and primitive nature. Within the most civilised of human beings are latent possibilities of violence and infantile egotism. This recognition of common involvement in the most savage as well as the more noble of human urges has made possible a psychological humanism which has been regarded by many as one of Freud's major contributions to Western culture. As Freud himself remarked, 'nothing human is alien to me'; his attitude to the unconscious elements at work in his patient's personality was essentially nonmoralistic and nonjudgmental.

Although Freud set out to be nonmoralistic, there is of course nothing amoral about this approach — nor is its ethical stance necessarily permissive, as Lapiere[5] seems to argue: this is a travesty of the Freudian position[6]. On the contrary, it can be held (and this was certainly Jung's view) that psychological insight and the elucidation of the darker aspects of the personality to which psychoanalysis points presents man with a new moral challenge; the greater his awareness of the potentialities for destructiveness within himself, the more difficult does his ethical task become. For Jung, integration of the personality involves not only the achievement of adult object-relationships, but the development of the ethical as well as the psychological components of man's nature. What the analyst does not attempt to do, however, (whatever his persuasion) is to solve the patient's moral dilemma for him, or to assume the role of mentor. His job is to help the patient to increased self-understanding, not to prescribe for him what his actions should be; to increase his area of choice, not to determine those choices for him[7]. To achieve true neutrality is in any event impossible, since value assumptions are invariably present in the concepts of mental health and illness, and in terms such as flexibility, rigidity, maturity; nevertheless, this remains an aspiration of psychoanalytic practice and as such forms an essential element in its ideology.

At its best, Freudian humanism has lent powerful support to liberalising and reforming influences in social affairs, particularly in relation to mental illness and crime. Within the penal field this influence can be seen particularly clearly. The basic rationale which guided penal policy in Victorian times was, according to Robertson,

> a belief in the efficacy of rational self-assessment and a programme which taxed and strengthened the offender's character, as means to the eradication of criminal tendencies.[8]

Thus in penal ideology as in social work the concepts of rationality and moral responsibility played an important part. Regimes designed to increase responsibility and strengthen character were often tough and authoritarian. In recent years, a more tolerant value-system owing much to Freudian influence has begun to emerge, manifest in such innovations as the psychological treatment of offenders. Geoffrey Gorer in particular has stressed the humanitarian consequences of psychoanalysis, claiming that

> Freud has profoundly modified our attitudes to children, child-rearing and education, to the sick, the criminal and the insane. Because Freud lived and worked, the weak and the unhappy are often treated with a gentleness and charity and attempts at understanding which constitute one of the few

changes in the climate of opinion in this century of which one need not be ashamed.[9]

Nevertheless, there is another, less liberal, face to the picture. While psychological humanism has undoubtedly tempered the harshness of social institutions concerned with the sick and the deviant, the illness model can also, on deeper analysis, be shown to provide a rationale for far less humane and altruistic forms of 'treatment'. It can be more degrading to be removed from the responsibility for one's behaviour than to be punished for it, and a diagnosis of 'illness' may itself lead to a form of dehumanisation based on the assumption that the patient must be cared for and can no longer be held responsible for his actions — an essential part of being human[10].

Social work has been strongly influenced by the values implicit in Freudian theory and these have been assimilated into its professional culture. The analytic attitude of moral neutrality has found its way into the basic value-framework as the principle of nonjudgmentalism and client self-determination and has strongly reinforced a conviction which was also expressed by earlier social workers — notably Octavia Hill[11]. Nevertheless, in earlier days, social workers, while recognising the influence of one personality on another, had viewed it primarily as *moral* influence, and the persistence of Victorian modes of thought was seen in the stress on 'character'; it was the essence of casework to attempt to build and strengthen in the individual the capacity for morally responsible action.

Psychoanalysis offered then a new perspective on man. It presented an alternative to the Victorian view of man as rational and morally autonomous, with its associated notions of blame and culpability. What social work derived from Freud was in effect a new stance towards those seeking help — indeed, a new ideology[12]. Halmos maintains that this ideology is characteristic of a professional counselling role far wider than social work, which operates on the basis of certain shared values and assumptions deriving ultimately from psychoanalysis. It may have been that this new ideology was no unintended consequence; Erich Fromm has asserted that Freud himself had an unconscious Messianic wish, a hope of founding a philosophical-scientific religion which should form 'a movement for the ethical liberation of man, a new secular and scientific religion for an elite which was to guide mankind'[13].

Social work has been affected by a number of emphases which derive from psychoanalysis, and have become part of its way of looking at recurrent professional problems and activities; part, in short, of its professional belief system. Although a number of different psychodynamic persuasions have had influence on social work, certain central features of the psychoanalytic paradigm are common to all these systems, and have contributed to characteristic directions of interest. These are, most importantly:

1. the primacy given to affective (rather than cognitive) elements of behaviour;

2. the central role ascribed to unconscious psychological determinants of behaviour;
3. the greater emphasis given to inner psychological processes than to social factors in explaining behaviour;
4. the stress on infantile life and its importance for the development of personality;
5. a heightened sensitivity to psychopathology;
6. a belief in rationality, and a reliance on insight as a major strategy of intervention in therapeutic change.

These will be considered in turn, the last somewhat briefly, since it has been examined in greater detail elsewhere[14].

6.1 The Primacy Given to Affective Life

Freud himself wrote:

> Psychoanalysis unhesitatingly ascribes the primacy in mental life to affective processes, and it reveals an unexpected amount of affective disturbance and blinding of the intellect in normal no less than in sick people.[15]

This emphasis has considerably affected social-work practice, and particularly the extent to which attention is given to the emotional rather than material or situational aspects of problems, for example in diagnostic assessments. The closer attention paid to the emotional aspects of a problem has had mixed consequences. It should mean a greater awareness of the emotional implications of life experiences and a greater sensitivity to the feelings, preferences and views of the client. But as Mayer and Timms[16] have found, it may also lead to a concentration on emotional problems which does not accord with the client's own perception of his problem or his expectation of the agency.

The tendency inherent in a psychotherapeutic orientation towards a preoccupation with feelings and emotional problems has been explicitly recognised by many social workers; and Winnicott, in particular, has stressed the dual function of the social worker as concerned with outer reality as well as inner experience. The social worker concerned with children, unlike the psychotherapist,

> starts off as a real person concerned with the external events and people in the child's life... She can never become entirely the subjective object which the psychotherapist becomes, she is bound to external reality because she is part and parcel of the child's real world, and often is responsible for maintaining that world. The social worker with children is therefore in a strategic position in their lives because she is in touch with a total situation representing a totality of experience.[17]

The psychodynamic emphasis on affective life may have contributed to a tendency towards discounting cognitive and rational elements in human activity. Elsewhere I have suggested that in actual social work interviews a cognitive type of insight in which connections between or patterns of events are recognised may play an important part[18]; this however has been somewhat neglected in discussion of practice because 'thought' or rationality has on the whole been regarded as less important than 'feeling', though it may have powerful effects on behaviour.

The emphasis on feeling may also have hampered the development of social-work theory. Although some of the early social workers such as Helen Bosanquet[19] stressed the need to think out and give some account of professional actions, later social workers nurtured in more psychodynamic pastures have tended to regard cognitive activity with some suspicion as 'intellectualisation' and theory as somewhat irrelevant to the social worker's proper concern with feeling. Intellectual activity may of course represent a flight from feelings; but it is equally true that an overemphasis on feeling may represent a flight from the effort of grappling with important theoretical issues. Bartlett has commented on a double resistance in social work to a rigorous intellectual approach associated with scientific thinking:

> It is perceived on the one hand as a threat to the uniqueness of the individual. On the other hand, since it seems cold and impersonal, it is perceived as a threat to the skill of the social worker, to the sensitivity and the artistic element that are regarded as important in social work.
>
> The psychiatric orientation of many social workers, with its emphasis on understanding the irrational aspects of behaviour, has probably furthered the anti-intellectual attitude. Thus, for some social workers, direct intellectual approaches to understanding and working with people may be dismissed with the derogatory term 'intellectualisation'.[20]

Paradoxically, while stressing the affective in human life, psychoanalysis has also laid emphasis, in the clinical situation, on the *affective neutrality* of the analyst. Here the appropriateness of the psychoanalytic model for social work is clearly open to question, and there is some evidence that self-disclosure on the part of the professional helper contributes to the establishment of rapport and may be a potent factor in providing an effective model from which the patient (or client) can learn different ways of handling situations or experiences that present him with difficulty[21].

6.2 The Central Role Ascribed to Unconscious Psychological Determinants of Behaviour

The theory of unconscious determinants of human behaviour has seemed particularly relevant to social workers, who frequently find themselves baffled by repetitive, blind and self-defeating actions. This has been a central concept drawn from psychoanalysis, but one which is specially liable to misuse. The

123

concern of psychoanalysis is with nonrational emotional elements in human behaviour, and the unravelling of hidden motives; it is concerned with the processes that lie behind overt actions and that lead up to them. It does not set out to investigate or analyse logical, purposive, rational behaviour.

> Psychoanalysis investigates the nature of the processes behind conscious thought and purposive action but not the characteristics and qualities of rational processes in themselves. It attempts to answer the question of what nonrational factors enter into the conscious behaviour of the individual, and it stops there. It does not attempt to explain the nature of external reality but rather deals with those factors which cause different individuals to apprehend this reality differently... Its field lies in the exploration of the effect of inner reality on the ways in which individuals relate to external reality.[22]

In any given situation, both internal and external factors are operative, and an explanation of 'causes' of behaviour in terms of either alone is likely to be misleading. While one or other may predominate, neither can be excluded theoretically. The psychoanalytic position here can be grossly distorted. To borrow an example from Peters[23], explaining a dentist's choice of profession in terms of unconscious sadism is only legitimate when more commonsense explanations do not hold, or where inner reasons predominate; even then, it is not an assertion but an hypothesis to be used with caution and tested against clinical material in the analytic situation. Peters[24] maintains that it is clear from *The Psychopathology of Everyday Life* that Freud never intended unconscious reasons to be adduced where commonsense explanations were adequate and sufficient, but where (as in the case of parapraxes) these explanations were unconvincing and 'deeper' reasons made more sense. Freud himself protested that 'psychoanalysis has never dreamt of trying to explain *everything*'. As the science of the unconscious mind it has 'its own definite and restricted field of work'[25]. Psychoanalysis, he said, has but a single aim, 'namely, to arrive at a consistent view of one portion of reality'[26]. The problem is to know when psychoanalytic explanations are appropriate and when they are not. Pumpian-Mindlin has observed:

> It is my feeling that much of the misunderstanding surrounding psychoanalysis stems from the fact that it is expected to furnish a total answer to human behaviour, which it does not presume to do. Psychoanalysis may, for example, be able to demonstrate the emotional basis for the interest of a particular scientist in his particular field, but it does not presume to explain his actual scientific activity in this field. The significance of the influence of external reality upon the rational activities of the individual lies in other disciplines than psychoanalysis. Parenthetically it might be added that unfortunately some psychoanalysts themselves do not always fully appreciate the nature of the subject matter in their chosen field, so that they at times wander into strange pastures and express opinions in areas beyond the province of their specialised competence

and knowledge. Because psychoanalysis has emphasised the importance of unconscious forces, it does not follow that they are the *only* factors or, in a given situation, the predominant factors involved. This is particularly true with regard to the application of psychoanalysis to related fields.[27]

Thus it is always necessary to bear in mind that psychoanalytic explanations of behaviour are only one possible kind of explanation, and exceptionally difficult to validate in any individual instance. They must therefore be used with great circumspection. A frequent and not ill-founded criticism levelled at the social worker is the apparent ease and certainty with which he makes psychodynamic inferences on the basis of sometimes very slender evidence.

⟶ Burdan patriarchy, control & power

6.3 A Diminution of Emphasis on the Social Environment

Psychoanalysis has made an important contribution to the understanding of social problems, for example crime and delinquency. Its special subject matter, however, concerns only a part of the total field, and what it deals with are the individual and psychological determinants of criminal behaviour; it will perforce tend towards individualist explanations of social phenomena, particularly of social problems. In recent years the research activities of psychoanalysts have extended to such areas as motoring offences, industrial disputes, organisational problems and international relations. Because of the special perspective of the psychoanalyst and the subject matter with which psychoanalytic theory has been concerned, it is the psychological aspects rather than the social determinants or external realities with which he is primarily concerned. In the industrial field, for example, it has been a criticism of the human relations type of approach that it tends to explain conflict in personal and psychodynamic terms, explaining away rather than accounting in structural terms for the real conflicts of interest which may be the major determinants of strained labour-management relations. To use a social work instance, we noted that in the 1950's explanations of the poverty of certain families were often made in personality terms — failure to develop ego strength, immaturity and so on — rather than in regard to the situational realities with which they had to cope and which may well have represented the more crucial factors. This discussion is of course highly reminiscent of the poverty debates at the end of the 19th century and it has recurred all through the history of social work. It has flared into open conflict recently, and the issue now centres on the extent to which many of the severe and distressing problems with which social workers have to deal (homelessness, inadequate housing, poverty) are to be explained (and therefore treated) in individual terms, and how far they are to be seen as rooted in a destructive social system and the deprivations (in broad cultural terms) that it allows to persist. As Miller and Riessman put it: 'The pathology approach does not lead to institutional or structural change, but rather to an emphasis on changing

125

personally disturbed deprived individuals so that they can utilise the inadequate services and opportunities inappropriately offered by the educational and social service systems'[28]. While a psychoanalytic perspective tends towards an individualist stance it is not of course the case that the analyst is interested only in inner psychological events, though this is his area of special expertise. Particularly with the development of ego psychology and its concern with the 'reality principle' psychoanalysis has become increasingly interested in social and environmental factors in psychological illness, and views behaviour (and psychological disorder) as the result of a complex interplay of psychological, social and cultural factors. It must be stressed however that the focus of ego psychology is still the *individual* and the way in which he copes, or fails to cope, with pressures. It is not a dynamic theory of interaction between the individual and the social system of which he is part. Equally, the strategies of intervention to which it leads are primarily focussed on the individual or on his immediate environment such as the family: it does not lead to strategies of change directed at the broader social environment. This is very evident from the two Smith College volumes, edited by Howard Parad, *Ego Psychology and Dynamic Casework*, and *Ego-Oriented Casework*.

The psychoanalytic direction is thus towards a minimising rather than a maximising of interest in social and structural change, and this is certainly the implication of classical Freudian psychology. Thus Rycroft writes: 'psychoanalysis interprets human behaviour in terms of the self which experiences it, and not in terms of entities external to it'[29]. It therefore becomes difficult to blend a social change with a psychoanalytic orientation — interest in one direction or the other tends in practice to predominate and to reflect the primary direction of theoretical interest[30]. Koestler[31] has suggested that there are two basic attitudes towards change, represented by the viewpoints respectively of the Yogi and the Commissar. The Yogi is primarily concerned with change from within, through introspection and self-improvement; the Commissar with change from without, through the altering of systems and structures. There is a tension between these two approaches, and synthesis (though both are obviously necessary) seems in practice extremely difficult to achieve; pendulum swings from one to the other tend to characterise succeeding phases.

All this is of course far more than an interesting theoretical argument and has very practical consequences; the perspective within which certain problems such as poverty or crime are viewed will determine the kinds of strategy devised for dealing with them. Probably very few of the distresses that the social worker encounters are to be seen exclusively in terms of one or the other: public ills still have personal effects — and, indeed, it has frequently been the lot of the social worker to try to ameliorate the personal distress caused by attempts to alter the structure of the social environment, for example dislocation resulting from housing or urban planning programmes. It is widely believed however that since the Second World War British social work has tended to withdraw from policy issues, and has failed to appreciate the socio-cultural determinants of the problems it is called on to deal with. This was the burden of Barbara Wootton's[32] well known indictment of casework in 1959, which was taken up as an issue of 'Reform or Therapy' at the Keele Interprofessional Conference of that year[33]. Earlier, T.S. Simey, an equally abrasive though more friendly critic, had insisted that 'the client's emotional disposition has become more and more the object of attention, and his environment less and less a matter of serious concern. This has increasingly widened the gulf that had begun to yawn between casework theory and sociology and anthropology'[34]. The subsequent discussion, it was reported, reflected some feeling among participants 'that psychiatric social work had been too dependent on the psychiatrist and had preferred the pursuit of ever deeper psychological knowledge to the exploration of social needs and social forms of treatment'[35]. More recently, Parker[36] has referred to the insulation of social work from issues of social reform, which in his view was a consequence of the new directions in social work training after the war.

If true, this is a serious indictment. Theoretically, the dual focus of social work — in assisting the individual and in social change — has always been present and was stressed by C.R. Attlee (then a lecturer at the London School of Economics) as long ago as 1920. The practical job of the social worker, however, has not given much opportunity for intervening at other than an individual level, and it is only in recent years with the growing strength of professional social work associations and the greater status of social workers in senior positions in local authorities and central government that intervention at a political and social planning level has become possible. While the issue is by no means a new one, it has for this reason taken on a new urgency. The problem at the present time is not so much that of awareness of socially-induced stresses (for social workers are brought starkly up against problems of lack of basic resources and social inequality every day of their professional lives) but of finding ways of solving urgent problems of social policy, such as those that relate to housing and the problems of the inner cities. These solutions do not lie within the competence of the social worker, but ultimately with decision-makers in central and local government with power to control the flow of resources. One of the consequences of a sharpened awareness of situational stresses, however, is the attempt now being made to find ways of sharing in and influencing these political processes, whether through informed study of these issues or through conflict strategies involving the explicit use of coercion.

The criticisms so far discussed have to do with social work's relation to broad social issues. The diminishing importance of the social environment can, however, also be detected in the emphases which casework theory has developed, particularly in the 1950's. In contrast to the dynamic view of the individual, there has been characteristically a restricted, static and limited view of the social environment and the practitioner's concern with it which must be regarded as a serious weakness[37]. The conception of casework that emerged in the 1950's placed in central focus the relationship between worker and client. The term came to be used to mean work with individuals in situations of personal and social stress. In this sense *casework is a continuous professional relationship, a process of dynamic interaction between the worker and client consciously used for social treatment purposes,* defined by a study of the particular person in his situation, the problems which most concern him and the ways in which he could be helped to meet these by the use of his own and the community's resources.

What matters is. . . *the concept of casework as the conscious use of the process of interaction between people to bring about certain beneficent results.*[38]

The emphasis here is placed on what is without doubt a central conception in any form of social work, not only casework; that is, its interpersonal aspect. As a *definition* of casework, however, it is limiting. For one thing, it seems to exclude all those briefer contacts (such as occur in intake and assessment procedures) which could hardly be called 'a continuous professional relationship' but which most would agree call for very skilful casework. For another — and more important in the present context — it seems to exclude all those areas of work traditionally called 'indirect treatment', where the focus of activity is other than the client; in particular, work with other professionals or organisations which may, in the military language of unitary approaches, constitute the target of intervention. The emphasis on relationship, as *an* important factor in casework, has thus tended in practice to lead to an over-emphasis on direct treatment of the kind that takes place within the social work interview and to a lessening of interest in situational measures designed to benefit the client indirectly, for example by working with significant others in his environment, whether these 'others' are the family, the work, or the educational system of which he is part. Thus it is an exclusive rather than an inclusive view of casework, and, if it is accepted, it is difficult to know how to classify all those other important (and no less skilled) activities in which the caseworker becomes involved but which do not form part of his direct inter-action with his client.

The restricted view of the environment and situationally focussed work can be detected in both British and American work. Moffatt, for example, describes casework in this way:

Casework is mainly concerned with helping people who are susceptible to the sort of help that caseworkers can give by means of personal contact. It consists mostly of talking and listening, aided when appropriate by money, goods or services. Its aim is to help the client to manage in the community either simply with the aid of encouragement from the worker or also by changing some of the client's attitudes if they are proving harmful.

And again:

Central to the whole discussion of casework treatment is the relationship between client and caseworker and either explicitly or implicitly any

128

discussion of treatment is a discussion either of how to cultivate this relationship or of what to do with it.[39]

He points out that environmental treatment is not given the same status as other methods in Hollis' book[40] (on which he largely draws) and he himself devotes only four paragraphs to this aspect, most of which is concerned with the provision of material aid.

A similar emphasis can be seen in the two volumes of the Smith College School of Social Work concerned with ego psychology and social work[41]. Although it is acknowledged (and indeed emphasised) in the foreword to the first of these that the 'person-in-situation' is the only sensible focus for social work activity, in fact there is very little reference to 'the situation', and only four references to 'social environment' can be found in the index; the text therefore seems to belie the focus outlined in the foreword. The second volume carries an excellent essay by Herman D. Stein, concerned with these very issues, but apart from this the focus is again almost wholly on direct therapeutic work with the client.

The major weaknesses resulting from theoretical treatment of the concept of the social environment and of environmental work seem to be these:

1. *Environmental work is assigned a low status and is often referred to, significantly, as 'environmental manipulation'.* It ranks low in the hierarchy of procedures used in casework. As far as the British literature is concerned, this is no doubt largely a reaction from the long association of social work with poverty and 'charitable doles' of one kind or another, from which social workers were understandably only too eager to escape.

2. *It is seen as an adjunct to counselling work, and as essentially peripheral to other more important aspects of casework treatment.* Much of the work which is now recognised as an important and integral part of the caseworker's total activity in relation to his case — for example, acting as advocate in relation to official bodies, negotiating with social security officials, housing departments, health authorities and the like, all of which calls for great ability and skill in working with professional colleagues and in mobilising and coordinating resources — came to be regarded as rather minor aspects of professional activity, and were given little theoretical treatment.

3. *From a diagnostic point of view, the social environment has been seen in somewhat static terms.* Social diagnosis has always included facts about schools, employment, family situations, leisure activities and so on, often very thoroughly garnered in the Mary Richmond tradition. In the 1950's, diagnosis came to be influenced more by psychoanalytic models. From a psychoanalytic point of view, the individual is the product of his past; his behaviour is historically determined and can best be understood through a vertical or historical approach; the social history thus became the main diagnostic instrument. As Dollard put it, the worker will 'peer down the long avenue of the client's past life to see how the present event matured'[42]. More recently, diagnostic emphasis is changing yet again, particularly as a result of systems

theory. There is much greater emphasis on the here-and-now and the social worker attempts to view the individual in his current life situation, in the context of the family as a social system, and as part of a complex network of role relationships and interactions. Furthermore, with increasing recognition of the effects on behaviour of the social systems of which he is part — in the family, at school, at work, in the institution — assessment has to be increasingly broadened to include the possibility of interventive action at points excluded by the more traditional casework frame of reference, and calls for what has been termed 'a broad diagnostic sensitivity'.

Assessment now needs to take account also of the effects of the social agency itself, which, as Carel Germain observes, may itself become a target of change rather than be taken as a 'given' in the situation. For example, from the point of view of newer concepts of family functioning, it seems likely that the more traditional models of intervention in child guidance work (in which parents and child were seen separately) may themselves have perpetuated or even created problems of communication. It is also obvious with hindsight how many difficulties were created by the removal of children in the earlier days of child care practice, so that administrative practice too may of itself represent an important 'problem' element.

6.4 Infantile Life

Fundamental to psychoanalysis is its exploration of the formation of personality in the very early years, and its explanation of behaviour as determined (in large measure) by the experience of the childhood past. This emphasis has, as we have seen, given rise to a great deal of research relating to personality development (and mal-development) which it is of fundamental importance for the social worker to take into account. The practical implications of this research for the care of children and the handling of separation experiences are too obvious and well known to need further elaboration here. Further, in the discussion of object-relations theory, it was suggested that, by its illumination of certain aspects of behaviour rooted in childhood, psychoanalytic work had contributed usefully to the worker's understanding of his own and other's actions.

More complex questions relate, however, to the extent to which the social worker uses knowledge of this kind not only to increase his own understanding, but in his actual interventive work with clients. A major part of psychoanalytic treatment is concerned with bringing into the open those hidden but persistent infantile elements which coexist with more adult attitudes within the personality, and which greatly affect his responses, particularly in interpersonal situations. Psychoanalytic therapy tries to cure 'by rolling the neurotic process back along the road of its development'[43]. Transference reactions, dream material, free associations, all contribute to the patient's gaining a new understanding of aspects of himself of which he was

130

previously unaware but which contribute to present difficulties — particularly feelings connected with painful or anxiety-laden events which have been split off from conscious awareness through repression but which remain dynamically active. The work of British analysts such as Balint, Fairbairn and Winnicott have been particularly concerned with elucidating the nature of early experiences which may greatly affect the whole development of personality, particularly where a neurotic defence develops which then becomes a characteristic mode of response. Winnicott's 'false self', Balint's 'basic fault' and Fairbairn's schizoid and depressive personality types all have to do with the development of faulty defensive reactions in the very early years which then become part of the personality structure.

But the social worker's job is different in nature; it is not his function, as Wittenberg puts it, 'to dig into the past'.

> The client comes because he is *at present* in some difficulty. There is therefore no need to dig into the past; the past is only relevant in so far as it is still active and influencing him today. It is therefore something traceable in the here-and-now, although it may have its roots far back in childhood.[44]

The more useful focus for the social worker is in terms of the present, and the difficulties or problems that the client is experiencing now. In terms of actual social work intervention, therefore, the psychoanalytic emphasis on the past may be misleading and inappropriate.

It must be added that from the point of view of the kinds of intervention which are open to the social worker, the psychoanalytic view has basically pessimistic implications. On this view, adult neuroses are rooted in the personality and developed in the early years; they are not easily susceptible to change. While the analyst may help the patient to achieve insight into early events through re-experiencing them in the transference and in the long and arduous process of analysis, to the social worker this therapeutic route is barred. He can only work with persons as they are, and he can do little more than attempt to understand the distortions which childhood events may superimpose on present-day experience and to recognise with patience and compassion sufferings which he cannot expect ultimately to change. The belief in the importance of the past for understanding behaviour in the present is nowhere more clearly demonstrated than in the centrality afforded to the concept of transference in social work literature. Yet we do not know how important or pervasive transference actually is as a feature of social work by contrast with psychotherapeutic practice. Theoretically it has been given great emphasis and it is assumed that the client will bring to the relationship deep and intense feelings of love, hatred, envy and rivalry characteristic of his earliest relationships. Carl Rogers, however, considered that transference was much less important in counselling situations than it was believed to be, and was mainly to be met in clients with persistent neurotic needs (those most likely to be found as analytic patients)[45]. Some analysts also have taken the view that manifestations of transference are to be seen as a consequence of the special conditions of the analytic situation when the distance and nonresponsiveness of the therapist, and his decision not to play by the ordinary social rules, creates frustration and encourages regressive behaviour which may not necessarily occur in situations structured in a different way.

> The psychoanalytic situation (writes Wolman) provides ideal conditions for reliving infantile emotions. The patient comes asking for help, and this fact puts him into a dependent, child-versus-parent relation with the analyst. The analyst's amiable, yet nonparticipative listening contributes to the patient's feeling of having found a friendly, benevolent, omniscient parental substitute. Free associations and the reclining position facilitate emotional regression. The patient lets his defences down and, in a regressive mood, weaves emotional fantasies around the silent analyst (who represents, as indicated, a parental figure). Past feelings and conflicts reemerge in the patient's mind and he relives the family drama as he experienced it in his childhood. The patient transfers his past emotional attachments to the psychoanalyst.[46]

At a commonsense level, it is evident that perception and expectations of present situations are likely to be coloured by past experience. As Wolman puts it, in this sense

> transference is a universal phenomenon, for everyone carries within his memory residues of past feelings and experiences. Transference elements influence one's choice of colors, preferences in music and art, and choice of a love object. Transference elements colour human ambitions and desires, for no-one can completely get rid of his past.[47]

While the effects of the past on present behaviour are undoubted, not all psychologists would accept the psychoanalytic account of how this occurs. The behavioural psychologist, for instance, would explain this simply as the generalisation of learned responses. The psychoanalyst, however, usually means much more than this by the term transference, and is referring to strong feelings originating with early relationships, which have a compulsive quality and of whose nature the patient is unaware. For Greenson and Wexler[48] the essential elements in transference are that it is a repetition of the past in the present and that it is inappropriate. Even among analysts, however, the term is used with considerable variation in meaning, and occurs in both technical and commonsense versions. The most useful as well as one of the most authoritative statements is that of Sandler et al. who regard it as

> a specific illusion which develops in regard to the other person, one which, unbeknown to the subject, represents, in some of its features, a repetition of a relationship towards an important figure in the person's past. It should be emphasised that this is felt by the subject, not as a repetition of the past, but as strictly appropriate to the present and to the particular person involved.[49]

Social workers do encounter transference manifestations and it is useful to recognise them for what they are. It is likely, however, that the extended discussions in the casework literature reflect the central importance which transference and its interpretation hold for psychoanalysis, rather than a true assessment of their importance for the caseworker. The structure of the casework relationship, its deliberate attempts to discourage dependency and regression, and its focus on strengths, coping capacities and the here-and-now, all serve to minimise the role that transference will play in social work. In other words, what is of far *greater* importance are the 'real' aspects of this relationship, about which psychoanalysis has so far had much less to say, and about which the social work literature is also strangely silent.

In general, the terms transference and counter-transference are used loosely in social work, and very often indicate no more than a feeling of attraction or hostility, whether rationally based or not. The whole point about transference, of course, is that it is *not* a reflection of the real properties of a situation; it operates quite independently of the actual qualities or behaviour of the other, and reflects entirely a subjective perception that is distorted and unreal. Further, analysing a relationship solely in terms of the analytic categories of transference and counter-transference can deflect attention from other important ways of thinking about relationships, particularly as a transactional process between two or more persons.

6.5 Psychopathology

Although psychoanalysis as a psychology gives an account of normal and not only abnormal mental processes, as a method of treatment its primary concern is with sick, disturbed or troubled individuals. It is the neurotic elements in the personality which are its primary focus and which it has done most to illuminate. The 'home base' of psychoanalysis, as Waelder puts it, is the neuroses. The function of the analyst tends to structure his observations in certain ways and to give him, as a clinician, a particular sensitivity to the undeveloped, weak or infantile aspects of his patient's personality. This is where his special function lies. The patient, for his part, acknowledges a need for help, or some incapacity to cope with his difficulties unaided, and thus defines himself as a patient, with all the connotations implicit in that term.

Social work has tended to take over this concern with psychopathology into its own nonclinical field of work, and in the literature of social work in the 1950's and early 1960's can be found extensive use of such terms as sick, immature, disturbed. An example has already been given of the approach to 'problem families'; many others could be cited, from the unmarried mother (typically depicted in the literature as unstable, neurotic or disturbed)[50] to the delinquent. My object here is not to examine the clinical validity of this approach, but simply to point out how the social worker's perception of the situations he encounters may be structured by his theoretical perspective — in this case a theory of human behaviour stressing psychopathology. This has had two significant consequences. First, it uses the analogy of disease entities, and locates the 'fault' or the problem within the individual, the so-called medical model; some of the implications of this have already been examined[51]. Second, it directs attention to the areas of weakness or difficulty, rather than to the strengths and coping abilities which the individual also has. Crisis theory has to some extent rectified this, bringing in a new way of thinking about human tribulations which has reduced the dangers inherent in the older approach. This conceives of life as presenting a series of demands (or tasks) which call for a response. Many of these are the ordinary life-tasks (entering school, getting a job, marriage, parenthood) which are part of the normal human lot, which have to be coped with, and through which (by successful adaptation) identity is formed. Others may involve more exceptional stress (bereavement, divorce, a car accident, imprisonment). What is important is the balance achieved between the person and the demands on him; the degree of stress involved, and his capacity for coping. Many people cope from their own resources, or with the help of friends or others in their immediate environment. For others, the severity of stress or disturbance may necessitate outside help, aimed at reducing strains and facilitating and strengthening the capacity to cope.

The task-coping concept is an extremely useful one for social work, since it focuses on what is normal, rational and capable, rather than on what is sick and disturbed. For example, much social work writing on single mothers in the past has sought links between psychopathology and extramarital pregnancy. Thus an experienced psychoanalyst puts forward the hypothesis that 'unmarried motherhood is rarely accidental and is usually the expression of extreme emotional difficulties'[52]. Such an approach directs attention to personality factors, to the effects of the past, and to the disturbed aspects of behaviour. It takes no account at all of the *context* in which such a pregnancy occurs, and by implication it diverts attention from the stresses (emotional, physical, material) involved for the single parent in today's society, and the degree to which the demands made on such a parent may be inordinate. In fact, as Jehu notes, there is strong evidence that behaviour may be much more situation-specific than we have supposed[53], and this further adds to the need to take situational factors much more into account. The capacity to cope — the important factor — is a function of many variables, including personality, life experience, constitutional factors (intelligence, health) and current resources (friends, partners, workmates, etc.); and what matters is the *balance* that is achieved between the task and the capacity to cope, the ability to master the task without breakdown in functioning.

6.6 Strategies of Insight

It is often pointed out that the term psychoanalysis refers to (a) a body of theory and (b) a method of treatment. While the social worker makes selective use of the first he is not, it is said, concerned with the second. Thus the major contribution of psychoanalysis has been to the understanding of behaviour,

134

and not to the interventive techniques or methodology of social work. Although this is in general true, it must still be the case that the beliefs the practitioner holds as to the nature and causes of the problems with which he is confronted will affect the direction of his efforts and the action that he takes; thus the models and direction of intervention may be affected in a subtle and indirect way.

The fundamental analytic method is interpretation leading to insight. Through this, particularly interpretation of transference reactions as they occur in the analysis, the patient is helped to gain a new understanding of how and why he behaves and feels as he does, and of the ways in which the emotional residues of the past affect his present behaviour. One of the major discoveries of Freud was to show that the personality is not unitary, but that coexisting with the adult that the patient believes he is are other aspects of himself of which he may be quite unaware — often childish, irrational, unacceptable, but often also rich in potential for new growth. Through re-experiencing early events in the transference but under new conditions and with the help of an understanding analyst, a new attitude becomes possible through the acquisition of insight, thereby enabling the patient to understand and alter his characteristic modes of response. Although, as I shall argue, the term insight is used with different meanings in social work and psychoanalysis, what social work has taken over from the analyst is a conviction of the value of insight and a reliance on this as one of the major means of helping a client to alter his situation of difficulty.

The same therapeutic primacy is not given to insight by all analysts. In Britain, the work of Fairbairn, Winnicott and others has drawn attention to the importance of other therapeutic factors and, in particular, emphasis has been placed not only on what is re-enacted in the analytic situation (the infantile residues present in the transference) but on what is new — the development of an authentic relationship with the analyst. In a paper given to the 1969 Congress of the International Psycho-analytical Association, Sacha Nacht laid emphasis on the importance of the analyst's personality and his 'deep inner attitude' towards the patient, though this he saw not as a substitute for insight, but as a prerequisite[54]. It is the analyst's capacity to provide the acceptance and kindness that the patient has not had, and his ability to *be* the good object the patient is seeking, that enables the patient to learn new patterns of relationship.

Nevertheless, at the same Congress, Hannah Segal took her stand firmly on the conviction that insight is at the root of all lasting therapeutic personality change, and that this is the *sine qua non* of analytic treatment[55]. She maintained that psychoanalytic insight differs from all other forms of insight (for example, that possessed by the ordinary well integrated intuitive person, or the perceptive historian or artist).

It involves a conscious knowledge of archaic processes, normally inaccessible to the most intuitive person, through reliving in the transference the very processes that structured one's internal world and conditioned one's perceptions.

Insight into the deepest layers of the unconscious and the primitive fantasies with which Kleinian theory is concerned comes primarily through experience of the transference and, says Segal, it is not retained after the termination of the analysis. Elsewhere[56] I have noted that the term insight may refer to:

(a) *a quality of mind,* or psychological attribute of the person ('possessing insight');
(b) a specific *act* of understanding of a special kind ('the achievement of insight', 'to have gained an insight'); or
(c) a particular kind of psychological *process* ('experiencing insight').

Thus the concept is by no means easy to define. There are however three main senses in which the word is commonly used.

1. *Insight* in its most general sense (and as it characterises the work of scientists, poets, critics, biographers, or any other activity of human understanding) involves the capacity to see below the surface, and to apprehend truths that are normally hidden from sight; it requires the ability to 'see into the heart of things'. In relation to scientific work, it is usually connected with problem solution, and thus refers to an essentially intellectual or cognitive activity. Insight is more than simply observation; it includes an appreciation of the relationships between or underlying observed phenomena (and thus some form of explanatory theory), but seems to depend more on intuition than on reasoning. While the *process* by which insight occurs is mental or psychological in nature (and thus has been a particular area of study for psychologists) the *phenomena* with which it is concerned may be of any kind. Literary and historical criticism, for example, may demonstrate varying degrees of insight in this sense.

2. *Psychological insight* is concerned with the understanding of psychological processes. It is related primarily to self-knowledge, but may be concerned with the understanding of others or of interpersonal relationships. It involves the same capacity to perceive or infer patterns of relationship or hidden significance behind manifest phenomena as described above. When used *psychodynamically,* however, it has reference to the appreciation of feelings by experiencing them, and thus is not a predominantly intellectual process. In relation to self-knowledge, therefore, insight includes affect as well as cognition, and it is this affective element (emotional insight) which is held to distinguish insight from other forms of understanding. In relation to others or to interpersonal dynamics insight may also have an affective component and is often said to involve the capacity for empathy. At the same time, the special characteristic of insight is that it links events or feelings in some explanatory way, and thus has an intellectual as well as an emotional component.

3. *Psychoanalytic insight,* as a special type of insight, has reference primarily to those aspects of behaviour that are unconsciously determined;

in particular, intrapsychic conflicts or unconscious fantasies and their infantile roots. The special characteristic of psychoanalytic insight is its linking of the present with the past, and its appreciation of the contribution of early experiences to contemporary behaviour. The achievement of this kind of insight is not restricted to the analytic treatment situation, it comes in the main through interpretation, especially of transference phenomena, and through the use of specialised techniques such as free association and the analysis of dreams and fantasies. A good deal of the material with which psychoanalytic insight is concerned therefore is not accessible to consciousness nor to ordinary introspection since it is subject to some form of censorship or is repressed. It is concerned with aspects of mental functioning which are buried and are dynamically unconscious rather than merely temporarily out of mind or unrecognised (preconscious).

The role that insight actually (rather than theoretically) plays in casework interviews has been greatly illuminated by the work of Florence Hollis. In her *Casework* (1964) she discussed specifically the relation between casework and the unconscious. While she holds that a knowledge of unconscious processes is essential to effective casework practice, she considers that generally case-workers do not deal with unconscious material, in the psychoanalytic sense.

> There was a time in the late 1940's when many of us believed that casework in 'insight development' has as its aim the bringing of true unconscious material to consciousness. I am inclined to think that for the most part we were confusing 'unconscious' with 'not conscious' and were actually dealing with preconscious suppressed material.[57]

Her own attempts, and those of the FSAA Committee on classification, to locate instances of 'insight development' in the strict sense produced very few indeed, even when agencies were asked for examples of their 'deepest' work. Thus Hollis does not see caseworkers as concerned with psychoanalytic insight in the sense defined above.

Her classification of casework procedures has a sixfold division, viz. sustaining procedures; direct influence; exploration — ventilation — description; person-situation reflection; reflection on personality dynamics; and reflection on developmental factors. Of these the last three are concerned with the development of insight or self-understanding, though research evidence suggests that very little casework intervention is in fact carried on at the level of the last two categories and that discussion of current patterns of interpersonal functioning is likely to be more central. Hollis' book is widely used on social work training courses, and indicates the very minor role which insight seems to play in social work practice. In her later analysis of 15 marital cases[58] this was confirmed, and it was evident that insight-oriented work was not characteristic of these cases.

In Britain interpretative work leading to insight has always enjoyed a special prestige among clinically oriented psychiatric social workers. With the spread of psychoanalytic influence more widely after the Second World War, and with

137

the development of new forms of training which were psychodynamically based (such as the generic courses and that at the Tavistock Clinic), even greater interest was generated in work of an interpretative nature, and the development of skill in the use of this technique came to be equated with 'advanced casework skill'. It is clear in retrospect that there was much confusion. Despite the attempts of some writers[59] to maintain a balance between 'inner' and 'outer' (or psychological and environmental) needs and not to get too seduced by the attractions of therapy, other aspects of the social worker's activity tended to be regarded as 'chores' and of lesser status than therapeutic work. Useful clarifications were made by Brown[60] in 1966 and by Elizabeth Irvine[61] (then Senior Tutor at the Tavistock Clinic) in 1964 which helped to place insight and interpretative work into perspective as one of a range of possible kinds of helpful activity. Nevertheless, there still appears to be confusion as to the kind of animal casework is, and insight is still stressed as a major aim of practice. A more recent study by Mayer and Timms noted that there is 'a positive, although possible decreasing, tendency in the field of social work to rely on psychodynamic concepts in explaining behaviour. As a consequence, cognitive elements (beliefs, thoughts, opinions) receive little attention and are apt to be viewed as epiphenomena, as derivatives of something deeper, and therefore unlikely to produce any decisive effects of their own on behaviour'[62]. This tendency was evident in the workers' predilection for methods involving the development of insight in their clients, regardless of whether or not this fitted the client's own definition of his problem and expectation of help, or of its appropriateness to working-class clients. The impression is gained that these workers (admittedly from an agency regarded as psychoanalytically oriented and therefore atypical) were greatly concerned with the development of insight as a primary treatment objective.

In recent years, the effectiveness of change strategies based upon insight has been called into question, notably from those concerned with the use of behaviour modification techniques based upon learning theory, and this will be discussed more fully in the next chapter. Nevertheless, it is likely that insight-oriented techniques even though directed towards a general psychological rather than a psychoanalytic understanding will retain an important place in casework.

Although the preceding discussion has been mainly concerned with insight as an aim of intervention, it should be said that the importance of insight for the social worker has been regarded first and foremost as having to do with self-understanding, in order to develop intuitive awareness of another's feelings — the capacity for empathy. The need for the social worker to have knowledge of himself and his own motivations has long been regarded as important in social work, but has been strongly reinforced by psychoanalytic influence. For the analyst to understand his own blind spots, biases and predilections was regarded as essential to analytic practice by Freud and hence the development of the training analysis in order to gain self-awareness at a deeper level than that possible through ordinary introspection.

In the last two decades the development of insight has come to be strongly emphasised as an aim of training for social work. It is a consequence of a conception of social work in which the personal relationship between client and worker is placed in central focus. The primary aim in the teaching of personality development is, according to Halmos, not the transmission of a body of relevant theory but 'that our students acquire insight'[63]. Several papers at the 1958 Keele Conference[64] emphasised the personal and emotional involvement of the student in learning about personality development, and the acquisition of insight as a primary aim of such teaching; the whole approach to teaching in this area in fact reflected an orientation which owed much, ultimately, to psychodynamic psychology, in teaching method and aim no less than in content.

The development of insight — 'the crux of which is the ability to recall the affects of one's own experiences when confronted with similar experiences in clients or pupils' — was discussed again the following year by Clare Winnicott[65]; indeed, she regarded the capacity for insight as the basic question in the selection of students for social work training. Although selection is normally based on a number of criteria — including intellectual ability and certain other personal qualities — there can be little doubt that the capacity for self-understanding has become a major element in the professional culture of social work no less than of psychoanalysis. Whether or not insight is to be an explicit aim of social work education, and if so how it is to be fostered, raises many difficult and thorny ethical questions which constitute a continuing (though by no means uncreative) source of tension and debate within educational institutions.

Although the Freudian view of man and the 'psychiatric world view' to which it leads has become a part of contemporary culture and has had pervasive effects on our value-system, it has certainly not gone without challenge. Some of the most fundamental and far-reaching criticisms have come from Szasz who has pointed to the disease model implicit in the concept of mental health and to the quasi-medical nature of psychiatric practice. Psychiatric medicine, he argues, is not 'like' physical medicine. The problems with which the psychiatrist deals are not primarily those of illness, for which clear medical causes can be discovered, but are primarily problems of living. The stuff with which psychiatry deals lies in the area of social and interpersonal relations, and the norms by which certain forms of behaviour are judged to be 'illness' and to need psychiatric treatment are in his view not physical but psychosocial and ethical ones. The practice of psychiatry is therefore inextricably tied to questions of value, in the face of which a claim to ethical neutrality is patently absurd. Szasz' proportion is that the whole concept of mental illness is a myth

whose function is to disguise and render more palatable the bitter pill of moral conflicts in human relations.[66]

This point of view has been taken to a more extreme position by Mowrer, who equally rejects the disease model of behaviour disorders and argues for viewing them as manifestations of sin rather than disease[67] — a view not surprisingly bitterly attacked by his psychological colleagues. Although criticisms of the so-called medical model are various and often surprisingly inexplicit, the main burden of concern seems to be that little place is left for choice and moral responsibility: issues such as these cannot be seen as the prerogative of the medical profession.

Among social workers too there are indications that the 'counselling ideology' referred to by Halmos does not involve such consensus as the term would imply, though perhaps for somewhat different reasons. It is a remarkable paradox that what was so eagerly embraced by social workers in the 1950's as offering an escape from the paternalism inherent in earlier social casework is beginning to acquire, in the eyes of the contemporary social worker, the very defects of the outlook it replaced. There is not much difference, it is said, between a moral inadequacy hypothesis and a psychological casualty hypothesis: both ascribe misfortune to individual causes, be they moral or psychological, and both assign a position of superiority to the social worker, whether in terms of his moral and cultural advantages or his psychological expertise. It is this paternalism to which Barbara Wootton has directed some of her most telling broadsides, and against which a considerable reaction can be detected in some of the professional literature today[68].

Thus the 'shared assumptions' to which Halmos refers are no longer being shared to the same extent, and there are signs that the therapeutic perspective is failing to provide social workers with a convincing and satisfactory way of perceiving their primary function. The major reason for this is probably to be found in the weakness of the Freudian view of society and of his account of the relationship between man and society. Freud's system of thought, once radical in terms of the psychiatric thought of his day, is no longer so[69]; it tends towards the maintenance of the existing social order, and reflects a deep pessimism as to the possibilities of constructive social change. It is, as Professor Bantock has observed, in the end a tragic view, and there remains a fundamental and insoluble conflict between instinctual demands and those of social life[70]. As he went on to point out, the types of action represented respectively by 'therapy' and 'social reform' are both necessary, and both psychological and sociological frames of reference are needed at different times. Nevertheless, it is probably true that the influence of psychoanalysis on social work has served to deflect attention from social towards individual change[71]. At a time when the inequalities of the distribution of resources in a wealthy society are becoming increasingly evident, it is not surprising that as a social theory the Freudian view is seen as unsatisfactory and that social workers are looking for approaches which will allow for the possibility of achieving constructive social change, without loss of that personal care which has been social work's distinctive and traditional concern.

140

Finally, it must be emphasised that what this chapter has been concerned with is the logical implications of certain aspects of psychoanalytic theory. It has attempted to identify some of the theoretical and value components that enter the professional ideology of the social worker, and whose source is to be located in psychoanalytic theory. It is no part of the argument to assert that, from this type of analysis, certain necessary characteristics of social work practice can be deduced; they are merely some among other influences on practice. Although psychoanalytic theory has undoubtedly *had* such influence, to determine its extent would require an analysis that took into account other quite different and perhaps countervailing theoretical and value components. Sorokin[72] has observed that culture is made up of interacting individuals and groups. The ideological aspect of culture consists of 'the totality of meanings, values and norms possessed by the interacting individuals and groups'. These meanings and values, like other cultural phenomena, stand to each other in one of three relationships: they may be integrated (or consistent), unintegrated (neutral, unrelated, neither consistent nor inconsistent), or contradictory (antagonistic). Thus, at both the individual and the group level of analysis, ideological culture reflects a complex relationship between systems of ideas which may be consistent, unrelated or antagonistic. Although the individual has several sets of meanings which are more or less consistent (thus enabling him to act in a more or less consistent way), these sets are also partially unintegrated or contradictory. Such contradictions occur when a political or national ideology (especially in time of war) conflicts with a Christian ideology of 'love thine enemy'. Similar contradictions may occur for the social worker who holds both a Freudian view of human behaviour and a Marxist view of society. Where such inconsistencies occur it is difficult to say how conflict will be resolved in terms of action, or with which set of beliefs behaviour is most likely to accord. In the same way, professional ideologies may be more influenced by political or ethical values which are not derived from, and may even be inconsistent with, the specific theories on which professional interventions are based.

7
Psychoanalysis and Social Work Education

An attempt will be made now to assess the importance of psychoanalysis for contemporary social work education, in the light of other significant developments in the social and behavioural sciences which offer alternative perspectives.

Since the 1950's psychoanalytic theory has formed an important part of the knowledge normally acquired by the social worker on professional and post-professional courses in Britain. On professional courses it is most often incorporated in sequences on human growth and development[1] (often forming the core of such a course) and to some extent in casework teaching. It also occurs in sequences on psychiatry and psychopathology in relation to the aetiology of the neuroses and methods of treatment. On some courses, a sequence of lectures may be devoted specifically to an account and critique of the major aspects of Freudian theory, or it may form part of a more broadly focussed course on theories of personality.

American textbooks such as Hollis[2] and Perlman[3] used on British courses show clearly this debt to Freud (though Perlman acknowledges an even greater debt to Dewey) and a recent account[4] of the major schools of American casework thought demonstrates how seminal psychoanalytic theory has been to most theoretical accounts of casework. Of the six theoretical stances reviewed in that book only one (that on 'Behavioural Modification and Casework') does not regard a knowledge of psychoanalytic theory as essential to effective casework practice. British textbooks also show evidence of psychoanalytic influence, though not to the same extent. Among those which reveal this influence most strongly are Ferard and Hunnybun[5], which offers a specifically psychodynamic account of the casework process, and the publications of the Family Discussion Bureau (now the Institute of Marital Studies). Timms[6] deals broadly with the sociological and psychological knowledge needed by the social worker, and under the heading of psychological knowledge lays special emphasis on that of a psychoanalytic nature; while his account is of course intentionally selective, the nature of his selection may be taken as reflecting his view of what is important. Other textbooks still in use such as Moffatt[7], Davison[8] and Monger[9] show some use of psychoanalytic concepts, though they also make use of sociological concepts such as role and interaction.

Post-professional trainings have been an important channel of psychoanalytic influence. In recent years, the training programme for social workers at the Tavistock Clinic and Institute has been greatly expanded and in most years some 300 social workers take part in day, evening and short courses run by its staff. The Tavistock Clinic, as we have seen, has always been eclectic in its approach, and seminars on such areas of work as family therapy and family and marital interaction are likely to draw on a range of theories (for example, communication and systems theories); nevertheless, a psychodynamic approach remains the essence of the Tavistock's teaching in these areas. A further source of post-professional influence have been various courses of group study which have developed in recent years such as those run by the Tavistock Institute, the Association of Psychotherapists, the Institute of Group Analysis, and the Grubb Institute of Behavioural Studies. All these use psychoanalytic personality theory.

The use made of psychoanalytic theories and concepts in the British social work literature has been selective and, on the whole, pragmatic. The theoretical aspects most commonly referred to are the psychoanalytic account of personality development and structure, especially the concepts of ego functions and ego development through object relations[10]. This includes the defensive processes. Particular use has also been made of concepts concerned with interpersonal relationships, such as ambivalence, resistance and transference. In general, it would appear that clinical concepts of this kind have been found to shed light on familiar aspects of behaviour, and there is far less interest in the metapsychological theories developed to account for the clinical observations. Considerable use is also made of the theory of unconscious motivation in explaining behaviour, and this has contributed to an alertness for its underlying psychodynamics. In particular, symptoms are held to have meaning: thus it may be hypothesised that the child who steals is seeking a substitute satisfaction for the love of which he has been deprived. As far as casework intervention is concerned, however, the social worker does not generally deal with unconscious material in the dynamic sense, though he may be alert to its presence; actual interviews are more likely to be concerned, as the work of Hollis has shown[11], with what is preconscious and relatively easily accessible.

Although psychoanalytic theories and concepts are used to label familiar behavioural phenomena and to explain behaviour, there is little reference in the literature to the clinical techniques of the analyst — free association, transference interpretation, dream analysis. It is sometimes suggested that social workers are taught to use psychoanalytic methods, but this is a patent misconception, at least as far as basic courses are concerned; some social workers do of course undergo further training in analytic psychotherapy, but this is atypical. Psychoanalysis is both a body of theory and method of treatment, and it is the contribution of some of its theories and its particular approach to human problems to the understanding of behaviour, rather than the application of its techniques to social work practice, which has been stressed in training. Although there seems to have been a predilection among some workers for the kind of casework aimed at the development of insight, it has been argued that this is not insight in the true psychoanalytic sense but is

143

rather a more general self-understanding concerned with events and interactions in the present.

Some distinguished American social work educators (notably Annette Garrett and Werner Boehm) have argued that the kernel of the psychoanalytic contribution to social work lies in ego psychology[12]. Garrett holds that many of the concepts of ego psychology can be of help in deepening the social worker's understanding of the human situations he encounters and in providing him with conceptual tools for use in his work[13]. Ego psychology, as must again be emphasised, is a development of psychoanalysis, and is not concerned exclusively, or even mainly, with conscious rational processes; at the same time it is particularly focussed on the development of the ego's capacity to relate to the outside world, to appreciate reality factors, to anticipate consequences, and to find solutions to adaptive problems. This includes the ability to postpone satisfactions and to tolerate frustration. The term 'ego strength' is used to indicate this capacity; for Garrett, it connotes particularly that capacity for free independent choice which is not determined by irrational and unconscious needs such as the need to win approval from others, or to prove something to oneself.

Werner Boehm also stressed the importance of ego psychology to social work, for similar reasons. Social work, he argues,

> focuses upon the social relationships which express the interaction between man and his social environment. Or, to put it differently, social work proceeds on the assumption that the nature of any problem in the area of social interaction has two dimensions which are interrelated; the individual's potential capacity for the performance of his social roles and the social resources available to satisfy his needs for self-fulfilment.[14]

Ego psychology, which is concerned with deepening understanding of the relationship between personality and social role performance, is one area of theory which is relevant and can illuminate this interaction.

> It is the concepts of the ego, its function and dynamic relationships with the other personality concepts, the id and superego, and their linkage with the theory of sexuality and the unconscious which constitute the core of the contribution of psychoanalysis to social work.[15]

It is the function of the ego, he observes, to 'orchestrate' the complexity of physical, psychic and social factors which impinge upon the individual. To do this effectively, he must perceive them realistically, relate them to each other, and himself act in relation to them.

> Thus, it is these attributes of the individual — perception, integration, orchestration and execution — which are the functions of the ego and are utilised in the process of social functioning.[16]

The emphasis of ego psychology on the integrating factors in the personality and on the identification of strengths and potential for personality growth, together with its appreciation of the social demands with which the individual has to cope has thus seemed operationally useful to social workers; further, its focus on strengths and coping capacity, rather than on pathology, makes it ideologically appealing.

But certain problems arise from it, both theoretical and practical. In particular, what relative weight is to be given to primary experiences of infancy in the etiology of neuroses, and what to later learning (during, for example, school and adolescence) in the development of characteristic behaviour patterns, more especially those of a maladaptive kind? From a classical psychoanalytic point of view, the experiences of the first five years are clearly crucial, and all later events are to be seen as secondary, only marginally affecting the personality structure laid down in the early years. To other psychologists (particularly those with a behavioural orientation) behaviour is constantly shaped by the environment in which it occurs, and is not so much an expression of enduring personality characteristics as a response to stimuli, the sources of which are often significant persons in the individual's immediate environment. This issue, which lies at the root of differences in viewpoint between psychoanalysts and learning theorists, will be considered more fully below. As this point, however, we may observe that these accounts are not necessarily mutually exclusive, and both can be valid; what is of great theoretical importance nevertheless (and indeed practical significance for social workers) is the *emphasis* to be attached to these different factors, for example, in relation to deviant or delinquent behaviour. Psychoanalysts themselves are undoubtedly broadening their frame of reference to include later environmental factors influencing behaviour; thus, for example, an interactional perspective is combined with a psychoanalytic view of personality in the work of group analysts such as Foulkes and Anthony, and family therapists such as Skynner. In practice, some of these recent developments in group and family therapy imply a recognition of the powerful therapeutic potential inherent in the immediate interpersonal environment, and a focus on contemporary rather than past events.

While ego psychology provides the worker with conceptual tools to use in assessment (for example, degree of ego strength, characteristic modes of defence and adaptation) and helps to sharpen his perception of the individual's ways of coping, the relation between such assessment and actual intervention is not always clear. Terms such as 'ego strength' (variously defined as the capacity to bear frustration, to postpone satisfactions, to cope with stress and conflict) are nebulous, and it is by no means clear what precisely the worker should be doing in building up ego strength. Thus the relationship between ego psychological explanations of behaviour and social work interventions can be somewhat tenuous.

In recent years the knowledge sources on which social work practice draws has expanded greatly in a number of directions. In particular, social work has been affected by other very different psychological perspectives, such as those introduced by behavioural approaches based on theories of learning. A behavioural orientation is growing in influence and poses challenges to the psychodynamic orientation which strongly coloured training perspectives in the 1950's and early 1960's; in particular it is widely claimed that behavioural approaches are more effective in achieving therapeutic benefit than those directed towards the achievement of insight.

7.1 Behavioural Approaches

Such measures, based mainly on theories of learning, have the object of altering maladaptive behaviour by modification techniques using principles drawn from experimental work. An important feature of behaviourally oriented social work is an emphasis on contemporary events, on the here-and-now, rather than an historical approach (characteristic of older psycho-analytically derived models) which sees the essence of present difficulties as rooted in the past. As Jehu observes, this may be a practical and appropriate approach for many social work problems[17]. In clinical psychology, the use of behaviour modification techniques has been exceptionally well documented, and it can point to considerable treatment successes, particularly perhaps in relation to phobias. For this reason it is being extensively used in the psychiatric field, and its potentialities for social work practice are also beginning to be systematically explored. Some of the most promising possibilities for social work would seem to lie less in the more clinical application of behavioural principles — such as may be applied in the treatment of addiction, for example, or sexual deviations — than in the use of techniques of behaviour modification in the natural environment.

Attempts to identify and modify environmental conditions which control problem behaviour are very much in line with the renewed emphasis in social work on social and environmental (rather than individual) change; furthermore, this approach offers an alternative to the illness model of problem behaviour which seeks for the causes and cures of problems within individuals. A consequence of the illness model is the emphasis placed on the therapeutic role of the professional 'expert'. This is associated with the belief that therapeutic activities must only be engaged in by very highly trained professionals, to the exclusion of other people in the patient's immediate environment, whose involvement in the helping enterprise is viewed as only peripheral. The point of view implicit in the illness model places a premium on professionalism, and on the development of ever greater skills on the part of highly trained professionals.

By contrast, the natural environment approach seeks instead to utilise the powerful influence of those closest to the patient in attempting to alter 'disturbed' behaviour; it uses to the full the goodwill and therapeutic potential of those involved in close everyday contact rather than viewing 'treatment' as a function of the clinic or the designated therapeutic specialist; the role of the later becomes instead that of 'a coordinator of these natural therapeutic

146

forces'[18]. The involvement of the nonprofessional is not sought for ideological or economic reasons alone, but derives from a theoretical model which sees disturbed behaviour as a function of the environment, often of the immediate interpersonal environment. Help is therefore most logically and effectively directed to the modification of that environment rather than by withdrawing the individual from it in order to treat him. Of particular interest is work now developing in the Child Treatment Research Unit in Leicester, which is applying behavioural methods to behaviour disorders of children. These methods are also being successfully used to assist mothers of hyperactive children, for whom the cumulative and unrelieved strains of coping with such a child can lead to wellnigh intolerable stresses[19].

In such situations more traditional psychotherapeutic approaches oriented towards understanding the underlying emotional problems (often thought to be those of the parents rather than the child) may not be helpful in actually achieving some beneficial change in a fraught situation. The chief failure of contemporary therapeutic practice, according to Tharp and Wetzel, is

the failure to guide the nonprofessional person in helping people. Professional mental health personnel simply do not know what to tell people to do. They neither have the data at hand on which to make clear-cut recommendations, with faith in the outcome, nor do they have strong theoretical principles dictating specific lay behaviour. There has developed in most therapeutic techniques a strong prohibition against giving direct advice and telling a patient what to do and how to manage his life. There are several theoretical rationales for this. The probable reason, however, is that no techniques produce a reliable result. The net result is passivity in therapist behaviour.[20]

There is now a very considerable body of literature available to the social worker dealing with the use of behavioural methods in relation to delinquency, to children's problems (particularly school and other phobias and problems such as enuresis) and to sexual and marital problems; in addition, relevant work deals with the use of token economies in institutional settings such as psychiatric hospitals, prisons and community homes[21]. The potential range is thus very wide, although, as Jehu has been at some pains to emphasise, there are large areas of practice to which this type of approach has no direct relevance, and it concerns only certain aspects of social work rather than the whole field. Among the attractions of behavioural approaches are their concern with present difficulties, their focus on observable behaviour rather than inferred states, and the specificity of the assessment process and the treatment or intervention procedures which follow from it. Behavioural work starts from a clear change objective. The assessment (in which the patient is closely involved) attempts to identify precisely what are the behaviours to be changed and to plan a modification programme designed to achieve this. 'Before treatment is attempted, it is necessary to identify and specify the client's problems and the conditions controlling them, to ascertain the resources available, to select and specify therapeutic goals, and to plan a treatment programme'[22]. The specification of desirable outcome means that progress can be measured and stress is laid on monitoring the process throughout. Most attractive of all, however, is the accumulating evidence for the effectiveness of behavioural methods; this alone should give them a strong claim to attention by social workers. They are however likely to complement rather than replace the other methods on which social workers have traditionally relied; counselling, for example, and the provision of needed resources. Despite the cumulative evidence for the effectiveness of behavioural approaches, they are nevertheless regarded with extreme suspicion by social workers, and so far very few attempts have been made to incorporate these techniques systematically in training. That this should be so in itself raises extremely interesting questions.

Social work, it has been suggested, has been strongly influenced in its understanding of man and of behaviour by psychoanalytic explanations, and thus by the model of man which is implicit in this account; the major features of this have been delineated in the preceding chapter. Despite some attempts at synthesis such as that of Alexander[23], classical psychoanalytic and behaviourist explanations are in sharp contradiction; the behaviourist wholly rejects the psychoanalytic assumption of the unconscious and the role of unconscious processes and ideas as behavioural determinants, and regards many of its explanations as speculative and of dubious validity. The differences between the behaviourist and the psychoanalyst are not merely semantic, nor are they simply differences of emphasis; they involve very different accounts of the origin of neurosis, very different approaches to treatment, different vocabularies, and, at root, very different conceptions of man as the object of psychological study and therapy.

The differences are most sharply pointed in relation to neurosis. The psychoanalyst views man as essentially the product of his past. Despite the concern with the 'reality principle' and with adaptation to the demands of the environment which characterises ego psychology, the psychoanalytic account of neurosis is essentially a biographical one; it seeks to understand and account for the present in the light of the events of the past. For the behaviourist, the past and the origins of neurotic behaviour are relatively unimportant; what matters more are the conditions in the present which control it. An extremely critical stance towards psychoanalytic therapy has been taken by Rachman in *The Effects of Psychotherapy*, and by Eysenck and Wilson in *The Experimental Study of Freudian Theories*. In the view of the latter authors, the experimental evidence does nothing to confirm psychoanalytic theory, and as a method of treatment they regard it as quite unproven; the lack of confirmatory evidence in itself, they argue, goes some way towards demonstrating that the theory upon which its treatment is based is false. Not only do they regard it as an ineffective form of treatment for neurotic disorders, but they consider that the psychoanalytic paradigm is

148

outdated and misleading and should be replaced. This replacement, they suggest, should be behaviour therapy.

> We have here a situation which... is ripe for a new paradigm to arise and such a paradigm is indeed in the process of completion in the form of behavioural therapy and the theories associated with it.[24]

But what of the conception of man implicit in the behavioural paradigm? Is this any more satisfactory, or does it too have limitations as a basis for social work practice?

The evidence leaves no doubt that certain aspects of human behaviour (those that are the result of learning) are very well articulated by the behavioural paradigm, and that the research traditions and much of the therapy which have developed from it have been fruitful. Nevertheless, many writers (and not only psychoanalysts) have felt that there is something inherently unsatisfactory, and indeed fallacious, in some of its assumptions. This seems to be a consequence of its origin in the laboratory and in experimental psychology, and of the natural science models that it emulates. As a result, behavioural theory focusses on what is observable and quantifiable but has been little concerned with affect, cognition, perception, or such important areas of human activity as creativity, except in so far as these have observable (and preferably physiologically measurable) referents. Susanne Langer, in *Mind: An Essay on Human Feeling*, has argued that the characteristically human element in cognition is the concept of symbolism, and it is this which sets man apart from the animal world. What she calls 'the vast and special evolution of feeling' in man which is expressed in one of its highest forms in symbolism and art 'adds up to the total qualitative difference which sets human nature apart from the rest of the animal kingdom as a mode of being that is typified by language, culture, morality and consciousness of life and death'[25]. It is precisely modes of this kind, involving important areas of human feeling and experience, about which behavioural analysis in terms of stimulus-response sequences fails to provide insight or illumination. That the emphasis on observable behavioural referents may exclude other aspects of human psychology — ideas, intentions, images, fantasies — has been acknowledged by several psychologists, and Bandura has observed that in learning theory the symbolic and higher-order processes are areas of significant neglect. Asch has commented, writing as a social psychologist, on the limitations of behavioural data alone. Also important, he maintains, is the place of experience in psychological investigation:

> The place of experience in human social psychology has been settled in a purely practical way. It is not possible, as a rule, to conduct investigation in social psychology without including a reference to the experiences of persons. The investigator must, for example, take into account what the person under investigation is saying; and such utterances have to be treated

149

in terms of their meaning, not as auditory waves, or sounds, or 'verbal behaviour'. One can hardly take a step in this region without involving the subject's ideas, feelings and intentions. We do this when we observe people exchanging gifts, engaging in an economic transaction, being hurt by criticism, or taking part in a ritual. The sense of these actions would disappear the moment we subtracted from our description the presumed mental operations that they imply.[26]

The limitations of behavioural concepts and what are regarded as legitimate areas of psychological study are a result of the adoption of the methods and models of the physical sciences (particularly physics) and their application to the very different subject matter of psychology. The consequence has been the erection of what Langer calls 'the Idols of the Laboratory' — physicalism, methodology, jargon, objectivity and mathematisation. All this, she maintains, has led to a real fiasco in the programmatic sciences, 'that in worshipping their picture of science they have rarely come to grips with anything important in their own domain'[27].

The scientific ideology which especially characterises behaviourist theory Koch regards as part of the ideology of psychological science generally during what he calls the Age of Theory, which reached its zenith in the 1940's. He has mapped out some of the major features of this ideology, among which has been a firm commitment to the observation base of psychological science. By this he means that 'all lawlike statements of psychology containing dependent variables not expressible in, or reducible to, publicly verifiable and thus 'objectively' observable *behaviour* are to be excluded as illegitimate'[28]. He points out that a telling measure of the strength of this ideology is that researchers whose interests are clearly compatible with a quite different epistemological rationale have often made a point of squaring their interests with such commitments; for example, speaking of perceptual behaviour, cognitive behaviour, fantasy behaviour and the like.

The dilemma facing the behavioural sciences is pointed up by the difficulty of developing concepts and language which can at one and the same time be used in research and yet make sense of the notions with which the practitioner — psychologist, psychiatrist, social worker — has to operate. The latter cannot restrict himself to the categories regarded as legitimate objects of scientific study in the laboratory; he has to concern himself with subjective experiences, with sentience, and with 'introspective data, fantasies, dreams and alleged memories which cannot be empirically checked'[29]. Yet between the behaviourist and the psychodynamic psychotherapist there is as yet no common language, no common universe of discourse. They use not only different languages, different concepts, but different modes of knowing. The one is concerned with a limited range of observable phenomena; the other with subjective experiences, with intentions, affect, images and the like which cannot be directly observed but only known or inferred from the communications of the subject.

150

Nevertheless, these differences may be diminishing. Koch, in his analysis of the trends represented in the first three volumes of *Psychology: A Study of a Science* observed that one of the striking features there revealed was 'the presence of a widely distributed and strong stress against behaviourist epistemology', demonstrated in: (i) the radical reanalysis of perception and central process; (ii) the generally increased interest in perception and central process; and (iii) the evidence for a new concern with experiential analysis. In relation to the first of these he points out that in the early days the search for objectivity led to the use, as behavioural indicators, only of physical or chemical events. But this was increasingly found to be insufficient. Not only did the stimuli sometimes fail to stimulate, but the real problem was that

> the patterns of physical change that occasion response we find ourselves initially describing in perceptual terms. It is not enough that they be available in the physical situation nor is it enough that the organism's attention orient sense organs to receive them; *it is further necessary that they have meaning for the responding organism.* [30]

In other words, behavioural psychologists, and particularly those concerned with modification, have become increasingly concerned not only with cause, and the linkages between stimulus and response, but the *meaning* of the stimulus to a particular individual. This has great significance. 'If the requirement is asserted that S be specified in a way that includes its inferred meaning for the organism, then any basis for a difference in epistemological status between an S—R language and what has been called 'subjective' language is eliminated'[31].

In the last two decades there has been increasing recognition that fidelity to the models of natural science as the central commitment of psychological science has led to some strange and unhappy results, and that there are other ways of proceeding and other approaches to knowledge. Koch's comment (1959) is of great significance:

> From the earliest days of the experimental pioneers, man's stipulation that psychology be adequate to science outweighed his commitment that it be adequate to man. From the beginning, some pooled image of the form of science was dominant: respectability held more glamour than insight, caution than curiosity, feasibility than fidelity or fruitfulness. A curious consequence... was the everwidening estrangement between the scientific makers of human science and the humanistic explorers of the content of man. It is, for instance, significant that a Freud, when he arrived, did not emerge from the laboratories of 19th century experimental psychology, nor was the ensuing tradition of work particularly hospitable to his ideas until rendered desperate by the human vacuum in its own content. [32]

What is important for social work is that it should be based upon an adequate image of man, and it is doubtful if the behavioural paradigm alone can provide this.

7.2 Psychoanalysis and the Social Work Curriculum

The major questions raised by the relation of psychoanalysis to social work education centre around three key issues, and can usefully be discussed under the headings of relevance, validity and utility.

7.2.1 Relevance

In the author's view psychoanalysis has much to offer in terms of its particular insights into the development of personality, human behaviour and emotional suffering. First, reference has been made in Chapter 6 to the developments in British psychoanalysis in the 1940's and 1950's which made important contributions to understanding of *child development*. Since then much further work has taken place both within and outside the analytic tradition which has important implications for services concerned with family and child care, particularly in their preventative aspects. A convenient summary of some of the general findings of psychological work relating to human development can be found in Kellmer Pringle[33]. Psychoanalysts have been most interested in the emotional aspects of development, and in the processes by which children interact and form relationships with others (object-relations); they have also studied the effects of separation and interrupted relationships on the growing personality.

A significant finding is that certain 'sensitive' periods occur in a child's development when there is 'heightened susceptibility to specific experiences such as stimulation or isolation, which may have a lasting and irreversible effect'[34]. Such a critical or sensitive phase is the period from about 6 to 24 months, when a child develops strong emotional attachments, particularly to the mother; early childhood experience is therefore of great importance and its effects may be lasting and extremely difficult to modify. The work of Bowlby, Robertson, Winnicott and others has contributed greatly to knowledge both of the conditions for normal emotional development and the possible noxious consequences for the child of particular experiences such as separation from the parent[35]. For example, a child whose family environment is apparently favourable may suffer from the effects of even a brief separation at a critical age. Of special relevance for social work are the studies of the Robertsons[36] which have been directed not only to understanding these emotional effects, but also to the practical task of how they may be lessened: for instance, by introducing a child to a fosterhome gradually; by ensuring that familiar objects, particularly those to which he is attached and which have symbolic significance for him (transitional objects) go with him; by maintaining so far as possible the continuance of familiar routines; and by keeping alive the contact with his own family by visits and photographs. Thus this is of direct relevance to much of the bread and butter work of the social worker in dealing with enforced separation and substitute care. Some of these children are part of 'ordinary' intact families. But others of the children with whom the social services come into contact have been grossly deprived, and the utmost sensitivity and care, as well as knowledge, is needed if the effects are to be mitigated and the best possible conditions provided for healthy development. When substitute care (fosterhome, day nursery, child minding) has to be provided, constant concern for the *quality* of such provision is necessary to ensure that the physical and emotional needs of the children are met so far as is humanly possible, and psychoanalysts have also turned their attention to the practical aspects of child care such as these.

Social services are not only concerned with the child needing some form of care outside his own family, but also with preventive work, with safeguarding and promoting the healthy development of the child who is part of a family unit. From the work of analysts in the object-relations tradition, a clear consensus seems to emerge as to the significance of the very early interpersonal experience of the infant (particularly with the mother) in developing a sense of identity, or what Fairbairn calls the 'self', the central core of the ego. This consensus is remarkably striking, even though there is disagreement as to precisely what factors are important and how impairment of this development can occur. Identity and how it is formed is a theme central to most current psychoanalytic thinking. Bowlby's more recent work[37], with its newer notion of instinct drawn from ethology, suggests that attachment to the mother may be as primary as sexual behaviour, and the result of inbuilt mechanisms in the human no less than the animal organism. It emphasises the mother or primary caregiver as a consistent, supportive figure providing that security against which the child can develop his own sense of worth and significance. While the physical proximity and accessibility of the mother is one essential factor, her emotional responsiveness to the needs and signals of the child is also important and the interaction between mother and child can be seriously impaired by depression or anxiety. One very important implication for social work, therefore, is the attempt to relieve those stresses which may adversely affect the mother's enjoyment of the child and render it difficult for her to respond adequately to him. Stresses of this kind may arise in many ways, but parents in certain common situations (such as single parent families, now on the increase) are likely to be particularly vulnerable. Psychological study in the field of child development has therefore clear relevance and importance for preventive social work, and psychoanalysts have made a major contribution to this area.

Second, psychoanalysis has an important contribution to make to the social worker's understanding of *human behaviour*, in adults as well as children. Considerable attention was given earlier to the concepts of ego psychology, as a fruitful field of development, and here psychoanalytic work has thrown much light on the characteristic ways in which people adapt to and cope with the normal as well as the more traumatic crises of living. Among the concepts of ego psychology which have particular relevance for social work practice are the defences and coping techniques — the ways in which people characteristically

153

deal with threat, pain and loss by anger, by projection, by denial, by displacement and so on. Many of these concepts (particularly perhaps that of projection) are now part of ordinary psychological currency and have been widely accepted.

Third, psychoanalysis has immeasurably deepened our understanding of *psychological suffering* and distress. It arose from the attempt to help people affected by emotional and nervous disorders; thus it was born out of human suffering, and throughout it has addressed itself, as the ground of its studies, to those crucial and central experiences — loss, separation, pain, anxiety, despair — which are the lot of mankind; these, as Bowlby observes[38], are the 'stock-in-trade' of psychoanalysis; and equally of social work. Bowlby's own work on loss is well known, but also valuable for social workers is other work linked with the object-relations tradition, such as that of Murray Parkes[39] on bereavement. Both the care assistant in the home for the elderly and the social worker in the terminal ward of a hospital can glean insights from work such as this which will enable them to understand more fully and enter more deeply into the experience of those faced with such situations. The work of the psychoanalyst, above all, points to dimensions of such experience which are more than common sense; in particular, to the way in which earlier experiences of loss and their repressed affects may be reactivated by similar experiences in later life.

The particular form of brief social work treatment known as crisis intervention[40] illustrates the way in which a psychodynamic view of personality may be usefully combined with other theories (stress theory, crisis theory, learning theories concerned with cognition) as a basis for intervention. Crisis intervention is concerned with the short-term treatment of individuals or families who are undergoing some form of crisis; by a crisis is meant a hazardous event (perhaps illness, loss, or the birth of a premature or handicapped child) which precipitates a state of emotional disturbance and in which accustomed problem-solving or coping mechanisms no longer serve. The state of crisis is produced by three interrelated factors: (i) one or a series of hazardous events which pose some threat; (ii) a threat to current or past instinctual needs which are symbolically linked to earlier threats that result in vulnerability or conflict; and (iii) an inability to respond with adequate coping mechanisms. Treatment (normally of three to six sessions duration) is directed towards helping the individual to resolve or master the present crisis by developing new and adaptive ways of coping, not only in relation to the immediate events, but to anticipate future stresses.

Crisis treatment differs in many of its emphases from more traditional forms of work. Among these emphases are that the focus is on the present, with the past explored only in so far as it relates dynamically to the present situation; that the worker acts in a more directive and active fashion; that there is less emphasis on insight — 'in brief treatment the goal is foresight — the enhancement of anticipatory awareness to be used in problem-solving'[41]. Finally, the brevity of the treatment is itself an indication that a high value is placed on the restoration of autonomy at the earliest possible moment, even though later life-crises may require further intervention later on.

These represent some of the ways in which psychoanalysis is relevant to social work and can make an important contribution to it, but it will be noted that the approach has been selective; while there are certain points at which the concerns of the psychoanalyst and the social worker touch closely, there are others (particularly the whole area of psychoanalytic techniques) where there is little common ground, and where the psychoanalyst would not only be an inappropriate but a misleading mentor; Meyer has pointed out the unhappy results for American social work practice which followed the presentation of inappropriate models by psychoanalysts who illustrated their teaching in schools of social work by reference to their own clinical work[42].

7.2.2 Validity: Psychoanalysis as Science

In the development of modern psychodynamic psychology, two apparently contradictory and opposing trends can be distinguished. The one attempts to establish psychoanalysis on surer scientific foundations and to anchor it ever more firmly within the sciences; this is epitomised in the work of Bowlby, who seeks to link his psychological work on attachment and loss with findings in related scientific fields such as ethology. The other looks in the direction of religion and philosophy and would in effect move psychoanalysis out of the orbit of the sciences and place it rather within the humanities.

The precise status of psychoanalysis, and whether or not it is to be regarded as a science, has been the subject of longstanding debate. Is it a science, or is it something *sui generis*? If a science, then the validity of its central propositions becomes a crucial issue; if they are confirmed by experimental work and research, then clearly they have an important place in the social work curriculum; if they are not, then they should be treated with caution.

Certainly Freud himself regarded psychoanalysis as a science, and most modern analysts would agree with this view, regarding it as firmly rooted in biology:

> For the psychoanalyst psychology is a branch of biology. The importance of somatic or organic influences on mental functioning is always borne in mind, particularly with relation to the instinctual drives which, according to psychoanalytic theory, are assumed to be the basic motivational forces in mental life.[43]

For Eysenck, a noted critic of psychoanalysis, the issue of the precise status it should be accorded resolves itself into the question 'whether the Freudian system is sufficiently determinate to permit testable deductions to be made'[44]. In his view, it is; and the result of experimental studies of deductions from Freudian theories can go a considerable way towards confirming or failing to confirm the major propositions. After a searching examination of some 20 empirical studies, Eysenck and Wilson conclude:

We would say that the studies looked at in this volume give little if any support to Freudian concepts and theories...; that several of the studies dealing in particular with treatment and with 'single case' investigations give results powerfully challenging Freudian hypotheses, and that the quality of the studies allegedly supporting psychoanalytic views is so poor that very little of interest can be gleaned.[45]

They add that

for the most part 'disproof' (of the fundamental tenets of Freudian theory) is too strong a term; all that can be said is that studies which were widely believed to support and prove Freudian theories fail, on examination, to provide any such proof.[46]

A much more sympathetic conclusion was reached in a comprehensive review of the experimental evidence by Paul Kline, whose general conclusion was that 'far too much that is distinctively Freudian has been verified for the rejection of the whole of psychoanalytic theory to be possible'; 'any blanket rejection of Freudian theory as a whole simply flies in the face of the evidence'[47]. Kline's position is that Freudian theory can be viewed as a premature synthesis offered in advance of the evidence, 'a huge collection of empirical hypotheses and propositions, some of which may be true'[48]; and what he has done is to attempt to distinguish those hypotheses for which the evidence provides some support from those for which it does not: the theory as a whole is complex and has neither been confirmed nor falsified *in toto*. He summarises his survey of the evidence in this way:

From a study of the objective evidence we are left with some confirmation of a tripartite division of mental activity into ego, super-ego and id. Developmental theory is supported in that oral erotism, Oedipus and castration complexes appear to occur. Furthermore adult personality patterns like the oral and anal character can be generally observed. There seems no doubt that the defence mechanism repression is commonly used and sexual symbolism is a verified phenomenon both within and outside dreams which do indeed seem concerned with basic human conflicts. In addition to this certain Freudian hypotheses concerning neuroses have been supported.[49]

An even more recent study of empirical evidence bearing on the validity of Freud's theories by Fisher and Greenberg (1977) has also found impressive evidence tending to substantiate some of his major hypotheses. In particular:

1. Important aspects of his developmentally based oral and anal personality types emerged as reasonable propositions. Clusters of traits in children and adults are found which correspond to the oral and anal personality 'types', the one tending to have a significant investment in establishing and maintaining dependent ties with others as a means of obtaining security, the other displaying a marked pattern of parsimony, compulsive and resistive bahaviour.

156

2. The etiology of male homosexuality as described by Freud stands up well to the known facts.

3. His views as to the origins of paranoid delusions, while far from confirmed in every detail, are generally substantiated by the available data, in particular the link with homosexual anxiety.

4. Some aspects of the complex oedipal theory are partially confirmed.

On the negative side, there is little confirmation that the dream is primarily a camouflaged fulfilment of an unconscious wish, though there is little doubt that dreams do provide an outlet for tension and disturbance and thus are valuable material for therapeutic exploration. Freud's views on female psychology also appear to be wide of the mark in a number of respects, particularly the belief that sexual maturity is marked by a shift from clitoral to vaginal erogenicity, now shown to be physiologically impossible. Finally, as regards psychoanalysis as therapy there is little evidence to suggest that it produces more profound or lasting changes than do other less expensive and lengthy forms of therapy.

In sum, Freud's theories are a rich store of hypotheses on the dynamics of personality, and in many respects the current evidence indicates that Freud was right and his theories are confirmed by impressive empirical support, much of it derived from nonpsychoanalytical sources; in other respects, he was clearly wrong. Quite apart from the intrinsic value of the conclusions which Fisher and Greenberg are able to draw from their review of the evidence, of equal interest and significance is their clear demonstration that Freudian theories *are* testable; not only that, but the relevant evidence is far more substantial than has been generally believed. It is in fact quite incorrect that there is little evidence for or against the validity of Freud's theories; on the contrary, Fisher and Greenberg claim that there is far more than for most other personality theories and that what is really remarkable is that, with a very few exceptions, this evidence has been virtually ignored both by supporters and detractors of psychoanalysis.

Also relevant to the relationship of psychoanalysis to social work education are the findings as to the relative inefficacy of psychoanalytic therapy. There may be a number of reasons for this, not least that there seems to be no clear unified identifiable practice which can be labelled 'psychoanalytic'; the term encompasses a wide variety of individual practices and approaches to treatment. This point is well illustrated by Frank's *The Human Dimension in Psychoanalytic Practice* (1977), where a number of distinguished analysts talk about their personal experience, attitudes and involvement in therapy, which, it is suggested, may in fact constitute the core of effective therapy though it is little discussed in the psychoanalytic literature. What is strikingly absent from this collection of essays is the 'blank screen' to which the analyst has sometimes been compared; rather, a picture emerges of a diversity of approaches which yet share a common concern and respect for the patient, a genuine and deep involvement in the caring process, and a readiness to meet new challenges in new ways, even playing chess with the patient when it seems indicated. On the

157

whole the psychoanalytic *literature* stresses the role of interpretation and insight in leading to growth and change, and social work has reflected this in its own writing. But other psychotherapy research suggests that may what be of greater salience are the personal attitudes and involvement of the therapist, and his capacity for warmth, empathy, genuineness and specificity, and it is these core attributes which may be of equal significance in casework, and which should receive detailed consideration in preparation for social work practice.

In so far as Freud's theories contain (as there is substantial evidence that they do) insights into the underlying dynamics of human behaviour and personality development, there is clearly a strong case for the inclusion of such teaching on social work courses, providing that it is clear which aspects can attract empirical support, which are unsupported or disproved, and which are imaginative but still speculative hypotheses that remain unproven one way or the other.

The question remains, however, whether the approach of Kline, Eysenck and Wilson, and Fisher via the logic of natural science is the only or even the most appropriate one. Is what is distinctive about psychoanalysis examinable in this way? It is difficult to avoid the impression that psychoanalysis belongs to a different order of knowledge, and what is peculiar to it escapes even the most careful scientific scrutiny. Freud himself, deeply influenced as he was by his own training as a neurologist, undoubtedly saw psychoanalysis as a science, and the need to make it respectable as a medical specialism has given further impetus to its claims to scientific status. Nevertheless the scientific is not the only way of knowing, and it may be that the language of the laboratory is neither the most useful nor the most appropriate to apply to psychoanalysis.

This is the position taken by several philosophers of science. Popper holds the view that psychoanalysis cannot be regarded as a science because it does not measure up to the criterion he regards as demarcating the scientific from the nonscientific, namely the principle of falsifiability.

I found that those of my friends who were admirers of Marx, Freud and Adler were impressed by a number of points common to these theories, and especially by their apparent *explanatory power*. These theories appeared to be able to explain practically everything that happened within the fields to which they referred, The study of any of them seemed to have the effect of an intellectual conversion or revelation, opening your eyes to a new truth hidden from those not yet initiated. Once your eyes were thus opened you saw confirming instances everywhere; the world was full of *verifications* of the theory. Whatever happened always confirmed it. Thus its truth appeared manifest; and unbelievers were clearly people who did not want to see the manifest truth; who refused to see it, either because it was against their class interest or because of their repressions which were still 'un-analysed' and crying aloud for treatment.[50]

158

It was the very ease with which confirmations of the theories came (even confirmations of opposing interpretations of the same phenemonon, say, a Freudian and an Adlerian interpretation) which caused him most concern.

It was precisely this fact — that they always fitted, that they were always confirmed — which in the eyes of their admirers constituted the strongest argument in favour of these theories. It began to dawn on me that this apparent strength was in fact their weakness.[51]

Popper concludes the psychoanalysis is like myth. The theories contain interesting psychological suggestions, but not in a form which can be tested or refuted; that does not mean, however, that they are of no value, and they may contain important anticipations of scientific theories.

Farrell has studied psychoanalysis over many years, again from the vantage point of a philosopher of science, and has written extensively on the theme of its scientific status. Like Popper, he does not regard it as a science, though for rather different reasons; first, that most of the supporting evidence comes from the use of psychoanalytic method whose own validity is in doubt; and, second, that the theory is not sufficiently determinate.

Freud's own intention undoubtedly was to establish a scientific psychology which could explain mental phenomena in terms of the interaction of forces which were discoverable, though unconscious and thus not accessible to direct observation. Throughout its history, psychoanalysis, with its principle of psychic determinism, has been commonly regarded as a causal-explanatory theory of human behaviour; like other sciences, its aim has been to establish general laws through which, given certain conditions, certain consequences necessarily follow and can be predicted. But, in recent years, some analysts have themselves expressed dissatisfaction with this view; they have held that psychoanalysis is not an *eklartung* psychology (concerned with explanation) but a *verstehende* psychology (concerned with understanding). It is best regarded, they would hold, as a semantic rather than a causal theory, concerned essentially with meaning and with the intuitive understanding of the individual's perceptions and values and the intensely subjective and personal world in which he moves, which is shaped in part by his biographical experiences. The task of the analyst is to enter this subjective world, and he can be seen as a specialist in the symbolic language of dream and fantasy. This point of view has been strongly argued by Rycroft, a practising analyst, who sees many advantages in regarding psychoanalysis as a semantic rather than a causal theory. Above all, for him, as a therapist,

If psychoanalysis is recognised as a semantic theory not a causal one, its theory can start where its practice does — in the consulting room, where a patient who is suffering from something in himself which he does not understand confronts an analyst with some knowledge of the unconscious — i.e. who knows something of the way in which repudiated wishes, thoughts, feelings and memories can translate themselves into symptoms, gestures and dreams, and who knows, as it were, the grammar and syntax

159

of such translations and is therefore in a position to interpret them back again into the communal language of consciousness. According to the scientific analyst this can only be done by elucidating and reconstructing the history of the illness and of its infantile origins, but even he agrees that this is useless unless the analyst has made contact (rapport) with the patient, and it seems to me that it makes better sense to say that the analyst makes excursions into historical research in order to understand something which is interfering with his present communication with the patient (in the same way as a translator might turn to history to elucidate an obscure text) than to say that he makes contact with the patient in order to gain access to biographical data.[52]

The most careful and reflective exposition of this point of view is to be found in the work of Ricoeur, unlike Rycroft a philosopher with no direct psychoanalytic experience. For Ricoeur, also, psychoanalysis is essentially about language and meaning. His central thesis is that Freud's greatest work, *The Interpretation of Dreams*, can be seen less as a scientific treatise than as an examination of the role of language and of symbol; dreams are seen as 'a model of all the disguised, substitutive, and fictive expressions of desire'; essentially, dreams express the 'semantics of desire'. He writes:

The scientific status of psychoanalysis has been subjected to severe criticism, especially in countries of British and American culture. Epistemologists, logicians, semanticists, philosophers of language have closely examined its concepts, propositions, argumentation and structure as a theory and have generally come to the conclusion that psychoanalysis does not satisfy the most elementary requirements of a scientific theory.

The analysts have answered either by flight, or by the adduction of additional scientific criteria for their discipline, or by attempts at 'reformulation' aimed at making it acceptable to men of science. By so doing, they have skirted the 'agonising revision' called for, I believe, by the logicians' critique and which I will express as follows: 'No, psychoanalysis is not a science of observation; it is an interpretation, more comparable to history than to psychology'.[53]

From this point of view, psychoanalytic interpretations are neither true nor false; their justification lies entirely in their subjective significance for the patient, and whether for him they make sense, in that they present his experience to him a new and revealing light.

In analysis (Ricoeur observes) the real history is merely a clue to the figurative history through which the patient arrives at self-understanding; for the analyst, the important thing is this figurative history.[54]

To Ricoeur, therefore, the question of whether or not psychoanalytic propositions are empirically verifiable or not is irrelevant; it is not a science.

Kline has pointed out that a further important issue is whether other theoretical accounts of the origins of maladaptive or neurotic behaviour are of and by themselves sufficient. He argues[55] that certain psychoanalytic findings for which good empirical support exists (such as oral erotism) could not be predicted on the basis of learning models alone. This is for the reason that learning theory is not concerned with phenomenology; that is, what does or does not act as a reinforcer or conditioned stimulus for an individual requires elucidation in the light of other theories concerned with its symbolic significance. Thus, to take an example, while the learning theory model fits the treatment of phobias well (leading to strategies designed to modify inappropriate avoidance responses to particular stimuli such as snakes or spiders) it does not adequately explain why *these* stimuli, rather than others, should elicit such a response. Psychoanalysis and learning theory, Kline suggests, can be viewed as complementary in that psychoanalysis is particularly concerned with the important task 'of examining the fundamental nature of the learning process in particular phobias'[56]. In sum, therefore, Kline regards the learning theory model as inadequate without propositions of a phenomenological nature such as those provided by psychoanalysis, and he regards psychoanalysis as 'in fact concerned with the details of the maladaptive learning processes underlying neurotic behaviour'[57]. Without it, he maintains, 'learning theory models of human behaviour would seem futile'. He thus favours the retention of those aspects of Freudian theory which can be shown to have empirical support. While the evidence at present may be slight and inconclusive, too much that is characteristically Freudian has received support for it to be rejected, and further research should provide progressively stronger confirmation or disconfirmation of its main propositions. It may be added that the very slenderness of the existing evidence can of itself support an argument for the retention of the teaching of psychoanalytic theory on social work courses: conclusive evidence on which a case for its abandonment could be based simply does not exist at the present time.

7.2.3   Utility

The knowledge explosion of recent years in the social and behavioural sciences has markedly affected the status of psychoanalytic theory within social work education, and has posed major problems of selection for the social work curriculum. Social work education must now be concerned with a range of knowledge drawn from various fields, involving very different levels of analysis and requiring the capacity to appreciate the contribution of different disciplines at these different levels. The breadth and complexity of this task is well illustrated by Thomas[58]. In discussing the potential relevance of behavioural science knowledge for social work (itself only one area of relevant knowledge) he identifies four areas which, considered at five levels of aggregation, yield no less than 20 cells (see table). Psychoanalysis mainly contributes to the first three of these cells, and, to a lesser extent, the fourth.

Thus psychoanalysis is only one source of relevant knowledge, and

Level to which subject matter applied	Normal behaviour	Abnormality and deviation	Growth, maturation and change	The helping process
Individual	1	2	3	4
Group	5	6	7	8
Organisation	9	10	11	12
Community	13	14	15	16
Society	17	18	19	20

contributes to our understanding of personality and primarily at the individual level of analysis. This must be combined with an openness to the assimilation and use of relevant and potentially fruitful knowledge from many other sources. Increasingly, social work has been looking to behavioural science (that is, that area of knowledge 'in which scientific approaches are employed to understand human behaviour and social life') for help with its professional tasks. But within the main relevant disciplines of psychology and sociology so rapid has been the growth of knowledge that very difficult problems of selection are inevitably posed. Recently, particularly in the United States, work has begun on examining and systematising for social work use possible contributions from these disciplines. Thomas suggests a number of provisional criteria on which selection might be made; these include content relevance, knowledge power (the potency of the knowledge in relation to practice, including validity and predictive power) and certain practical referent features such as identifiability, accessibility, manipulability and ethical suitability. The application of behavioural science knowledge, he suggests,

> is not a direct, simple importation, but rather calls for detailed thoughtful appraisal of the relevance of the content, the power of the knowledge, as well as of many practical considerations relating to the knowledge referents.[59]

If this kind of approach were to be more widely adopted in curriculum planning, then the contribution of psychoanalysis would have to be assessed in the light of the same kind of criteria.

A crucial argument of this chapter has been that Freud's theories are a rich source of hypotheses in regard to the dynamics of behaviour and the development of personality, and as a *verstehende* psychology it has lost none of its significance; if anything, it attracts stronger empirical support than a decade ago. Despite its awkwardness and its relative neglect by academic psychologists, psychoanalysis will not go away, and too many distinguished and intelligent people have been convinced of its fundamental importance to an adequate understanding of man for it to be ignored or dismissed. As an *action* theory for social work, however, it has less value. Apart from the high value placed on insight and interpretation, it is difficult to draw behavioural prescriptions for the social worker from it. Too often, it seems, the social worker is able to make excellent and perceptive diagnoses, and even attach all the right labels (schizoid, oedipal fixation and the like) but the relation between diagnosis and treatment is extremely difficult to specify. What must be done in order to ameliorate the situation that has been so carefully labelled? Labelling, in fact, may itself lead to the illusion that, once named, a problem is not only understood but practically cured. This point can be made particularly in regard to the concepts of ego psychology. What, in precise behavioural and operational terms, should the social worker do in attempting to strengthen a weak ego? This weakness becomes apparent by contrast with the approach of the behaviourist, for whatever the limitations of behavioural theory and epistemology, it does offer the practitioner quite clear guidelines as to precise behavioural assessment leading to clear strategies of change.

Further, if psychoanalysis is to be taken as the basis of a practice theory, its implications are extremely pessimistic. For the psychoanalyst — particularly perhaps the Kleinian analyst — the foundations of personality are laid in the very early months of life, and the roots of behaviour lie in phantasies (mental representations of the instincts) which are deeply buried in the unconscious and only become accessible and open to insight and rational control in the course of a long analysis. From the point of view of the social worker, though Kleinian theory may give an added understanding of the very primitive unconscious wishes that affect the behaviour even of the supposedly mature adult (particularly the masked aggressive and destructive wishes) the message in the end is a profoundly pessimistic one. The basic structure of the personality cannot be altered except at great cost and by the use of techniques that are beyond the social worker's competence and professional brief. If social work is indeed about change, then the kind of change strategy implicit in Kleinian theory has little relevance to social work, and it has little to offer as a theory of change. Jungian psychology, it might be thought, (with its teleological perspective and its central idea of individuation) counterbalances the reductive trend inherent in Freud's own theories; it looks rather to what the personality is becoming, to the hidden potentialities and possibilities for growth latent in the psyche; on the face of it, it is a far more optimistic system of thought. But again, Jungian psychotherapy demands of the patient a total, long and arduous commitment; it is simply not applicable to the very different circumstances of nonclinical social work practice.

The conclusion, then, must be that while psychoanalysis has much of value in terms of insights into human behaviour and personality, as an 'action theory' for social workers it has little to offer, and social work must draw upon other psychological and, even more, social theories of action as a basis for practice. Its significance for the social worker lies primarily in the insights it offers into important areas of human experience, particularly his own.

In sum, a great deal of work is developing in disciplines other than psychodynamic psychology which offer the social worker different perspectives on his work and new possibilities of effective helping. These are already reflected in the expansion of the knowledge base of contemporary social work, and in the face of such rapid and promising developments, the credal approach to theory for which social work has been criticised can have no place. Theory has to be regarded as transitional, as the best we have for the moment, rather than as a creed or an orthodoxy which must be held to at all costs and for all time[60].

For the future, psychoanalysis seems likely to make its greatest contribution to social work and related professions in those areas where its findings are systematically related to those in other disciplines. This kind of approach has led to very fruitful collaboration in the organisational field where a number of disciplines (sociology, anthropology, social psychology, psychoanalysis) bring different perspectives to bear on problems of common interest. In the area of personality also the same kind of integrative approach is to be found. Thus Bowlby sets out to relate psychoanalytic work to ethology, and Lidz, whose work is psychodynamically based, seeks to

> achieve a conceptualisation which is not only internally consistent but which is also compatible with both the biological and the behavioural science with which personality theory must interdigitate.[61]

Guntrip has recently staked a claim for the establishment of a psychodynamic science, and he too stresses the need for interdisciplinary collaboration and for the establishment of stronger relationships between psychoanalysis and general psychology:

> The organic, behavioural and psychodynamic sciences must learn to recognise each other's contributions and their own limitations, and learn to cooperate. Within the narrower ambit of the psychodynamic field any tendency to preserve exclusive schools of theory as closed in-groups must spell the death of open-minded scientific enquiry and gravely hinder progress.[62]

With developments such as these, the boundaries of psychoanalysis are now less easy to draw in any clear-cut way; and they have contributed to a desire within psychoanalysis itself to strengthen its scientific foundations through research, and have also made for a readier acceptance, in other circles, of established psychoanalytic findings.

It is important to note that the precise scientific status of psychoanalytic propositions is still under review and that the evidence for its central propositions is if anything growing stronger. Kline expresses the hope that his work:

> will help to put psychoanalysis back among the sciences and encourage imaginative researchers to investigate with methodological precision those areas of human thought and behaviour that Freudian theory has attempted to illuminate and which behaviourist psychologies seem unwilling to study or even to contemplate.[63]

164

This is in line with the current trend away from the development of comprehensive, over-arching theoretical systems towards more partial and limited systematisations; and it should lead, in the future, to a much clearer identification of precisely which aspects of psychoanalytic theory should be incorporated in the education of social workers.

8
Postscript

One of the major premises of this book has been that it is essential to draw a clear distinction between the contribution of psychoanalysis to the understanding of human behaviour and emotional life, and its contribution to the methodology of social work. Its impact on the former has in my view been by far the greatest; the treatment techniques of psychoanalysis lie well outside what social work regards as its territorial waters. It must be acknowledged however that counselling methods intended to promote growth and greater autonomy through self-awareness (ultimately psychoanalytically derived) have been given special weight, and it appears to be the case that the treatment model has been given special eminence[1].

There is some evidence from the United States that the theoretical weight given to psychoanalytic theory on training courses has declined in recent years, and on some it is not taught at all[2]. There are two main reasons for this; the first is that social work is looking for theoretical foundations which will lead to effective practice, and it has been strongly argued (for example by Eysenck and Rachman[3]) that counselling and psychotherapy conducted on psychodynamic lines is ineffective, and that behavioural methods lead to much more satisfactory results in changing behaviour; in so far as individual behavioural change is a function of social work the results of behavioural approaches, particularly those which capitalise on the resources of the natural environment, are undoubtedly promising.

8.1 The Limitations of the Treatment Model

This objection to psychoanalysis is still within the context of the treatment model. There is, however, a second and very cogent objection; that with the fresh recognition of the impact of interpersonal, organisational and structural factors on human behaviour, a theory which is primarily intrapsychic is of limited relevance, and that change efforts may more profitably be directed towards the situation rather than the person. Thus the relevance of a treatment model (whether behaviourally or psychodynamically based) to the mainstream of social work practice is itself at issue. The case for social and situational change has been strongly put by Meyer *et al.*:

> Rather than concentrate almost entirely on self-understanding, attitudes and feelings, might not professional efforts be directed to the situations of

family, peer-group, school and work place which form, or at least sustain, the psychological conditions of these 'clients'? Should we expect weekly interviews with caseworkers, or weekly counselling sessions in groups, to have critical effects when situational conditions were hardly touched?[4]

Similar criticisms have been advanced by social workers in this country. Bond writes that it is his view that

social workers persistently overestimate personality factors in explaining their clients' behaviour; that they consistently fail to recognise the constraints imposed on their clients' behaviour by the situations in which they find themselves; and that they tend to underestimate the influence on their clients of the expectations that others have of them. I believe that this failure in diagnosis leads many social workers to treat their clients by the inappropriate methods of 'supporting' or 'insight-giving' casework instead of focussing their action on their clients' external situation.[5]

It would I think be fairly generally recognised now that an individual treatment model (particularly one which stresses insight) has limitations in its application to social work at large. Some of these limitations are:

1.   *It is only appropriate in relation to a limited number of clients* and is best adapted to those with good ego strengths who value self-understanding. Miller and Riessman suggest that it is more appropriate to middle-class than to working-class clients whose expectations of psychiatric or social work help may be in more concrete terms than verbal communication and insight — for example, clear guidance on what to do[6].

2.   *It is not inclusive enough for many social work activities*; for instance, those involving work with significant persons other than the nominated client, the fostering of community resources, or social advocacy or broker functions. In actual day-to-day work, the dominance of the treatment model creates considerable anxiety amongst practitioners, who wonder whether the kinds of activities they are daily involved in (which may not involve therapy at all but are of no less importance to the individual on whose behalf they are undertaken) are really 'proper' casework. And in terms of a treatment model these activities (for example work with collaterals) *are* of course to be seen as peripheral or ancillary rather than as focal activities. Further, the treatment model tends to lead to a predetermined professional response, a particular set, when the problems actually encountered may demand new and creative answers — answers that do not form part of the traditional repertoire. To the development of such responses, on which professional advance depends, traditional and circumscribed models may act as a brake.

3.   *It defines the role relationship between social worker and client in an inappropriate way*, blurring the distinction between social work and therapist roles. The organisational context of social work practice is the crucial factor here. As an instance, the nature of the contract between client and social worker, whether explicit or not, is normally very different from that between

patient and therapist. Contrast the contract between client and social worker in a social services department with that between patient and therapist in a clinical setting. In the first case, the contract is generally with the agency rather than the individual social worker, and it is limited in scope to certain problems which are jointly recognised, and which the agency has both the statutory powers and the resources and competence to tackle. In the second place, the implicit agreement is that no area of personal and emotional life is excluded from discussion in the therapeutic sessions.

A further difference is that the social worker may be invested with considerable powers of statutory authority — to bring a client before the court or to remove a child from home. As Winnicott[7] has pointed out, he may be a central figure in the drama of his client's life, with power to influence profoundly the course of a person's life experience. The exercise of this kind of authority would normally lie outside the boundaries of the therapist's role (certainly that of the analyst) and would be regarded as incompatible with the therapeutic function.

Again, a much greater degree of mutuality, informality and equality may be desirable in social worker-client as distinct from therapist-patient relationships. From a therapeutic point of view, the patient is the object of treatment, and the classical psychoanalytic model tends to stress the impersonality and distance of the therapist as a means of increasing and thereby more readily identifying transference. Such a model is not easily transferable to social work, and has been developed to further the very particular purposes of psychoanalysis. These are very real differences, rooted in differences of function and organisational context which make the therapeutic relationship an inappropriate guide for most social work in nonclinical settings.

Thus the treatment model tends to promote a view of the social work process as separate and distinct from the social service context of which it forms part. The professional competence the social worker has traditionally claimed by virtue of his knowledge of social resources and of the complex world of local government or the penal system has been played down in favour of a professional competence grounded in psychological knowledge and human relations skills. It is now becoming again apparent that this first area of expertise has been under-rated and is one which on the whole is not shared by related professions such as doctors and clergy, and which can be of great value to those who are socially impotent, unaware of their rights, or unable to gain access to the resources which might be made available to them. Thus the appropriateness of the model has been questioned in the light of the kinds of core functions social workers actually carry out in present-day society. Typically they are located in areas of high social stress, in urban areas with their problems of poverty, housing, unemployment, with their complex institutions and accompanying bureaucracies. Carole Meyer, in an invigorating book, has argued that to assist people to find their way in the complex jungle of urban life is itself a major and legitimate function. If, she argues, the aim of practice is to enable people to get resources, to make their

168

own choices, and to be in command of their own lives so far as possible, then practice must include

> ways of connecting people with goods or services by arranging pathways, promoting accessible organisations, advocating and strengthening individuals to cope with a confusing array of urban structures and diffuse relationships which are symptomatic of the modern world.[8]

The social worker, located as he is at the interface of consumers and welfare systems, is in an unrivalled position to try to ensure that large-scale provision is tailored to individual needs, and similarly to recognise ways in which these welfare systems may themselves operate in dehumanising ways ('diswelfare') thus negating their own explicit purposes. Such a view, which retains the traditional personal focus of social work and is essentially client-centred but at the same time tries to see him in relation to all those complex systems which go to make up the context of his life, has been termed the ecological model. In place of the role-specificity of the treatment model, such a conceptualisation stresses role-diffusion: the social worker may act variously and at different times as friend, teacher, therapist, enabler, resource mobiliser, resource generator, social broker, advocate, coordinator and catalyst. All this calls for a flexibility of response for which the treatment model is an inadequate guide, and reflects a movement away from notions of pathology and therapy (implicit in terms such as diagnosis and treatment) towards a view of social work as concerned with the person in his social milieu, and with ways of increasing his control and effectiveness in relation to his environment.

Concerns such as this have led to a number of publications in recent years which attempt to present a broader and more holistic view of social work as concerned with change not only at the individual and interpersonal level, but also at organisational, community and (perhaps more exceptionally) socio-political levels. The impetus has come from a wish to integrate different methodologies (casework, groupwork, community work) into a more broadly defined professional social work role, and to identify common principles and concepts which can be applied to any form of social work activity. While this should have the effect of broadening the perspective within which the social worker approaches a problem and sensitising him to the possibility of *choice* between different targets and methods of intervention, it does not claim to add anything methodologically very new. Nevertheless, a change of stance can of itself create a climate of innovation in which new responses to familiar problems can be tried out, thus leading to perhaps more effective ways of helping.

The dilemma for social work seems to be how to retain the insight which psychoanalysis has to offer without at the same time adopting its narrower frame of reference which is clearly inadequate for understanding the range of phenomena with which the social worker must deal. It seems to be the case that psychoanalysis, once radical in its day, is coming to be viewed as inherently conservative, in contrast to the 'radicalism' associated with certain social and political theories. Since radicalism has powerful ideological appeal and no-one likes to be thought reactionary, individual psychology and the concern with micro-worlds is currently unfashionable. A recent critique of psychoanalysis from a Marxist point of view[9] argues that it is detached from any real social base, and divorces the study of the human being from the material world which shapes his consciousness. To Freud, human personality was rooted in biology rather than created, or at least powerfully moulded, by the particular modes of production characteristic of capitalist economy. Thus psychoanalysis can itself be viewed as a product of capitalist society and as an expression of its ideology; it serves as an expression of capitalist hegemony. In the view of the authors, psychoanalysis fails even to begin to approach an adequate understanding or account of man as a social being, reflecting in his personal consciousness the real contradictions and conflicts inherent in the productive system. They acknowledge that there is, at the present time, no Marxist psychology, no satisfactory way of relating the world of individual consciousness and insight to the material context in which it is rooted, but suggest some lines on which this might be developed. The main bulwarks of such a theory would be the proposition that individual consciousness is a product of social relations, which are in turn shaped by the dominant mode of production; and that such a psychology must be able to incorporate an understanding of the dialectical relationship between individual psychology and specific historical contexts.

Is it possible, however, that psychoanalysis may be not merely a repressive ideological instrument, but a route to liberation? Despite the limitations of classical Freudian theory, concerned as it is with the relationship of intrapsychic systems, psychoanalysis can also be viewed as a means of gaining insight into the social as well as the psychological chains which keep man captive. For the hegemony which maintains a particular social order is not only 'out there' but 'here'; is not an abstract conception, but a deeply personal experience, of suffering, pain, conflict, frustration. Freud's views on women illustrate this most aptly. In one sense his theory of feminine psychosexual development can be seen as an account of how women not only are but should be, and thus as a way of putting women in their place; this is the traditional feminist critique of Freud. But from another standpoint it can also be viewed as a powerful analysis of feminine psychology as shaped by male hegemony in early 20th century Vienna, and this is how Juliet Mitchell sees it in her penetrating book. The very realisation that a personal predicament may reflect political reality can itself be profoundly liberating and enable the individual to gain a sense of suprapersonal consciousness which frees him to become a participant in a dialectical process; to shape, not merely to suffer, the events of history. The blanket rejection of Freud and the dichotomy in recent social work literature between personal and political has created a false division and prevented that exploration of the relationship between man's view of himself and the social order in which he breathes which could provide new insight into the ways in which personal consciousness is moulded by economic and political relations. This exploration, pointed to by Corrigan and Leonard, has so far been undertaken by few authors (notably Fromm and Marcuse) and represents an urgent and immediate task.

Despite all the reservations to which the discussion of the relationship between psychoanalysis and social work must give rise, and which have been examined at various points in this book, there is likely to remain an important place within social work for ways of working aimed at increasing self understanding, autonomy and growth. Other considerations aside, psychoanalysis and related systems retain a very powerful appeal for many social workers which seems to have nothing very much to do with questions either of effectiveness or validity. At one level, this appeal is related to what Curle has termed 'belonging-identity'[10]. The individual can define himself, at least in part, by reference to the societies to which he belongs or the labels he attaches to himself; that is, his sense of value and of his place in the world is derived from things external to himself (social position, professional societies, academic honours) and not what he himself is. This gives him some feeling of security, a location within the social and intellectual world, especially desirable if that location is seen as status-enhancing. To be an analyst, or involved in the analytic world (or for that matter to be a member of the Association for Behavioural Psychotherapy) has symbolic significance. It is one way of defining oneself. But it is an uncertain form of identity, for it is only solid to the extent that the social order from which it derives persists. It follows that to maintain 'belonging-identity' there is great investment in perpetuating the institutions which confer it, and a strong resistance to change. It is an immature orientation which makes growth, adaptation and receptivity to new ideas slow and difficult.

At another level, the appeal of psychoanalysis is akin to the second type of identity which Curle calls 'awareness-identity'; this is essentially the recognition of what one *is*, accepting one's self with its strengths, its limitations, and its fulfilled or failed potentialities. It is a definition in existential terms, not of belonging but of being[11]. Psychoanalysis and related therapies are *par excellence* self-conscious and purposeful ways of achieving such awareness; through the provision of a consistent, understanding human relationship, the analyst enables the patient to know himself more fully, to make contact with the vulnerable, hidden, forgotten aspects of himself, and thus to achieve a sense of surely based inner identity and an expansion of his area of choice, action and imagination. Such an enterprise can perhaps be more meaningfully spoken of in religious or ethical terms than in those of behavioural science. For many, self-understanding is an ethical imperative, to be pursued for its own sake irrespective of its consequences or of other people's judgements of its validity. It is these who are most likely to find that the psychoanalytic perspective for them makes sense.

References

Introduction

1. Heraud, B. *Sociology and Social Work*, p. 278.
2. Lees, Ray. *Politics and Social Work*, p.1.
3. e.g. Hollis, F. *Casework: A Psychosocial Therapy*.
4. Woodroofe, K. *From Charity to Social Work*.
5. Alexander, L.B. 'Social Work's Freudian Deluge: myth or reality?'

Chapter 1

1. Ullmann, L. and Krasner, L. *Case Studies in Behaviour Modification*, p. 49.
2. See bibliography.
3. Rycroft, C. (ed.) *Psychoanalysis Observed*, p. 10.
4. *Ibid.*, p. 9.
5. Shakow, D. and Rapaport, D. *The Influence of Freud on American Psychology*, p. 10.
6. Bessell, R. *Interviewing and Counselling*.
7. Yelloly, M. 'The Concept of Insight' in D. Jehu *et al. Behaviour Modification in Social Work*.
8. Bessell, R. *op. cit.*, p. 61.
9. It may be observed in passing that many of the classical social work writers of the 1950's (Charlotte Towle, Jessie Taft, Gordon Hamilton) had acquired, through study and personal analysis, a grasp of psychoanalytic theory far superior in depth and intimacy to that of many of their later critics, and a disturbing feature of some of the current British debates about psychoanalysis and social work is the tenuousness of the theoretical understanding on which both attack and defence are based.
10. Fenichel, O. *The Psychoanalytic Theory of the Neuroses*, p. 7. When used as a noun the term seems to imply a reification of unconscious processes, and a specific location within the mind. This point of view has received much criticism. Thus Miles accepts that there are undoubtedly unconscious ideas and contents, but rejects the concept of 'the' unconscious. The term is used substantivally as well as adjectively by Freud himself (*der unbewusst*) but may be a form of shorthand to cover a variety of mental processes and events — wishes, ideas, fantasies, etc.

172

11. Whyte, W.H. *The Unconscious Before Freud*.
12. Wolman, B.B. *The Unconscious Mind*, p. 4.
13. Freud, S. *Introductory Lectures on Psycho-Analysis*, p. 240.
14. Freud, S. *Introductory Lectures on Psycho-Analysis*, p. 241.
15. Jung, C.G. 'Sigmund Freud in his Historical Setting'. C.W.**15**, p. 36.
16. Freud, S. *'The Unconscious'*.
17. Freud, S. *An Outline of Psychoanalysis*, p. 19.
18. Brenner, C. *'Psychoanalysis'*.
19. Freud, S. *An Outline of Psycho-Analysis*, p. 21.
20. Freud, S. *The Psychopathology of Everyday Life*, p. 239.
21. Freud, S. *New Introductory Lectures on Psychoanalysis*, p. 200.
22. Waelder, R. *Basic Theory of Psychoanalysis*, p. 253.
23. Freud, S. *An Outline of Psychoanalysis*, p. 270.
24. Waelder, R. *op cit.*, p. 37.
25. See Klein, G.S. 'Ego Psychology'.
26. *Ibid*.
27. Fairbairn W.R.D. *Psychoanalytic Studies of the Personality*.
28. For example, Murray Parkes, C. *Bereavement*; Bowlby J. *Attachment and Loss*; and the publications of James and Joyce Robertson.
29. Guntrip, H. *Psychoanalytic Theory, Therapy and the Self*.
30. The term object-relationship, with its impersonal connotations, is somewhat misleading, but is intended to refer to the infant's relationship not only to people, but in a more primitive stage, to parts or aspects of a person — particularly the breast.
31. *Ibid.*, p. 17.
32. Main works are cited in the bibliography. See also Segal, H. *An Introduction to the work of Melanie Klein*.
33. See bibliography.
34. See bibliography, especially *The Maturational Processes and the Facilitating Environment*.
35. Dr. J.D. Sutherland, in the Freud Memorial Lectures at the University of London 1974.
36. Tillich, P. 'Existential Philosophy', *Journal of the History of Ideas*, 5, 44, 44—70.
37. Sartre, J.P. 'Existentialism is a Humanism' in W. Kaufman (ed) *Existentialism from Dostoevsky to Sartre*, p. 289.
38. *Ibid.*, p. 300.
39. *Ibid.*, p. 301.
40. Buber, M. *I and Thou*.
41. Macquarrie, J. *Existentialism*, p. 82.
42. Binswanger, L. *Being-in-the-World*, p. 189.
43. *Ibid.*, p. 171.
44. Laing, R.D. *The Divided Self*, p. 23.
45. May, R. 'Dangers in the Relation of Existentialism to Psychotherapy'. In Ruitenbeck, H.M. *op cit.*, pp. 182—3.

46. Laing, R.D. 'Ontological Insecurity'. In Ruitenbeck H.M., *op cit.*, pp. 44—5.
47. Binswanger, L. *op cit.*, p. 4.
48. Laing, R.D. *op cit.*, p. 25.
49. *Ibid.*, p. 25.
50. May R. and Basescu, S. 'Existential Psychology'.
51. Tillich, P. *The Courage to Be*, p. 125.
52. Ruitenbeck, H.M. *Psychoanalysis and Existential Philosophy*, p. 20.
53. May, R. and Basescu, S. *op cit.*
54. Friedenberg, E.Z., *Laing*, pp. 93—4.
55. Bion, W.R. *Experiences in Groups*.
56. Rice, A.K. *Learning for Leadership*.
57. Ackerman, N. *Treating the Troubled Family*, p. 54.
58. *Ibid.*, p. 55.
59. *Ibid.*, p. 56.
60. Schafer, R. *Language and Insight*.
61. Waelder, *op cit.*, p. 51.

Chapter 2

1. *Brain,* **19**, 1896, 401—414.
2. Hart, B. 'A Philosophy of Psychiatry'.
3. Hart, B. 'The Psychology of Freud and his School'.
4. Hart, B. 'Freud's Conception of Hysteria'.
5. *Ibid.*
6. *Ibid.*
7. *Ibid.*
8. Murphy, G. *A Historical Introduction to Modern Psychology*.
9. Hart, B. *The Psychology of Insanity*. Preface to first edition 1912.
10. The book may have been responsible for some of the misconceptions which later filtered into popular versions of psychoanalysis. For example, among the concepts mentioned whose source can only be deduced are dissociation (Janet), complexes (Jung) and the herd instinct (Trotter). The term 'subconscious' which Freud abandoned as misleading in 1898, also occurs in the early edition. Nevertheless, this book together with Jones' *Papers on Psychoanalysis* may be regarded as the first systematic account of the major Freudian concepts to be published in England.
11. Brown, W. 'Freud's theory of Dreams', *The Lancet*, April 19th, 1913, 1182.
12. *The Lancet*, May 10th, 1913, 1327.
13. *The Lancet*, May 10th, 1913, 1345.
14. Dr. C.A. Mercier, *Brit. Med. Journ.* **2**, 1916, 897.
15. Dr. Robert Armstrong-Jones, *The Lancet*, I, 1916, 210.
16. Jones, E. *Free Associations*, p. 159.

17. *Ibid*, p. 160.
18. Jones, E. *The Life and Work of Sigmund Freud*, p. 328.
19. Jones, E. *Free Associations*, p. 166.
20. Burt, C. 'An Autobiographical Sketch'.
21. Brown, W. 'Freud's Theory of the Unconscious'. Pear, T.H. 'The Analysis of Some Personal Dreams, with reference to Freud's Theory of Dream Interpretation'.
22. Woolf, L. *Beginning Again*, pp. 167−8.
23. Hearnshaw, L.A. *Short History of British Psychology*, 1840−1940, p. 16.
24. Jones, E. *Free Associations*, p. 230.
25. Crichton-Miller, H. (ed) *Functional Nerve Disease*, p. 185.
26. *Ibid*. See the critical account in *Psychology and Psychoanalysis* (1924).
27. Crichton-Miller, H. *The New Psychology and the Teacher*, p. 18.
28. See Glover, E. *The Roots of Crime*.
29. Dicks, H.V. *Fifty Years of the Tavistock Clinic*, pp. 1−2.
30. *The Times*, December 31st, 1925.
31. Dicks, H.V. *op cit.*, pp. 38 and 61.
32. Loch, C.S. 'Charity and Charities', *Encyl. Britan.*, 11th edn.
33. Markham, V. *Return Passage*, p. 66.
34. Lindsay, A.D. Introduction to Green, T.H. *Lectures on the Principles of Political Obligation*, p. viii. It is a highly controversial issue: some modern historians see the utilitarians as strongly interventionist.
35. J.H. Muirhead (ed) *Bernard Bosanquet and His Friends*, p. 46.
36. Green, T.H. *Lectures on the Principles of Political Obligation*, p. 8.
37. Barker, Ernest, *Political Thought in England*, 1848−1914, pp. 4−5.
38. Quoted Barnett, S.A. 'Religion and Politics', p. 52.
39. *Ibid.*, p. 32.
40. See Abel, Emily: *Canon Barnett and the First Thirty Years of Toynbee Hall*, Ph.D. thesis, University of London, 1969.
41. Barnett, S.A. 'Settlements of University Men in Great Towns', in *Practicable Socialism*.
42. 'Settlements of University Men in Great Towns'.
43. Barnett, S.A. 'Class Divisions in Great Cities', p. 29.
44. 'Twenty-one Years of Settlement', in *Practicable Socialism*, p. 125.
45. *Ibid*.
46. Barnett, S.A. 'Vision and Service'.
47. Beveridge, W.H. *Power and Influence*, p. 17.
48. *Ibid.*, p. 29.
49. *Ibid.*, pp. 30−1.
50. Stedman-Jones points out that the COS included individuals of varying beliefs and it is thus difficult to situate it with any certainty in either the older or the newer traditions. Loch himself was greatly influenced by Green and Bosanquet, and his views were far more complex than the Spencerian individualist label often attached to him might suggest.
51. Barnett, S.A. 'The Failure of Charity', in *Perils of Wealth and Poverty*,

p. 64.

52. *Ibid.*
53. *Ibid.*, p. 138.
54. Professor Carr-Saunders was later Chairman of the Joint University Council and did much to develop and encourage social work training.
55. Urwick, E.J. 'Social Education of Yesterday and Today'. See Macadam, E. *The Social Servant in the Making*, for an account of early developments in training. The first university course was established at Liverpool in 1904, and Birmingham University was the first to award a Diploma in 1908.
56. Pinker, R.A. *Social Theory and Social Policy*, p. 30.
57. Beatrice Webb, quoted in Terrell, R. *R.H. Tawney and His Time*, p. 6.
58. Terrell, R. *op cit.*, p. 67.
59. This account of the origins of the Joint University Council is drawn from its early reports, viz: The Social Studies Committee for London. 'The Selection and Training of Welfare Supervisors in Factories and Workshops', 1917; The Social Studies Committee for London, 'Part-Time Social Study Courses for Social Workers and Adult Students', 1918; Joint University Council, 'Social Study and Training at the Universities'; Joint University Council, 'University Training for Welfare Work in Industry and Commerce', 1921; see also Joint University Council, 'A Review of Work During the Years 1918—1944'.
60. Attlee, C.R. *The Social Worker*, pp. 2—3.
61. *Ibid.*, p. 27.
62. *Ibid.*, p. 27.
63. Macadam, E. *The Equipment of the Social Worker*, pp. 55—6.
64. Heath, J. St.G. 'University Training Courses'. Conference of the Association for the Education of Women in Oxford, 1916.
65. Brown, S. Clement, 'Looking Backwards'.
66. Evelyn Fox's role in the development of social work has received little recognition from the profession. Her vigour and energy did much to advance the social care of the mentally handicapped. See Welfare, Marjorie U. 'Dame Evelyn Fox', *Social Service*, 28, 172—5.
67. *Studies in Mental Inefficiency*, 6th Jan 1925.
68. Central Association for Mental Welfare, *13th Annual Report*, 1926—7.
69. Memorandum on the Training of Social Workers, submitted to the Joint University Council for Social Studies by the Central Association for Mental Welfare, 1926 (unpublished).
70. Institute of Hospital Almoners, *Annual Report*, 1922.
71. Institute of Hospital Almoners, *Annual Report*, 1921.
72. I have been unable to discover a copy of this report, but it is summarised in the I.H.A. *Annual Report*, 1926.
73. Hospital Almoners Association, Minutes, 1.12.24.
74. Hospital Almoners Association, Minutes, 8.1.25 — 'This Association is alive to the importance of the new developments in medical psychology,

and is anxious to equip its members to carry out any new work the medical staffs may instruct them to do, and therefore asks the Council to include a course of elementary psychology in the latter part of the student's training and to consult the leading psychologists as to their views on the proper functions of almoners in special mental work, in order that a scheme of postgraduate lectures should, if found desirable, be immediately arranged'.

75. This information is drawn from the Executive Committee Minutes of the Hospital Almoners Council, 1925/1926.
76. Dicks, H.V. *Fifty Years of the Tavistock Clinic*.
77. Their perplexity was further sharpened by the visit of Dr. Cabot, who had done so much to develop medical secial work in the United States, to the High Leigh Conference in 1928. He expressed the view that the Freudian movement had done more harm than good, and that more could be learnt from a study of the great novels than from the psychology of the unconscious.
    Hospital Almoners Association *Year Book*, 1928.
78. Hospital Almoners Council, Executive Committee Minutes, 10.12.28.
79. Institute of Hospital Almoners, *Annual Report*, 1928.
80. Dr. Rees, Director of the Tavistock Clinic argued that, for the future, 'the policy required is one which will embody, in all social training, the point of view of the psychiatrist which emphasises the emotional values and inherent purposiveness of all human behaviour, and hence insists that treatment cannot be effective without understanding of the *real* (not only the apparent) meaning of a patient's symptoms as experiences to him. . .
    The great amount of *preventable* nervous trouble and faulty handling of life especially in the training of children, due to ignorance of mental hygiene principles, and the amount of serious mental disease and unhappiness which results from it, makes strikingly evident the need of more provision for early treatment; and an important feature of this is the employment, in all organisations dealing with individuals, of social workers qualified to recognise and understand the early signs of such trouble'.
    Rees, J.R. and Robinson, D.F. 'Modern Psychiatry and Social Work'. Hospital Almoners Association *Year Book*, 1930.
81. Shelling, J.M. 'The Contribution of the Institute of Medical Social Workers to Education for Social Work'.
82. Strachey, J. St. Loe, 'American Juvenile Courts and Children's Courts in England'.
83 *3rd Annual Report* of the National Council for Mental Hygiene, 1925—6. See also *13th Annual Report* of Central Association for Mental Welfare, 1926—1927, for accounts of these early negotiations.
84. A different facet is recorded by Cyril Burt which ascribes the establishment of the Child Guidance Council to the outcome of a meeting of psychologists and educationalists at the London Day Training College

(where he had that year taken the chair of Educational Psychology) under the chairmanship of Sir Percy Nunn, and at the request of Mrs. Strachey.

85. Burke, N. and Miller, E. 'Child Mental Hygiene — History, Methods and Problems'.

86. Shrubsall, F.C. 'Notes on the Investigation and Treatment of 'Difficult' Children in the United States of America'.

87. Mary Richmond also used the term 'treatment', but it was a social concept without the medical and clinical connotations (and the underlying assumption of illness) which it acquired in psychiatric settings.

Chapter 3

1. Timms, N. *Psychiatric Social Work in Great Britain*.

2. Brown, S. Clement, 'Looking Backwards'.

3. In 1938, for example, the course included: Psychology for Mental Health Workers (Dr. Blake Prichard); Introduction to Applied Social Psychology (Miss Clement Brown); Mental Health Course Seminar (Miss Clement Brown); General Psychology (Miss Fildes); Psychiatry (Dr. Aubrey Lewis); Mental Deficiency (Dr. Tredgold); The Psychology of Individual Differences (Professor Burt); The Psychology of Childhood and Adolescence (Professor Burt); The Legal and Administrative Provisions relating to Mental Disorder and Deficiency (Dr. Wilson); The Treatment of the Law Breaker, with special reference to Methods in Borstal Institutions (Dr. Methven); Elements of Human Genetics (Dr. Penrose).

4. See, for example, *Dreams and Nightmares* and *Psychology and Mental Health*.

5. Moodie, W. 'Child Guidance by Team Work'.

6. Lewis, Aubrey, 'Sigmund Freud: 1856—1939', in *The State of Psychiatry*. This gives his assessment of Freud's work.

7. In 1924 Dr. Tredgold reviewed Wohlgemuth's very critical assessment of psychoanalysis. In welcoming it he remarked: 'Although in this country the theories and practice of Freud have made appeal to very few leading psychiatrists, and even to fewer scientific psychologists, yet they have undoubtedly been seized on with avidity by a considerable number of the more junior and inexperienced practitioners, by still more educationalists, and by a large section of the general public and certain sections of the public press'.

He concluded: 'Personally, we have never read a more convincing or more damaging criticism, and we do not think the warning has come any too soon'.

Review of Wohlgemuth, A.A. 'A Critical Examination of Psychoanalysis' *Studies in Mental Inefficiency*, 5.3.1924.

8. Brown, S.C. 'Looking Backwards'.

9. At the same time, she stressed the importance of psychoanalysis

178

historically: 'This period of expectation and movement. . . with its heightened sense of individual and social needs, saw the beginning of various fruitful interchanges of experience and method. Of all that was then put into circulation, the discoveries of Freud, and those whose work derived from his, were incomparably the most important. Social workers were henceforth to feel, increasingly if unevenly, the influence of the main concepts of psychoanalysis. The special importance of this for social workers who were to train for work with the mentally ill and maladjusted can hardly be overstressed'.

Ashdown, M. and Brown, S.C. *Social Service and Mental Health*, p. 15.
10. 'Child Guidance', a pamphlet published by the Child Guidance Council, 1937.
11. Moodie, W. 'The Child Guidance Clinic', *The Magistrate*, **2**, 1930, p. 391.
12. Moodie, W. 'Child Guidance by Team Work' (not dated). Dr. Moodie's view of the psychiatric social worker was very much that of a psychiatric aide and the therapeutic aspirations of the early psychiatric social workers, we may deduce, did not receive very much encouragement from that source.
13. Moodie, W. *Ibid*.
14. The Child Guidance Council, *Annual Report*, 1936.
15. Goldberg, E.M. 'Some Developments in Professional Collaboration and Research in the USA', *Brit. J. Psychiatric Social Work*, III, **1**, 1955, 4−12.
16. In Ashdown and Brown's study of a sample of students trained on the Mental Health Course between 1935 and 1939, 17 out of 65 respondents indicated that they had had a personal analysis.
17. Brown, S.C. 'Looking Backwards'.
18. Association of Psychiatric Social Workers, *Annual Reports*, 1936 and 1941.
    After the Second World War, the mental health course increasingly came to serve as an advanced course, and in 1961, a high proportion were in nonpsychiatric work — 155, compared with 488 in mental health work of varying kinds.
19. Timms, N. *op cit.*, p. 68.
20. 'Lessons from Jung about Casework', *C.O. Quarterly,* **20**, 1927.
21. Jung, C.G. Letter to the Editor, *C.O. Quarterly*, 21, 1927. The anonymous writer had commented: 'Confronted as your workers are by a movement on a vast scale, away from individual casework to mass treatment of human necessity by huge State schemes of insurance and assistance, it will cheer you to find in Dr. Jung an unrepentant champion of elaborate individual casework'.
22. Crosse, Olive, 'American Experience', *C.O. Quarterly*, **4**, July 1930; Crosse, Olive, 'A study of Casework', *C.O. Quarterly,* **4**, October 1930,

172 — 0; Cosens, M. 'Psychology and Social Casework'. *C.O. Quarterly* 7, April, 1933; Brown S. Clement, 'Family Case Work and Mental Health'. *C.O. Quarterly,* **13**, January 1939.

Earlier articles with a psychological reference were Burt, C. 'Individual psychology and social work', *C.O. Quarterly,* **43**, 1918, 4 — 19 and 51 — 60; Reid, Mrs. 'The equipment of the social worker', *C.O. Quarterly,* July 1924; Raven, Alice, 'The use of psychology in social work', *C.O. Quarterly*, July 1925. Burt's work in particular, was much influenced by the idea of 'efficiency' — 'a place for everyman, and every man in his place'.

23. In a personal interview.
24. Brown, S. Clement, *op. cit.* Asked to give evidence before the 1936 Committee on Social Services in Courts of Summary Jurisdiction, Pringle interpreted the invitation as asking whether the COS had something to offer. He responded: 'We believe with a deep and passionate conviction that we have not only something, but the Pearl of Great Price. . . ' (Minutes of Evidence). His commitment to the COS conception of casework was absolute: 'The COS lays down without compromise that there is no force of human succour which is scientific other than casework of the COS type'. 'Charity Organisation, Science and Politics'. *C.O Quarterly*, July, 1927, p. 76.
25. Macadam, E. *The New Philanthropy*, p. 104.
26. British Federation of Social Workers. Meeting of Interim Committee, 1.4.1935.
27. Younghusband, E. *Social Work and Social Change*, p. 19.
28. *Social Casework: Generic or Specific* — Report of the Milford Conference, 1929.
29. The medical analogy was frequently used by COS workers much earlier than *Social Diagnosis*.
30. e.g. Sainsbury, E. *Diagnosis in Social Casework*.
31. Germain, C. 'Casework and Science: A Historical Encounter', in R.W. Roberts and R.H. Nee (eds.) *Theories of Social Casework*.
32. Neilson, W.A. 'The Smith College Experiment in Training for Psychiatric Social Work'. *Mental Hygiene,* III, **1**.,1919, 59 — 64.
33. Jarrett, Mary 'The Psychiatric Thread Running through all Social Casework'.
34. Taft, Jessie 'The Relation of Psychiatry to Social Work'.
35. Taft, Jessie 'Qualifications of the Psychiatric Social Worker'.
36. Taft, Jessie *Ibid*.
37. Robinson, V.P. *A Changing Psychology in Social Casework,* p. 184.
38. *Ibid.*, p. 184.
39. Austin, L. 'Trends in Differential Treatment in Social Casework'.
40. Kadushin, A. 'The Knowledge Base of Social Work'. In Kahn, A.J. *Issues in American Social Work*.
41. Hamilton, Gordon 'Methods of Family Social Work'. *Second Inter-*

national Conference on Social Work, Paris, 1932.
42. Colcord, Joanna 'The Significance of Unemployment for the Family and for the Social Treatment of the Family'. *Second International Conference on Social Work*, Paris, 1932.
43. Hamilton, G. *op cit*.
44. Alexander, L.B. 'Social Work's Freudian deluge: Myth or reality?'; Borenzweig, H. 'Social Work and Psychoanalysis'; Hellenbrand, S.C. 'Freud's Influence on Social Casework'.
45. Meyer, H.J. 'Social Work'.
46. Towle, C. Preface to Hollis, F. *Casework: A Psychosocial Therapy*.
47. Donnison, D.V. 'Observations on University training for social work in Great Britain and North America'.
48. Flexner, A. 'Is Social Work a Profession?'. *National Conference of Charities and Correction*, 1915. Reprinted Pumphrey, R.E. and M.W. *The Heritage of American Social Work*.
49. Bruno, F.J. *Trends in American Social Work*, p. 141.
50. Kadushin, A. *op cit*.
51. Sargent, V. 'Psychiatric Treatment'.
52. Levine, M. and Levine, A. *A Social History of the Helping Services*.
53. Cohen, N. *Social Work in the American Tradition*, p. 318.
54. 'It is perhaps impossible to say at the present time what part psychological methods will play in the Juvenile Court of the future, but the recent attention given to the science of psychology and the great developments that may confidently be expected cannot be neglected. If it is true, as certain psychological writers have recently said, that the hypothesis of the unconscious motive is one of the greatest discoveries of modern science, a great deal of light may eventually be thrown on the conditions which lead children to commit offences, and on the right methods of dealing with them. Even if the claims advanced for psychoanalysis as a means of treating juvenile delinquency prove to be extravagant, all who are responsible for the care and training of children must acknowledge the renewed stimulus thereby given to the subject of child study which is likely to lead to more enlightened handling of young people by parents, teachers and others'.
55. Macadam, E. *The New Philanthropy*, pp. 65−6.
56. Cohen, N. *op cit*., p. 126.
57. Cosens, M. Review of Aptekar, H. *Basic Concepts in Social Casework* and Robinson, V.P. *Training for Skill in Social Casework, Social Work*, January, 1943.

Chapter 4

1. Parker, R. 'Social Ills and Public Remedies'. In W.A. Robson (ed) *Man and the Social Sciences*, p. 116.

2. Murphy, G. 'The Current Impact of Freud upon Psychology'.
3. Dibble, V.K. 'Occupations and Ideologies'.
4. Heraud, B. *Sociology and Social Work*, p. 225.
5. *Ibid.*, p. 271.
6. *Ibid.*, *passim*.
7. United Nations. *Training for Social Work: Third International Survey*, Part 3.
8. Isaacs, S. *Social Development in Young Children*.
9. Burlingham D. and Freud A. *Young Children in Wartime* and *Infants Without Families*.
10. Bowlby, J. *Maternal Care and Mental Health*, p. 11.
11. Bowlby, *op cit.*, p. 11.
12. e.g. Goldfarb, W. 'Effects of early institutional care on adolescent personality'.
13. Spitz R.A. and Wolf K.M. 'Anaclitic Depression: an inquiry into the genesis of psychiatric conditions in early childhood'.
14. Burlingham D. and Freud A. *op cit*.
15. Isaacs, S. *The Cambridge Evacuation Survey*.
16. Winnicott, D.W. and Britton, C. 'The Problem of Homeless Children', in *Childrens Communities*. New Education Fellowship Monograph No. 4. 1944; Winnicott, D.W. and Britton, C. 'Residential Management as a Treatment for Difficult Children'.
17. Bowlby, J. *Child Care and The Growth of Love*.
18. Bowlby, J. *Attachment* and *Loss*.
19. Rutter has argued (in *Maternal Deprivation Reassessed*) that the maternal deprivation hypothesis is now seen to cover such a complexity and variety of conditions as to be too comprehensive to be useful, and suggests it should be abandoned altogether.
20. Bowlby, J. 'The Nature of the Child's Tie to the Mother'; Sluckin, W. *Imprinting and Early Learning*.
21. Sluckin, W. *The Impressionable Age*.
22. Powdermaker, F., Lewis, H.T. and Touraine, S. 'Psychopathology and Treatment of delinquent girls'.
23. Harlow, H.F. (1960), 'Primary affection patterns in primates', Amer. J. Orthopsychiat, **30**, 676.
24. *Young Children in Brief Separation: 'Kate'*. Film by James and Joyce Robertson.
25. A series under the title *Young Children in Brief Separation* by James and Joyce Robertson.
26. e.g. Home Office Circular No. 160/1948, Para. 5, reads: 'To keep the family together must be the first aim, and the separation of a child from its parents can only be justified when there is no possibility of securing adequate care for a child in his own home'.
27. Bowlby, J. *Maternal Care and Mental Health*, p. 157.
28. Ashdown, M. and Brown, S.C. *Social Service and Mental Health*.

29. Hunnybun, N.K. 'A Contribution to Casework Training'. *Case Conference*, 2(8) 1955.
30. This observation is based on an analysis of posts held by members of the Tavistock Social Workers Continuation Group, which includes many former Casework Fellows.
31. Notes on the Oxford Conference, *Social Work*, October 1941.
32. McIver, O. Alsager. 'Looking Forward', *Social Work* 1 (7) 1941.
33. Wilson, A.T.M. 'The Development of a Scientific Base in Family Casework'.
34. Wilson, A.T.M., Menzies, I. Eichholz. E. 'The Marriage Welfare Sub-committee of the Family Welfare Association'.
35. See Monger, M. *Casework in Marital Problems*: he draws extensively on theoretical approaches and models developed by the Institute of Marital Studies.
36. Mrs. Enid Balint (formerly Eichholz).
37. *The Departmental Committee on Children Deprived of a Normal Home Life*, chaired by Dame Myra Curtis.
38. Interim Report of the Curtis Committee.
39. See her series of articles in *Child Care and Social Work*.
40. Bowlby, J. *Forty-four Juvenile Thieves*.
41. Robertson, Alex. 'Penal Policy and Social Change'.
42. This account is based on Glover, E. *The Diagnosis and Treatment of Delinquency*, Institute for the Study and Treatment of Delinquency, 1944.
43. Friedlander, K. *The Psychoanalytic Approach to Juvenile Delinquency*.
44. Glover, E. *The Diagnosis and Treatment of Delinquency*.
45. Schmideberg, M. *Children in Need*.

Chapter 5

1. e.g. Greenwood, E. 'Attributes of a Profession', and Heraud, B.J. *Sociology and Social Work*, Chapter 10, 'The Professionalisation of Social Work.
2. Millerson, G.L. *The Qualifying Associations*, Chap. 1.
3. Shils, 'The Concept and Function of Ideology'.
4. Bendix, R. *Work and Authority in Industry*. New York. Wiley, 1956.
5. See Strauss, A. *et al.* 'Psychiatric Institutions and Ideologies'; Gilbert, D.C. and Levinson, D.J. 'Role Performance, Ideology and Personality in Mental Hospital Aides'; Gilbert D.C. and Levinson, D.J. '"Custo-dialism" and "Humanism" in Mental Hospital Structure and in Staff Ideology'.
6. Apter, D. *Ideology and Discontent*, p. 16.
7. Geertz, C. 'Ideology as a Cultural System', in Apter, *op cit.*, p. 64.
8. Marx, J.H. 'A Multidimensional Conception of Ideologies in Professional

Arenas: the case of the Mental Health Field'. *Pacific Sociol. Rev.*, **12**, 2, 75.

9. *Ibid*.
10. *Ibid*.
11. *Ibid*
12. Rogers, E.C. *The Diffusion of Innovations*, surveys work from most of these fields.
13. Katz, E. and Lazarsfeld, P.F. *Personal Influence: the Part Played by People in the Flow of Mass Communications.*
14. Dibble, V.K. 'Occupations and Ideologies'.
15. Katz, E., and Lazarsfeld, P.F. *op cit.*
16. Younghusband, E.L. *Report on the Employment and Training of Social Workers.*
17. *Ibid*.
18. *Ibid*., para. 143.
19. *Ibid*., para. 149.
20. *Ibid*., para. 194 ff.
21. See *New Trends in European Social Work, The Impact of Casework* (not dated), a series of essays dedicated to Marguerite Pohek by European social workers, for an indication of the influence of these seminars.
22. Snelling, J.M. 'The United Nations Seminar on the teaching and supervision of Social Casework'. *The Almoner*, 5 January 1953.
23. *Report on the Employment and Training of Social Workers.*
24. Morris, C. (ed) *Social Casework in Great Britain.*
25. Hamilton, G. *Theory and Practice of Social Casework*, second edition, p. 24.
26. Shenfield, B. 'Social Casework in Great Britain'.
27. McDougall, K. 'The Future of Casework in England Today'. *The Almoner*, 5 (6) September 1952, 243—250.
28. e.g. Pollak, O. *Integrating Sociological and Psychoanalytic concepts: an exploration in Child Psychotherapy.*
29. Hamilton G. *Theory and Practice of Social Casework*, first edition, 1946, p. 346.
30. Hamilton, G. *ibid*., p. 345.
31. Snelling, J.M. *op cit.*
32. *Op. cit.*, para 7.
33. *Social Work in Britain*, para. 461.
34. The Employment and Training of Social Workers, para. 85.
35. Morris, C. (ed) *Social Case Work in Great Britain*, p. 193.
36. *Ibid*.
37. *Social Work in Britain*, para. 462.
38. Brown, S.C. 'Training for Social Work'.
39. Brown, S.C. 'The Cinderella of the Professions'.
40. *Ibid*.
41. Black, E.I. Report to Members of the Joint University Council for Social

Studies on a visit to the United States in April/May 1948 (unpublished).
42. Joint University Council, Minutes, 13th May, 1950.
43. Draft outline for a One-Year Post-Certificate Course in Social Casework, prepared in January 1951 by a Sub-committee of the Training Committee of the Joint University Council (unpublished).
44. Institute of Almoners. Minutes of Training Committee, 19.1.51.
45. Not published.
46. Joint University Council, unpublished memorandum.
47. A sequence on 'Clinical Aspects of Child Development' was incorporated in the Mental Health Course. This was 14 lectures, compared with the proposed 40 on the Carnegie Course. This weighting indicates the differential importance attached to it.
48. One Year Course in Applied Social Studies (Social Casework) at the London School of Economics, May 1954, (duplicated).
49. *Ibid*.
50. 'Generic Training for Social Work' *Probation*, December 1956.
51. *Ibid*.
52. Towle, C. *The Learner in Education for the Professions*, Preface p. ix.
53. *Ibid*., p. 259.
54. Towle, C. 'New Developments in Social Case Work in the United States'.
55. Towle, C. 'Generic Trends in Education for Social Work'.
56. Prince, G.S. 'The Teaching of Mental Health in Schools of Social Work'. United Nations Educational Scientific and Cultural Organisation, UN Regional Seminars on Social Work Training Working Paper, 1957.
57. *Ibid*.
58. Titmuss, R.M. 'The Administrative Setting of Social Service'.
59. *Ibid*.
60. Analysis of examination questions during the first 10 years of the course shows that nearly as many were designed to test understanding at an organisational level of analysis as at the individual personality level.
61. Irvine, E.E. 'Renaissance in British Casework'.
62. Ratcliffe, T.A. in 'The Problem Family'. Report of a Conference at Worcester, October 1957. Institute for the Study and Treatment of Delinquency.
63. Bergman, I., Butrym, Z.T., Nicholson, A.K. and Watts, B.W. Letter on 'Psychology and Medical Social Work', *The Almoner*, 5 (1) April, 1952.
64. Rees, H.E. 'The United Nations Seminar on Teaching and Supervision of Social Casework in Europe'.
65. Snelling, J.M. 'The United Nations Seminar on the Teaching and Supervision of Social Casework'.
66. See *The Almoner*, 7 (10) January 1955 and 7 (12) March 1955.
67. Irvine, E.E. 'Some Implications of Freudian Theory for Casework'.
68. *The Almoner*, 9 (2) 1956.
69. Butrym, Z.T. 'An Open Letter'. *The Almoner*, 13 (12) March 1951.
70. Such articles included J.R. Rees, 'Mental Health and the Offender'

185

(1947); K. Soddy, 'Mental Health in Probation Work' (1948); W.L. Neustatter, 'Psychiatric Disorders and Crime' (1950).

71. *Probation*, 6 (18) 1952.
72. *Probation*, 8 (1) 1956.
73. Corner, E.P. Address to National Association of Probation Officers Conference. *Probation*, 8 (2) 1956.
74. 'Casework Supervision in the Probation Service', *Probation*, 8 (7) 1957.
75. *Probation*, 8 (9) 1958.
76. 'The Boundaries of Casework'. Association of Psychiatric Social Workers, 1956.
77. Hollis, E.V. and Taylor, A. *Social Work Education in the United States*, p. 151.
78. Janchill, M.P. 'Systems concepts in Casework Theory and Practice'.
79. Parsloe, P. 'Group Work in the Social Work Curriculum', In *Group Work*, National Institute for Social Work, 1977.
80. Wasserman, H. 'Social Work Treatment: An Essay Review'.
81. Filmer, P. (ed) *Recent Directions in Sociological Theory*.
82. Giddens, A. (ed) *Positivism and Sociology*, p. 1.
83. MacLeod, R.B. 'Phenomenology', *Encyclop. of the Soc. Sci.*, **13**, 1968, p. 70.
84. *Ibid*.
85. Parker, R.A. 'Social Ills and Public Remedies'.
86. Townsend, P. and Abel-Smith, B. *The Poor and the Poorest*.
87. Bailey, R. and Brake, M. (eds) *Radical Social Work*; Corrigan P. and Leonard P, *Social Work Practice under Capitalism*.
88. Kendall, K. 'Dream or Nightmare? : the future of Social Work Education'.

Chapter 6

1. See Kuhn, T.H. *The Structure of Scientific Revolutions*.
2. Rieff, P. *Freud, The Mind of a Moralist*.
3. Fromm, E. *The Crisis of Psychoanalysis*, p. 15.
4. Bruner, J.S. 'Freud and the Image of Man'. Bruner has observed: 'Freud's sense of the continuity of human conditions, of the likeness of the human plight, has made possible a deeper sense of the brotherhood of man. It has in any case tempered the spirit of punitiveness towards what once we took as evil and what we now see as sick. We have not yet resolved the dilemma provided by these two ways of viewing. Its resolution is one of the great moral challenges of our age'.
5. Lapiere, R. *The Freudian Ethic*. Freud reports similar criticisms in *Collected Papers*, V, p. 169.
6. Freud wrote: 'One can only characterise as simple-minded the fear which is sometimes expressed that all the highest goods of humanity, as they are

186

called — research, art, love, ethical and social sense — will lose their value or their dignity because psychoanalysis is in a position to demonstrate their origin in elementary and animal instinctual impulses'. *Collected Papers*, V, p. 128.

7. 'However much the analyst may be tempted to become a teacher, model and ideal for other people and to create men in his own image, he should not forget that that is not his task in the analytic relationship, and indeed that he will be disloyal to his task if he allows himself to be led on by his inclinations. If he does, he will only be repeating a mistake of the parents who crushed their child's independence by their influence, and he will only be replacing the patient's earlier dependence by a new one'.

Freud, S. *An Outline of Psychoanalysis*, p. 32.

8. Robertson, A. 'Penal Policy and Social Change'.
9. Gorer, G. 'Freud's Influence'.
10. See Tharp, E.G. and Wetzel, R.J. *Behaviour Modification in the Natural Environment*, p. 13.
11. Self-determination appears as an important value in Victorian social work and thus antedates Freud. Octavia Hill wrote: 'It is essential to remember that each man has his own view of life, and must be free to fulfil it; that in many ways he is a far better judge of it than we, as he has lived through and felt what we have only seen. Our work is rather to bring him to the point of considering the spirit of judging rightly, than to consider or judge for him'. 'The Management of a London Court'.
12. See Halmos, P. *The Faith of the Counsellors*.
13. Fromm, E. *Sigmund Freud's Mission*, p. 105.
14. See 'The Concept of Insight' in Jehu D., Hardiker P., Yelloly M. and Shaw, M. *Behaviour Modification in Social Work*.
15. Freud, S. 'The Claims of Psycho-Analysis to Scientific Interest'. *S.E.* XIII, p. 175.
16. Mayer, J. and Timms, N. *The Client Speaks*.
17. Winnicott, C. *Child Care and Social Work*, p. 45.
18. See Yelloly, M. 'The Concept of Insight'.
19. Bosanquet, H. 'The meaning and methods of true charity'.
20. Bartlett, H. *The Common Base of Social Work Practice*, p. 37.
21. For example, Skynner, A.C.R. 'A Group-analytic Approach to conjoint Family Therapy'; Bednar, R.L. 'Empirical Guidelines for Group Psychotherapy'.
22. Pumpian-Mindlin, E. 'The Position of Psychoanalysis in Relation to the Biological and Social Sciences'. In E. Pumpian-Mindlin (ed) *Psychoanalysis as Science*, p. 132.
23. Peters, R.S. *The Concept of Motivation*.
24. *Ibid*.
25. Freud, S. 'Psychoanalysis'. *Collected Papers*, V, pp. 127, 128.
26. *Ibid*., p. 128.
27. Pumpian-Mindlin, *op cit*., pp. 133—4.

187

28. Miller, S.M. and Riessman, F. *Social Class and Social Policy*, p. viii.
29. Rycroft, C. (ed) *Psychoanalysis Observed*, p. 21.
30. Nevertheless, Freud wished to see certain social changes; notably a greater accommodation to the demands of the sexual instincts.
31. Koestler, A. *Yogis and Commissars*.
32. Wootton, B. *Social Science and Social Pathology*, Chap. IX.
33. 'Moral Issues in the Training of Teachers and Social Workers'. *Sociological Review Monograph*, No. 3, 1960.
34. Simey, T.S. *The Boundaries of Casework*, p. 61.
35. *Ibid*.
36. Parker, R.A. 'Social Ills and Public Remedies'. In W.A. Robson (ed) *Man and the Social Sciences*, p. 116.
37. I am referring here to the 'textbook' view; whether actual practice reflected this I am not in a position to say.
38. United Nations: *Training for Social Work. Third International Survey*, pp. 57—59 (my italics).
39. Moffatt, J. *Concepts of Casework Treatment*, pp. 3—4.
40. *Ibid*., p. 62. See Hollis, F. *Casework, A Psychosocial Therapy*.
41. Parad, H.J. *Ego Psychology and Dynamic Casework* (1958); Parad, H.J. and Miller, R.R. *Ego-oriented Casework: Problems and Perspectives* (1963).
42. Germain, C. 'Social Study, Past and Future'.
43. Waelder, R. *Basic Theory of Psychoanalysis*, p. 46.
44. Wittenberg, I. Salzberger. *Psychoanalytic Insight and Relationships*, p. 9.
45. Rogers, C. *Client-centred Therapy*, p. 198 ff.
46. Wolman, B.B. *The Unconscious Mind*, p. 176.
47. *Ibid*., p. 179.
48. Greenson, R.R. and Wexler, M. 'The Non-transference Relationship in the Psychoanalytic Situation', *International Journal of Psychoanalysis*, **50**, 27—39.
49. Sandler, J. *et al. The Patient and the Analyst*, p. 47.
50. See, for example, Bernstein, R. 'Are we still Stereotyping the unmarried Mother?'
51. See p. 62.
52. Gough, D. 'Work with Unmarried Mothers'. *The Almoner*, March 1961.
53. Jehu, D. *et al. Behaviour Modification in Social Work*, p. 92.
54. Nacht, S. 'The curative factors in psychoanalysis'. The human face of psychoanalysis and the personal involvement and attitudes of the analyst have been given much more attention in recent years (Lomas 1973; Frank 1977) and the analytic process emerges from this as a much warmer, more caring and human encounter than might be thought from other psychoanalytic writing.
55. Segal, H. 'The Curative Factors in Psychoanalysis'.
56. Yelloly, M. 'The concept of insight'. In Jehu D. *et al. Behaviour Modifica-*

tion in Social Work.

57. Hollis, F. *Casework: A Psycho-social Therapy*, p. 138.

58. Hollis, F. 'Explorations in the development of a typology of casework treatment'.

    Hollis, F. 'The Coding and Application of a typology of casework treatment'.

    See also Reid, W.J. 'A Study of Caseworkers' use of insight-oriented techniques'.

59. For example, Bree, M.H. (1952).

60. Brown, M.A.G. 'A review of casework methods'. In Younghusband, E. (ed) *New Developments in Casework*.

61. Irvine, E.E. 'A new look at Casework'. In Younghusband, E. *op cit*.

62. Mayer, J.E. and Timms N. 'Clash in perspective between worker and client'.

63. Halmos, P. In 'Problems arising from the teaching of personality development'.

64. *Ibid*.

65. Winnicott, C. In 'Problems arising from the teaching of personality development'.

66. Szasz, T. 'The Myth of Mental Illness'.

67. Mowrer, H.O. '"Sin", the Lesser of Two Evils'.

68. e.g. Specht, H. 'The deprofessionalisation of social work'.

69. This point is made in Fromm, E. *The Crisis of Psychoanalysis*.

70. Bantock, G.H. Comment on 'Reform or Therapy' in 'Moral Issues in the Training of Teachers and Social Workers'. *Sociological Review Monograph*, No. 3, pp. 71 — 2.

71. See Plant, R. *Social and Moral Theory in Casework*, p. 79.

72. Sorokin, P. *Society, Culture and Personality*, p. 69 ff.

Chapter 7

1. Rayner, E.V., *Human Development*, is a frequently used text.

2. Hollis, F. *Casework: A Psychosocial Therapy*.

3. Perlman, H. *Social Casework*.

4. Roberts, R.W. and Nee, R.H. *Theories of Social Casework*.

5. Ferard, M.L. and Hunnybun, N. *The Caseworker's Use of Relationships*.

6. Timms, N. *Social Casework: Principles and Practice*.

7. Moffatt, J. *Concepts of Casework Treatment*.

8. Davison, E. *Social Casework*.

9. Monger, M. *Casework in Probation*.

10. See Chapter I.

11. Hollis, F. 'A profile of early interviews in marital counselling'.

12. See Chapter I for an account of this approach.

13. Garrett, A. 'Modern Casework: The Contributions of Ego Psychology'. In

Parad, H. (ed.) *Ego Psychology und Dynamic Casework*.

14. Boehm, W. 'The Contribution of Psychoanalysis to Social Work Education'. In E. Younghusband (ed.) *Education for Social Work*, p. 87.
15. *Ibid.*, p. 88.
16. *Ibid.*, p. 89.
17. Jehu, D. *et al. Behaviour Modification in Social Work*, p. 16.
18. Tharp, R.G. and Wetzel, R.J. *Behaviour Modification in the Natural Environment*, p. 14.
19. See Herbert, M. *Conduct Disorders of Childhood*.
20. Tharp and Wetzel, p. 12.
21. Ayllon, T. and Azrin, N.H. *The Token Economy*
22. Jehu, D. *et al.*, *op cit*. Introduction.
23. Alexander, F. 'The Dynamics of Psychotherapy in the light of Learning Theory'.
24. Eysenck, H.J. and Wilson, G.D. *The Experimental Study of Freudian Theories*, p. 393.
25. Langer, S. *Mind: An Essay on Human Feeling*, p. xvii.
26. In Koch, S. *Psychology: A Study of a Science*, p. 374.
27. Langer, S. *op cit*., p. 51.
28. Koch, S. *Psychology: The Study of a Science*, pp. 729—788.
29. Langer, S. *op cit*., p. 18.
30. In Koch, *op cit*., p. 165 (my italics)
31. Koch, *op cit*., p. 165.
32. Koch, *op cit*., p. 784.
33. Kellmer Pringle, M.K. *The Needs of Children*. For a fuller account see Herbert, M. *Emotional Problems of Development in Children*.
34. *Ibid.*, p. 22.
35. See Rutter, M. 'Parent-child separation: Psychological effects on the children'.
36. See bibliography.
37. Bowlby, J. *Attachment* and *Loss*.
38. Bowlby, J. Introduction to *Attachment*.
39. Parkes, C.M. *Bereavement*.
40. See Rapoport, L. 'Crisis Intervention as a Mode of Brief Treatment', in Roberts and Nee, *Theories of Social Casework*; Parad, H. *Crisis Intervention*.
41. Rapoport, L. *op cit*., p. 301.
42. Meyer, C. *Social Work Practice*, p. 141.
43. Brenner, C. 'Psychoanalysis'.
44. Eysenck, H.J. and Wilson, G.D. *The Experimental Study of Freudian Theories*, p. 4.
45. *Ibid.*, p. 392.
46. *Ibid.*, p. 392.
47. Kline, P. *Fact and Fantasy in Freudian Theory*, p. 346.
48. *Ibid.*, p. 3.

49. *Ibid.*, p. 350.
50. Popper, K.R. *Conjectures and Refutations* pp. 34—5.
51. *Ibid.*, p. 35.
52. Rycroft, C. *Psychoanalysis Observed*, pp. 18—19.
53. Ricoeur, P. *Freud and Philosophy: An Essay on Interpretation*, p. 345.
54. *Ibid.*, p. 369.
55. Kline, P., *op cit.*, p. 354.
56. *Ibid.*, p. 359.
57. *Ibid.*
58. Thomas, E.J. 'Selecting Knowledge from Behavioural Science', in *Building Social Work Knowledge*, NASW, 1964.
59. *Ibid.*
60. See Hearn, G. *Theory Building in Social Work*, p. 21.
61. Lidz, T. *The Person*, p. viii.
62. Guntrip, H. 'The Promise of Psychoanalysis'. In Landis, B. and Tauber, E.S. (eds.) *In the Name of Life*.
63. Kline, P., *Fact and Fantasy in Freudian Theory*, p. x.

Chapter 8

1. Cypher, J.R. 'Social reform and social work'. In Jones, H. (ed.) *Towards a New Social Work*.
   Hardiker, P. 'Social work ideologies in the Probation Service'. *Br. J. Social Wk.*, **7**, 2, 1977, 131—154.
2. Rockmore, M.J. and Conklin, J.J. 'Contemporary social work education and psychoanalysis'. *J. of Educ. for Social Work*, 10, 2, Spring 1974, 68—75.
3. Rachman, S. *The Effects of Psychotherapy*. The evidence is by no means conclusive, and the debate remains wide open.
4. Meyer, H.J. *et al.* *Girls at Vocational High*, p. 24.
5. Bond, N. 'The case for radical casework'. *Social Work Today*, **2**, 9, 1971.
6. Miller, S.M. and Riessman, F. *Social Class and Social Policy*.
7. Winnicott, C. *Child Care and Social Work*, p. 45.
8. Meyer, C. *Social Work: a response to the urban crisis*, p. 106.
9. Corrigan, P. and Leonard, P. *Social Work Practice under Capitalism*, p. 107 ff.
10. Curle, A. *Mystics and Militants*.
11. *op cit.*, p. 33.

Bibliography

ACKERMAN, N. *Treating the Troubled Family*. New York and London. Basic Books Inc. 1966.

AD HOC COMMITTEE ON ADVOCACY. 'The social worker as advocate: champion of social victims'. *Social Work*, **14**, 2, April 1969, 16—22.

ALEXANDER, F. 'Analysis of the therapeutic factors in psychoanalytic treatment'. *Psychoanalytic Quarterly*, **19**, 4, 1950, 482—500.

ALEXANDER, F. 'The voice of the intellect is soft'. In *The Scope of Psychoanalysis, Selected Papers of Franz Alexander, 1921-1961*, 244—275. New York. Basic Books, 1961.

ALEXANDER, F. 'The dynamics of psychotherapy in the light of learning theory'. *American Journal of Psychiatry*, 120, 1963, 440—448.

ALEXANDER, F.M. and FRENCH, T.M. *Psychoanalytic Therapy*. New York. Ronald Press, 1946.

ALEXANDER, F. and ROSS, H. (eds.) *The Impact of Freudian Psychiatry*. Chicago. University of Chicago Press, 1961.

ALEXANDER, F. and SELESNICK, S.T. *The History of Psychiatry: an evaluation of psychiatric thought and practice from prehistoric times to the present*. London. Allen and Unwin, 1967.

ALEXANDER, L.B. 'Social work's Freudian deluge: Myth or reality?'. *Social Service Review*, 1972, **46** (4), 517—538.

AMERICAN ASSOCIATION OF SOCIAL WORKERS. *Social Casework: Generic or Specific?* New York. AASW, 1929.

ARMOR, D.J. and KLERMAN, G.C. 'Psychiatric treatment orientations and professional ideology'. *Journal of Health and Social Behaviour*, **9**, 3, 1968, 243—255.

ASSOCIATION OF PSYCHIATRIC SOCIAL WORKERS. *The Boundaries of Casework*. London 1956.

ASHDOWN, M. and BROWN, S.C. *Social Service and Mental Health*. London. Routledge and Kegan Paul. 1953.

ASHDOWN, M. 'The Role of the Psychiatric Social Worker'. Association of Psychiatric Social Workers. 1935.

ASSOCIATION OF SOCIAL WORKERS. *Report of a seminar on supervision*, April 1955.

ASTBURY, B.E. 'Twenty-five years with the Family Welfare Association'. *Social Work*, **13**, 1, January 1956, 138.

ATHERTON, S.T. 'Locating points for intervention'. *Social Casework*, **52**, 3, March 1971, 131—141.

ATHERTON, S.T. 'Using Points for intervention'. *Social Casework*, **52**, 4, April 1971, 223—33.

ATTLEE, C.R. *The Social Worker*, London, G. Bell and Sons, 1920.

AUSTIN, L. 'Trends in Differential Treatment in Social Casework'. In *Principles and Techniques in Social Casework*. New York. Family Service Association of America. 1950.

AYLLON T. and AZRIN N.H. *The Token Economy: A Motivation System for Therapy and Rehabilitation*. New York. Appleton-Century-Crofts, 1968.

BALINT, M. *The Basic Fault*. London. Tavistock Publications, 1968.

BALINT, M. 'Changing therapeutic aims and techniques in psychoanalysis'. *International Journal of Psychoanalysis*, **31**, 1950, 117—124.

BANDURA, A. *Principles of Behavior Modification*. New York. Holt Rinehart and Winston, 1969.

BANKS, Charlotte. 'Research in child guidance'. *British Journal of Educational Psychology* **23**, 1, 1953, 1.

BANNISTER, K, *et al. Social Casework in Marital Problems*. London. Tavistock Publications. 1955.

BANNISTER, K. AND PINCUS, L. *Shared phantasy in marital problems: therapy in a four-person relationship*. Hitchin. Codicote Press. 1965.

BARKER, E. *Political Thought in England, 1848—1914*. London. Oxford University Press, 2nd edn. 1928.

BARNETT, H.O. *Canon Barnett, His Life, Work and Friends*. London. John Murray, 1918.

BARNETT, S.A. *Religion and Politics*. London. Wells, Gardner, Darton & Co. Ltd., 1911.

BARNETT, S.A. and H.O. *Practicable Socialism*. London. Longmans & Co., 1888.

BARTLETT, F.C., Ginsberg, M., Lindgren, E.J. and Thouless, R.H. *The Study of Society*. London. Kegan Paul & Co., 1939.

BARTLETT, H.M. *The Common Base of Social Work Practice*. New York. National Association of Social Workers, 1970.

BASNETT, M. *Voluntary Social Action: A History of the National Council of Social* Service, 1919—1969. London. National Council of Social Service. 1969.

BEECH, H.R. *Changing Man's Behaviour*. London. Penguin Books Ltd., 1969.

BELDOCH, Michael. 'The death of the hero: an essay on Max Schur's Freud: Living and Dying'. *Bulletin of the Menninger Clinic*, **38**, 6, 1974, 476—526.

BELL, E.M. *The Story of the Hospital Almoners: The Birth of a Profession*. London. Faber & Faber, 1961.

BENDIX, R. and Lipset, S. (eds.) *Class, Status and Power*. Illinois. The Free Press of Glencoe, 1954.

BERGIN, A.E. 'Implications of psychotherapy research'. *International Journal of Psychiatry*, **3**, 1967, 136—50.

BERGIN, A.E. and Garfield, S.L. *Handbook of Psychotherapy and Behaviour*

Change. New York. John Wiley & Sons, 1971.

BERGMANN, G. 'Psychoanalysis and experimental psychology'. *Mind*, **52**, 1953, 122—140.

BERGMAN, G. 'Ideology'. *Ethics* 61, 205—218.

BERNFELD, S. 'Freud's earliest theories and the school of Helmholtz'. *Psychoanalytic Quarterly*. **13**, 1944, 351—62.

BERNSTEIN, A. 'The psychoanalytic technique'. In B.B. Wolman (ed.) *Handbook of Clinical Psychology*. New York. McGraw-Hill Book Co., 1965.

BERNSTEIN, R. 'Are we still stereotyping the unmarried mother?' *Social Work*, **5**, 3, 1960, 22—28.

BESSELL, R. *Interviewing and Counselling*. London. B.T. Batsford Ltd., 1971.

BEVERIDGE, W.H. 'The place of the social sciences in human knowledge'. *Politica*, September 1937.

BEVERIDGE, W.H. *Power and Influence*. London. Holder & Stoughton, 1953.

BEVERIDGE, W.H. *Voluntary Action*. London. George Allen & Unwin, 1948.

BIBRING, E. 'On the theory of the therapeutic results of psychoanalysis'. *International Journal of Psychoanalysis*, **18**, 1937, 170—189.

BIBRING, E. 'The mechanism of depression'. In P. Greenacre (ed.) *Affective Disorders: Psychoanalytic Contributions to their Study*. New York. International Universities Press, 1953.

BIBRING, G.L. 'Psychiatry and Social Work'. In C. Kasius (ed.) *Principles and Practice of Social Casework*. New York. Family Service Association of America, 1950.

BIERMAN, R. *Therapist activity-passivity and affection-rejection in Therapeutic Psychotherapy*. New York. Holt Rinehard & Winston, 1967.

BIESTEK, F.P. *The Casework Relationship*. Loyola University Press 1957. British edition: George Allen & Unwin, 1961.

BINSWANGER, L. *Being-in-the-World. Selected Papers*. New York and London. Basic Books Inc., 1963.

BION, W.R. *Experiences in Groups*. London. Tavistock Publications, 1961.

BLACKER, C.P. *Neurosis and the Mental Health Services*. London. Oxford University Press, 1946.

BOCOCK, R. *Freud and Modern Society*. London. Nelson and Sons Ltd, 1976.

BOEHM, W.W. 'The Contribution of Psychoanalysis to Social Work Education'. In E. Younghusband (ed.) *Education for Social Work*. London. George Allen & Unwin,1968.

BOND, N. 'The case for radical casework'. *Social Work Today*, 2, 9, 1971.

BOOTH, Charles. *The Life and Labour of the People of London*. London. Macmillan & Co., 1892—97.

BORENZWEIG, H. 'Social work and psychoanalytic theory'. *Social Work*, **16**, 1, 1971, 7—16.

BOSANQUET, B. 'The philosophy of casework'. *Charity Organisation Review*, **31**, 1916, 117—135.

BOSANQUET, B. 'Politics and charity'. *Charity Organisation Review*, **38**, 1915,

380—395.

BOSANQUET, Benard (ed.) *Aspects of the Social Problem*. London. Macmillan & Co., 1895.

BOSANQUET, B. 'Idealism in social work'. *Charity Organisation Review*, New Series, **3**, 1898, 122—133.

BOSANQUET, C.P.B. The Organisation of Charity. London. Longman's, 1875.

BOSANQUET, Helen. See Dendy, Helen.

BOURDILLON, A.F.C. (ed.) *Voluntary Social Services: their place in the modern state*. London. Methuen, 1945.

BOWLBY, J. *Maternal Care and Mental Health*, Geneva. World Health Organisation, 1951.

BOWLBY, J. 'The nature of the child's tie to his mother'. *International Journal of Psycho-Analysis*, **39**, 1958, 350—73.

BOWLBY, J. 'The study and reduction of group tensions within the family'. *Human Relations*, **2**, 1949, 123.

BOWLBY, J. 'Separation anxiety'. *International Journal of Psychoanalysis*, **41**, 1960, 89—113.

BOWLBY, J. 'Processes of mourning'. *International Journal of Psychoanalysis*, **42**, 1961, 317—40.

BOWLBY, J. *Child Care and the Growth of Love*. London. Penguin Books, 2nd ed., 1965.

BOWLBY, J. *Attachment and Loss*. Vol. I *Attachment*. London. The Hogarth Press and the Institute of Psychoanalysis, 1969.

BOYERS, R. (ed.) *Laing and Anti-Psychiatry*. London. Penguin Books, 1972.

BRAGER, G. 'Advocacy and political behaviour'. *Social Work*, **13**, 2, 1968, 5—15.

BREE, Mollie. 'Staying the course'. *British Journal of Psychiatric Social Work*, X, **4**, 1970, 170—177.

BREGER, L. and McGaugh, J.L. 'Critique and reformulation of "learning theory" approaches to psychotherapy and neurosis'. *Psychological Bulletin*, **63**, 1965, 338—58.

BREMNER, R.H. 'Scientific philanthropy, 1873—93'. *Social Service Review*, **30**, 1956, 168—73.

BREMNER, R.H. *American Philanthropy*. Chicago. University of Chicago Press, 1960.

BRENNER, C. 'Psychoanalysis'. *International Encyclopaedia of the Social Sciences*, 1968 ed. Vol. 13.

BRENNER, C. *An Elementary Textbook of Psychoanalysis*. New York. Doubleday. Revised edn. 1974.

BREUER, J. and Freud S. Abstract of the 'Preliminary Communications'. *Brain*, **12**, 1894, 125.

BRIAR, S. and Miller H. *Problems and Issues in Social Casework*. New York. Columbia University Press, 1971.

BRIAR, Scott. 'The current crisis in social casework'. In *Social Work Practice*, National Conference on Social Welfare. New York. Columbia University

Press, 1967, 19—33.

BRIAR, Scott. 'The casework predicament'. *Social Work*, **13**, 1, January 1968, 5—11.

BRIERLEY, S. (afterward Isaacs). *An Introduction to Psychology*. London. Methuen & Co., 1921.

BRIERLEY, S. *Contributions to Modern Education*. London. Methuen & Co., 1941.

BRIERLEY, S. (ed.) *The Cambridge Evacuation Survey*. London. Methuen & Co., 1941.

BRIERLEY, S. *Social Development in Young Children*, London. Routledge & Kegan Paul, 1951.

BRISKIN, S. 'Casework and present day trends'. *Social Work*, **15**, 4, 1958, 521.

BRITISH ASSOCIATION FOR THE ADVANCEMENT OF SCIENCE. *Scientific Research on Human Institutions*. London, 1943.

BROWN, M.A.G. 'A review of casework methods'. In E. Younghusband (ed.) *New Developments in Casework*. London. George Allen & Unwin, 1966.

BROWN, S. Clement. 'The methods of social case workers'. In Bartlett, F.C., Ginsberg M., Lindgren E.J., and Thouless R.H. (eds.) *The Study of Society*. London. Kegan Paul, Trench, Trubner & Co. Ltd., 1939.

BROWN, S. Clement. 'Family casework and mental health'. *Charity Organisation Quarterly*, **13**, 1, 1939, 40.

BROWN, S. Clement and Crosthwaite, A.A. 'Notes from the BFSW'. *Social Work Today*, (U.S.A.), February 1942.

BROWN, S. Clement. 'Social casework'. *Sociological Review*, **33**, 3, 1942, 171—183.

BROWN, S. Clement. 'Training for social work'. *Social Work*, **3**, 8, 1945, 181—189.

BROWN, S. Clement. 'The Cinderella of the professions: Reflections on social work and training in the United States, 1947'. *Social Work*, **5**, 1, 1948, 125.

BROWN, S. Clement. 'Looking Backwards'. *British Journal of Psychiatric Social Work*, X, **4**, 1970, 161—169.

BROWN, William. 'Freud's theory of the unconscious'. *British Journal of Psychology*, **6**, 1914, 265—280.

BROWN, William. *Psychology and Psychotherapy*. London. Edwin Arnold, 1921.

BROWN, William. *Suggestion and Mental Analysis*. London. University of London Press, 1922.

BROWN, William. *Mind and Personality. An essay in psychology and philosophy*. London. University of London Press, 1926.

BROWN, William. *Personality and Religion*. London. University of London Press, 1946.

BRUNER, Jerome. 'The Freudian conception of man and the continuity of nature'. *Daedalus*, **87**, 1958, 77—84.

BRUNER, Jerome. 'Freud and the Image of Man'. *Partisan Review*, **23**, 1956, 340—7.

BRUNO, F.J. *Trends in Social Work, 1874—1956*. New York. Columbia University Press, 1957.

BUBER, Martin, William Alonson White Memorial Lectures, 4th series. *Hibbert Journal*, **49**, 1951, 105—113. Reprinted in *Psychiatry*, **20**, 1957, 97—129.

BUBER, Martin. *I and Thou*. Edinburgh. T. and T. Clark, 2nd edn., 1958.

BUBER, Martin. *Pointing the Way*. Collected Essays. Ed. and trans. M.S. Friedman. New York. Harper & Bros., 1957.

BURKE, N.H.M. and MILLER, E. 'Child Mental hygiene — its history, methods and problems'. *British Journal of Medical Psychology*, **9**, 3, 1929, 218—242.

BURLINGHAM, D. and Freud, A. *Young Children in Wartime*. London. George Allen & Unwin, 1942.

BURLINGHAM, D. and Freud, A. *Infants Without Families*. London. George Allen & Unwin, 1944.

BURNS, C.L.C. 'Critical notice of Stevenson G.S. and Smith G, Child Guidance Clinics'. *British Journal of Educational Psychology*, **4**, 1934, 317.

BURNS, C.L.C. 'Child guidance on the continent'. *British Journal of Educational Psychology*, **3**, 1933, 251—267.

BURROW, J.W. *Evolution and Society. A Study in Victorian Social History*. Cambridge. University Press, 1966.

BURT, C. 'The psychological clinic'. *Howard Journal*, **2**, 4, 1929, 290—4.

BURT, C. *Mental and Scholastic Tests*. London. Staples, 2nd edn. 1947.

BURT, C. 'The respective spheres of psychology and medicine'. *British Journal of Educational Psychology*, **19**, 1949, 39.

BURT, C. 'An autobiographical sketch'. *Occupational Psychology*, **22**, 1, 1949, 9—20.

BURT, C. 'The historical development of the guidance movement in education — England'. *The Year Book of Education*, 1955.

BURT, C. 'Individual psychology and social work'. *Charity Organisation Review*, **43**, 1918, 4—19 and 51—60.

BURT, C. *The Young Delinquent*. London. University of London Press, 1925.

BUTRYM, Z.T. 'An Open Letter'. *The Almoner*, **13**, 1, 1961, 501—507.

BURTYM, Z.T. *Medical Social Work in Action*. London. Bell, 1968.

BUTRYM, Z.T. *The Nature of Social Work*. London. Macmillan, 1977.

BUXBAUM, E. 'Psycho-sexual development: The oral, anal and phallic phases'. In M. Levitt (ed.) *Readings in Psychoanalytic Psychology*. London. Staples Press, 1959, 43—55.

CAPLAN, G. *An Approach to Community Mental Health*. London Tavistock Publications Ltd., 1961.

CAPPON, D. 'Values and value judgment in psychiatry'. *Psychiatric Quarterly*, **40**, 3, 1966, 538—554.

CARKHUFF, R.R. (ed.) *The Counsellor's Contribution to Facilitative Processes*. Urbana, Illinois, Parkinson, 1957.

CARKHUFF, R.R. *Helping and Human Relations*. Vols. I & II. New York,

Holt, Rinehart and Winston Inc. 1969.

CARKHUFF, R.R. and Berenson H.G. *Beyond Counselling and Therapy*, New York. Holt, Rinehart and Winston, 1967.

CARR-SAUNDERS, A. *1836—1966*. University of London, 1967.

'The Case for Casework'. *The Lancet*. April 4th, 1959, 719.

CAUTELA, J.H. 'Desensitization and insight'. *Behaviour Research and Therapy*, **3**, 1965, 59—64.

CHADWICK, W.E. *Social Work*. London. Longman's & Co., 1908.

CHILD GUIDANCE: Symposium on psychologists and psychiatrists in the child guidance service. *British Journal of Educational Psychology*, **21**, **22**, **23**, 1951.

CLARK, J. Michell. 'Review of *Studien uber Hysterie*', *Brain*, **19**, 1896, 401—414.

COHEN, N.E. *Social Work in the American Tradition*. New York, Dryden Press, 1958.

COLCORD, J.C. 'The significance of unemployment for the family and for the social treatment of the family'. Second International Conference on Social Work, Paris, 1932.

COLCORD, J.C. and Mann, Z.S. (eds.) *The Long View: Papers and Addresses of Mary E. Richmond*. New York, 1930.

CORMACK, U.M. 'Developments in casework'. In A.F.C. Bourdillon (ed.), *Voluntary Social Services*.

CORNER, E.P. Address to National Association of Probation Officers Conference. *Probation*, **8**, 2, 1956.

COSENS, M. 'Function: A book review'. *Social Work*, **6**, 3, 1949, 307—310.

CRICHTON-MILLER, H. (ed.) *Functional Nerve Disease: An Epitome of War Experience for the Practitioner*. London. Oxford University Press, 1920.

CRICHTON-MILLER, H. *The New Psychology and the Teacher*. London, Jarrold's, 1921.

CRICHTON-MILLER, H. *Psycho-analysis and its Derivatives*. London. Home University Library, 1933.

CRICHTON-MILLER, H. *Advances in Understanding the Child*. Home and School Council of Great Britain, 1935.

CROWLEY, R.H. 'Child Guidance Clinics, with special reference to American experience'. London. Child Guidance Council, 1928.

DAVIES, M. 'The assessment of environment in social work research'. *Social Casework*, 55, 1, 1974, 3—12.

DEED, D.M. 'Further considerations on the future of casework'. *The Almoner*, **6**, 6, 1953, 261—265.

DEED, D.M. 'The general principles of social casework'. *The Almoner*, **6**, 6, 1953, 305.

DENDY, H. (afterwards Bosanquet). 'The meaning and methods of true charity'. In B. Bosanquet (ed.) *Aspects of the Social Problem*. London. Macmillan & Co., 1895.

DENDY, H. *Social Work in London, 1869—1912: A History of the COS*

London. John Murray. 1914.

DEVEREAUX, George. 'Two types of modal personality models'. In Smelser, N.J. and Smelser, W.T. *Personality and Social Systems*. New York and London. John Wiley & Sons, 1963.

DIBBLE, V.K. 'Occupations and Ideologies'. In J.E. Curtis and J.W. Petros (eds.) *The Sociology of Knowledge*. London. Gerald Duckworth & Co., 1970.

DICKS, H.V. *Marital Tensions*. London. Routledge & Kegan Paul, 1967.

DICKS, H.V. *Fifty Years of the Tavistock Clinic*. London. Routledge & Kegan Paul, 1970.

DILMAN, I. 'The unconscious'. *Mind*, **58**, 1959, 272.

DONNISON, D.V. 'Observations on university training for social work in Great Britain and North America'. *Social Service Review*, **29**, 1955, 341—50.

DREVER, James. *An Introduction to the Psychology of Education*. London. Edward Arnold & Co., 1922.

DREVER, James, and Drummond, Margaret. *The Psychology of the Pre-School Child*. London. Partridge & Co., 1930.

DUMMER, Ethel S. 'Life in relation to time'. In L.G. Lowry and V. Sloane, *Orthopsychiatry 1923—48*. .

EDMINSON, M.W. 'Milestones: the story of the hospital almoners profession'. *Social Work*, **2**, 1, 1941, 16—27.

EDMINSON, M.W. 'The first fifty years. The Middle Period: Episode II, 1914—1938'. *The Almoner*, **6**, 8, 1953, 360—372.

EICHHOLTZ, E. 'The development of Family Discussion Bureaux Work'. *Social Work*, **8**, 1, 1951, 495.

ELLENBERGER, H.F. *The Discovery of the Unconsious*. London. Allen Lane, 1970.

ELLIOTT, P. *The Sociology of the Professions*. London. Macmillan, 1972.

ELLIS, Henry Havelock. *Studies in the Psychology of Sex*, Vol. I. London. Wilson & Macmillan, 1897.

EPSTEIN, I. 'Social workers and social action: attitudes towards social action strategies'. *Social Work*, **13**, 2, 1968, 101—8.

EPSTEIN, I. 'Professionaliz.ition, professionalism and social-worker radicalism'. *Journal of Health and Social Behaviour*, **2**, 1, 1970, 67—77.

ERIKSON, E.H. *Childhood and Society*. London, Imago, 1951. Revised edn. Penguin Books, 1965.

ERIKSON, E.H. *Insight and Responsibility*. London. Faber & Faber, 1966.

EYDEN, J.M.L. 'The professional social worker'. *Social Work*, **6**, 3, 1949, 246—251.

EYDEN, J.M.L. 'Training for social work'. *Social Work*, **7**, 3, 1950, 433—437.

EYSENCK, H.J. 'The effects of psychotherapy: an evaluation'. *Journal of Consulting Psychology*, **16**, 1952, 319—24.

EYSENCK, H. J. *Behaviour Therapy and the Neuroses*. New York. Pergamon Press, 1960.

EYSENCK, H.J. 'Psychoanalysis — Myth or Science?' *Inquiry*, 4, 1961, 1—36.

EYSENCK, H.J. 'The effects of psychotherapy'. *International Journal of Psychiatry*, **1**, 1965, 99—142.

EYSENCK, H.J. and Rachman, S. *The Causes and Cures of Neurosis*. San Diego. Robert R. Knapp, 1965.

EYSENCK, H.J. and Wilson, G.D. *The Experimental Study of Freudian Theories*. London. Methuen & Co., Ltd., 1973.

EZRIEL, H. 'The Scientific testing of psycho-analytic findings and theory'. *British Journal of Medical Psychology*, **24**, 1, 1951, 30—34.

FAIRBAIRN, W.R.D. *Psychoanalytic Studies of the Personality*. London Tavistock Publications, 1952.

FAIRBAIRN, W.R.D. 'A critical evaluation of certain basic psycho-analytic conceptions'. *British Journal for the Philosophy of Science*, **7**, 1956, 49—60.

FAIRBAIRN, W.R.D. 'On the nature and aims of psychoanalytical treatment'. *International Journal of Psycho-Analysis*, **39**, 1958, 374—385.

FAIRFIELD, L.D. 'Child Guidance in America'. London County Council, 1928.

FAMILY DISCUSSION BUREAU. *Social Casework in Marital Problems: The development of a psychodynamic approach*. London. Tavistock Publications. 1955.

'FAR AWAY AND LONG AGO'. Anonymous article. *British Journal of Psychiatric Social Work*, **2**, 10, 1954, 9—11.

FARBER, Leslie H. 'Introduction to Martin Buber'. William Alonson White Memorial Lectures, 4th series. *Psychiatry*, **20**, 2, 1957, 95.

FARRELL, B.A. 'The scientific testing of psychoanalytic findings and theory'. *British Journal of Medical Psychology*, **24**, 1951, 35—41.

FARRELL, B.A. 'Can psychoanalysis be refuted?' *Inquiry*, **4**, 1961, 16—36.

FARRELL, B.A. 'Psychoanalytic theory'. *New Society*, **38**, 1963, 11—13.

FARRELL, B.A. 'Psychoanalysis — II. The method'. *New Society*, **39**, 1963, 12—14.

FENICHEL, O. 'On the theory of the therapeutic results of psychoanalysis'. *International Journal of Psychoanalysis*, **18**, 1937, 133—138.

FENICHEL, O. *The Psychoanalytic Theory of Neurosis*. London. Kegan Paul, Trench, Trubner & Co., 1946.

FERARD, M.L. and Hunnybun, N.K. *The Caseworker's Use of Relationships*. London. Tavistock Publications, 1962.

FEVERSHAM COMMITTEE: *Report on the Voluntary Mental Health Services*. London, 1939.

FINE, Reuben. *Freud: A critical re-evaluation of his theories*. London. George, Allen & Unwin, 1962.

FISCHER, J.L. 'Is casework effective? A review'. *Social Work* (U.S.), **18**, 1, 1973, 5—20.

FISCHER, J.L. *Interpersonal helping: emerging approaches for social work practice*. Springfield, Ill, Charles C. Thomas, 1973.

FISHER, S. *The scientific credibility of Freud's theories and therapy*.

Hassocks. Harvester Press. 1977.

FLEXNER, A. 'Is social work a profession?' *National Conference of Charities and Correction*, 1915. Reprinted in Pumphrey, R.E. and M.W. *The Heritage of American Social Work*.

FLUGEL, J.C. *The Psycho-Analytic Study of the Family*. London. Vienna printed, 1921.

FLUGEL, J.C. *A Hundred Years of Psychology, 1833–1933*. London. Duckworth, 1933.

FLUGEL, J.C. *Man, Morals and Society. A psychoanalytical study*. London. Duckworth, 1945.

FOREN, R. and BAILEY, R. *Authority in social casework*. London. Pergamon Press, 1968.

FOULKES, S.H. and ANTHONY, E.J. *Group Psychotherapy*. London. Penguin Books, 1957.

FOULKES, S.H. and PRINCE, G.S. (eds.) *Psychiatry in a Changing Society*. London. Tavistock Publications Ltd., 1969.

FOX, Evelyn. 'Modern developments in work for mental defectives'. *Mental Welfare*, November 23, 1934.

(FOX Evelyn) *Dame Evelyn Fox, 1874–1955: Some Personal Tributes*. Letchworth, St. Christopher's Press, 1955.

FOX, Evelyn. 'The child guidance council and the Commonwealth Fund'. *Mental Welfare*, 8, 3, 1927, 79–80.

FRANK, J.D. 'The influence of patients' and therapists' expectations on the outcome of psychotherapy'. *British Journal of Medical Psychology*, **41**, 1968, 349.

FRANK, J.D. *Persuasion and Healing*. London. Oxford University Press, 1961.

FRANK, J.D. 'Recent American research in psychotherapy'. *British Journal of Medical Psychology*, **41**, 5, 1968, 5–13.

FRANK, K. (ed) *The Human Dimension in Psychoanalytic Practice*. New York. Grune and Stratton. 1977.

FRASER, Derek. *The Evolution of the British Welfare State*. London. Macmillan, 1973.

FRENCH, T.M. 'Insight and distortion in dreams'. *International Journal of Psychoanalysis*, **20**, 1939, 1.

FRENCH, T.M. *The Reintegration Process in a Psychoanalytic Treatment*. Vol. III 'The Integration of Behaviour'. Chicago. University of Chicago Press, 1958.

FREUD, A. *The Ego and the Mechanisms of Defence*. London. Hogarth Press and the Institute of Psychoanalysis, 1936.

FREUD, A. *Normality and Pathology in Childhood*. London. The Hogarth Press and the Institute of Psychoanalysis, 1966.

FREUD, A. *Research at the Hampstead Child-Therapy Clinic and Other Papers, 1956–65*. London. The Hogarth Press and the Institute of Psychoanalysis, 1970

FREUD, S. (1900). *The Interpretation of Dreams*. London. George Allen & Unwin, 1954, SE **4**—**5**.

FREUD, S. (1901). The Psychopathology of Everyday Life. SE **6**.

FREUD, S. (1905). Three Essays on Sexuality. London. Hogarth Press, 1962, SE **7**, 125.

FREUD, S. (1908). ' "Civilized" sexual morality and modern nervous illness'. SE **9**, 179.

FREUD, S. (1910). 'The origin and development of psychoanalysis'. *American Journal of Psychology*, **21**, 181—218.

FREUD, S. (1913). 'The claims of psychoanalysis to scientific interest'. SE **13**, 165.

FREUD, S. (1914). 'On the history of the psychoanalytic movement'. SE **14**.

FREUD, S. (1915) 'Observations on transference love'. SE **12**.

FREUD, S. (1915) 'The unconscious'. SE **14**, 161.

FREUD, S. (1916) *The History of the Psychoanalytic Movement*. Trans. A.A. Brill. New York. Nervous and Mental Disease Publishing Co.

FREUD, S. (1916) 'The history of the psychoanalytic movement'. *Psychoanalytic Review*, **3**, 406.

FREUD, S. (1916—17). *Introductory Lectures on Psychoanalysis*. London. George Allen & Unwin, 1954. SE **15**—**16**.

FREUD, S. (1919) 'Lines of advance in psychoanalytic therapy'. SE **17**, 159.

FREUD, S. (1920) *Beyond the Pleasure Principle*. SE **18**, 7.

FREUD, S. (1923) *The Ego and the Id*. SE **19**.

FREUD, S. (1925) 'The resistances to psychoanalysis'. SE **19**.

FREUD, S. (1925) *An Autobiographical Study*. SE **20**.

FREUD, S. (1926) *Inhibitions, Symptoms and Anxiety*. SE **20**.

FREUD, S. (1926) *The Question of Lay Analysis*. SE **20**.

FREUD, S. (1927) *The Future of an Illusion*. SE **21**.

FREUD, S. (1930) *Civilization and its Discontents*. SE **21**.

FREUD, S. (1933) *New Introductory Lectures on Psychoanalysis*. London. The Hogarth Press and the Institute of Psychoanalysis, 1967, SE **22**.

FREUD, S. (1935) 'Postscript to an Autobiographical Study'. SE **20**.

FREUD, S. (1937) 'Analysis terminable and interminable'. SE **23**.

FREUD, S. (1940) *An Outline of Psychoanalysis*. London. The Hogarth Press and the Institute of Psychoanalysis, 1969. SE **23**.

FREUD, S. (1940)(1938) 'Some elementary lessons in psychoanalysis'. SE **23**.

FREUD, S. (1940)(1938) 'Splitting of the ego in the process of defence'. SE **23**.

FREUD, S. (1950) *The origins of Psychoanalysis*. SE **1**.

FRIEDLANDER, K. *The Psychoanalytic Approach to Juvenile Delinquency*. London. Kegan Paul, 1947.

FRIEDLANDER, W.A. *Individualism and Social Welfare*. New York, Free Press of Glencoe, 1962.

FRIEDLANDER, W.A. *Introduction to Social Welfare*. Englewood Cliffs, New Jersey. Prentice-Hall. 3rd edn. 1968.

FROMM, E. *Sigmund Freud's Mission. An analysis of his personality and influence*. New York. Harper & Bros., 1959.

FROMM, E. *Beyond the Chains of Illusion. My encounter with Marx and Freud*. New York, Simon and Schuster, 1962.

FROMM, E. *The Crisis of Psychoanalysis*. London. Jonathan Cape, 1970.

FROMM-REICHMANN, F. *Principles of Intensive Psychotherapy*. London. George Allen & Unwin, 1953.

FRY, Margery. 'A Belgian psychological laboratory'. *Howard Journal*, **1**, 3, 1924.

GARRARD, Jessie. 'Some reflections on the philosophy of medical social work'. *The Almoner*, **12**, Nos. 4–6, 1959, 151–162.

GARRETT, A. 'Modern casework: the contribution of ego psychology'. In H. Parad (ed.) *Ego Psychology and Dynamic Casework*. New York. Family Service Association of America, 1958, 38–52.

GARRETT, A. 'Historical survey of the evolution of casework'. In *Principles and Techniques in Social Casework*, 1940–50. New York. Family Service Association of America, 1950.

GELDER, M.G., Marks, I.M., Wolff, H.E. and Clarke, M. 'Desensitization and psychotherapy in the treatment of phobic states: a controlled enquiry'. *British Journal of Psychiatry*, 113, 1967, 53–73.

GELDER, M.G. 'Desensitization and insight in psychotherapy research'. *British Journal of Medical Psychology*, **41**, 1968, 39.

GELLNER, E. 'Review of R.E. Money-Kyrle *Man's Picture of His World'*. *Inquiry*, **4**, 1961, 209–214.

GERMAIN, C. 'Casework and science: An historical encounter'. In R.W. Roberts and R.H. Nee (eds.) *Theories of Social Casework*.

GERMAIN, C. 'Social study: past and future'. *Social Casework*, **49**, 7, 1968, 403–409.

GERMAIN, C. 'An ecological perspective in casework practice'. *Social Casework*, **53**, 6, June 1973, 323–330.

'Generic training for social work'. Anonymous article by students of the first generic training course. *Probation*, 1952.

GILBERT, B.B. *The Evolution of National Insurance in Great Britain*. London. Michael Joseph, 1966.

GILBERT, D.C. and LEVINSON, D.J. 'Ideology, personality and institutional policy in the mental hospital'. *Journal of Abnormal and Social Psychology*, **53**, 3, 1956, 263–271.

GILBERT, D.C. and LEVINSON, D.J. '"Custodialism" and "humanism" in mental hospital structure and in staff ideology'. In Greenblatt *et al* (eds.) *The Patient and the Mental Hospital*.

GILL, Merton. 'Topography and system in psychoanalytic theory'. *Psychological Issues*, **3**, 2, 1963.

GINSBURG, Ethel. 'Freud's contribution to the philosophy and practice of social work'. *American Journal of Orthopsychiatry*, **10**, 1940, 877.

GLADD, D.D. *Operational Values in Psychotherapy*. New York, Oxford University Press, 1959.

GLOVER, E. *The Diagnosis and Treatment of Delinquency. Clinical Report on the Work of the ISTD, 1937—41.* Institute for the Study and Treatment of Delinquency, 1944.

GLOVER, E. 'The position of psycho-analysis in Britain'. *British Medical Bulletin*, **6**, 1949, 1—2, 27—31.

GLOVER, E. 'The uses of Freudian theory in psychiatry'. *British Journal of Medical Psychology*, **31**, 3—4, December 1958.

GLOVER, E. *The Roots of Crime.* London. Imago Publishing Co., 1960.

GLUECK, Bernard. 'The special preparation of the psychiatric social worker'. *Mental Hygiene*, **3**, 3, 1919, 409—426.

GOLDBERG, E.M. *Family Influences and Psychosomatic Illness.* London. Tavistock Publications 1958.

GOLDBERG, E.M. 'The function and use of relationship in psychiatric social work'. In E. Younghusband (ed.) *New Developments in Casework.*

GOLDBERG, E.M. 'Some developments in professional collaboration and research in the USA'. *British Journal of Psychiatric Social Work*, **3**, 1, 1955, 4—12.

GOLDFARB, W. 'Effects of early institutional care on adolescent personality'. *American Journal of Orthopsychiatry*, **14**, 1944, 441.

GOLDSTEIN, A.P. *Therapist-patient Expectations in Psychotherapy.* Oxford. Pergamon Press, 1962.

GOLDSTEIN, A.P., Heller K., and Sechrest, L.B. *Psychotherapy and the Psychology of Behavior Change.* New York. John Wiley & Co., 1966.

GOLDSTEIN, A.P. and Dean, S.J. *The Investigation of Psychotherapy: Commentaries and Readings.* New York. John Wiley & Co., 1966.

GOLDSTEIN, H. *Social Work Practice: A Unitary Approach.* University of South Carolina Press, 1973.

GOODSTEIN, Leonard D. 'Behaviour Theoretical views of counselling'. In Stefflre, D. *Theories of Counselling.* New York, McGraw Hill, 1965.

GORDON, W.E. 'Toward a social work frame of reference'. *Journal of Education for Social Work*, **1**, 2, 1965, 19—26.

GORDON, W.E. 'Basic constructs for an integrative and generative conception of social work'. In G. Hearn (ed.) *The General Systems Approach: Contributions towards a holistic conception of social work.* New York. Council on Social Work Education, 1969.

GORER, Geoffrey. 'Freud's Influence'. *The Encounter.* November 1958, 82—84.

GOUGH, Donald. 'Work with unmarried mothers'. *The Almoner*, **13**, 2, March, 1961, 490.

GRAY, B. Kirkman. *A History of English Philanthropy.* London. P.S. King & Son, 1905.

GREEN, T.H. *Lectures on the Principles of Political Obligation.* London. Longmans, Green & Co., 1941.

GREENSON, R.R. 'The working alliance and the transference neurosis'. *Psychoanalytic Quarterly*, **34**, 1965, 155—181.

GREENSON, R.R. and Wexler, M. 'The non-transference relationship in the psychoanalytic situation'. *International Journal of Psychoanalysis*, **50**, 1969, 27—39.

GREENWOOD, E. 'Attributes of a profession'. In Mayer N. Zald (ed.) *Social Welfare Institutions. A Sociological Reader*. New York. John Wiley & Sons Inc., 1965.

GUNTRIP, H. 'The therapeutic factor in psychotherapy'. *British Journal of Medical Psychology*, **26**, 2, 1953, 115—132.

GUNTRIP, H. *Personality Structure and Human Interaction. The developing synthesis of psychodynamic theory*. London. The Hogarth Press and the Institute of Psycho-Analysis, 1961.

GUNTRIP, H. *Schizoid Phenomena, Object-relations and the Self*. London. The Hogarth Press and the Institute of Psycho-Analysis, 1968.

GUNTRIP, H. *Psychoanalytic Theory, Therapy and the Self*. London. The Hogarth Press and Basic Books Inc., 1971.

GUNTRIP, H. 'The promise of psycho-analysis'. In B. Landis and E.S. Tauber (eds.) *In the Name of Life, Essays in honour of Erich Fromm*. New York. Holt, Rhinehart and Winston, 1971.

HADFIELD, J.A. *Psychology and Mental Health*. London. George Allen & Unwin, 1950.

HADFIELD, J.A. *Dreams and Nightmares*. London. Penguin Books, 1954.

HAGERSTRAND, T. 'The diffusion of innovations'. *Encyclopaedia of the Social Sciences*, Vol. 4, 1968.

HALE, N.G. *Freud and the Americans. The origin and foundation of the psychoanalytic movement in America, 1876—1918*. New York. Oxford University Press, 1971.

HALL, C.S. and Lindzey, C. *Theories of Personality*. New York. John Wiley & Sons, 1957.

HALMOS, P. 'Personal involvement in learning about personality'. *Sociological Review Monograph No. 1*, Keele, 1958.

HALMOS, P. *The Faith of the Counsellors*. London. Constable, 1965.

HALMOS, P. *The Personal Service Society*. London. Constable, 1969.

HAMILTON, G. *Theory and Practice of Social Casework*. New York. Columbia University Press. 1st edn. 1940; 2nd edn. 1951.

HAMILTON, G. *et al. Social Work as Human Relations*. New York. School of Social Work, 1949.

HAMILTON, G. 'Methods of family social work'. Second International Conference on Social Work, Paris, 1949.

HARDCASTLE, D.N. 'The child guidance clinic in America: its evolution and future development'. *British Journal of Psychology* (Medical Section) **13**, 1933, 328—353.

HARRIS, Jose. *Unemployment and Politics. A Study in English Social Policy, 1886—1914*. Oxford University Press, 1972.

HARRISON, B. 'Philanthropy and the Victorians'. *Victorian Studies*, **9**, 4, 1966, 353.

HART, Bernard. 'A philosophy of psychiatry'. *Journal of Mental Science*, **54**, 1908, 473—490.

HART, Bernard. 'The psychology of Freud and his school'. *Journal of Mental Science*, **56**, 1910, 431—452.

HART, Bernard. 'Freud's conception of hysteria'. *Brain*, **33**, 1919, 339—366.

HART, Bernard. 'The conception of the subconscious'. *Journal of Abnormal Psychology*, **4**, 1910, 351—371.

HART, Bernard. *The Psychology of Insanity*. Cambridge Manuals of Science and Literature, 1912.

HART, J. 'Nineteenth century social reform: A Tory interpretation of history'. *Past and Present*, **31**, 1965, 38—61.

HARTMANN, H. 'The Development of the ego concept in Freud's work'. *International Journal of Psycho-Analysis*, **37**, 1956, 425—38.

HEALY, W. *The Individual Delinquent*. Boston. Little, 1915.

HEALY, W. *Mental Conflicts and Misconduct*. London. Kegan Paul, Trench, Trubner & Co., 1917.

HEALY, W. and BRONNER, A. *New Light on Delinquency and its Treatment*. New Haven. Yale University Press, 1936.

HEALY, W. and BRONNER, A. 'The child guidance clinic: Birth and growth of an idea'. In L.G. Lowry and V. Sloane (eds.) *Orthopsychiatry 1923—1948*. American Orthopsychiatric Association, 1948.

HEALY, W., BRONNER, A., and BOWERS, A. *The Structure and Meaning of Psychoanalysis as related to personality and behaviour*. New York. A.A. Knopf, 1930.

HEARN, G. *Theory Building in Social Work*. Toronto. University Press, 1958.

HEARN, G. (ed.) *The General Systems Approach: Contributions towards a holistic conception of social work*. New York. Council on Social Work Education, 1969.

HEARNSHAW, L.S. *A Short History of British Psychology 1840—1940*. London. Methuen & Co., 1964.

HEIMAN, Marcel (ed.) *Psychoanalysis and Social Work*. New York. International Universities Press. 1953.

HEIMLER, E. *The Night of the Mist*. London. Bodley Head, 1959.

HEIMLER, E. *A Link in the Chain*. London. Bodley Head, 1962.

HELLENBRAND, S.C. 'Freud's Influence on social casework'. *Bulletin of the Menninger Clinic*, **36**, 4, 1972, 407—418.

HERAUD, B.J. *Sociology and Social Work*. Oxford, Pergamon Press, 1970.

HERBERT, Martin. *Emotional Problems of Development in Children*. London, New York. Academic Press, 1974.

HERBERT, Martin. *Problems of Childhood*. London. Pan Books Ltd., 1975.

HILGARD, E.R. *Theories of Learning*. London. Methuen & Co., 1958.

HILL, O. *Letters to my Fellow-Workers, 1872—1911*. (39 parts). London. James Martin, 1873—1912.

HILL, O. *Our Common Land, and Other Essays*. London. Macmillan & Co., 1877.

HILL, O. 'A more excellent way of charity'. In *Our Common Land and Other Essays*.

HILL, William T. *Octavia Hill*. London. Hutchinson & Co., 1956.

HOBBS, N. 'Sources of gain in psychotherapy'. *American Psychologist*, **17**, 1962, 741—747.

HOBSON, J.A. *The Crisis of Liberalism*. London. P.S. King & Son, 1909.

HOBSON, J.A. 'The social philosophy of charity organisation'. In *The Crisis of Liberalism*.

HOLDEN, H.M. 'Reply to Dr. Schmideberg'. *British Journal of Criminology*, **5**, 1965, 462—63.

HOLLIS, E.V. and TAYLOR, A.T. *Social Work Education in the United States*: The Report of a Study made for the National Council on Social Work Education. New York. CSWE 1951.

HOLLIS, F. 'The techniques of casework'. *In Principles and Techniques in Social Casework, 1940—50*. New York. Family Service Association of America, 1950.

HOLLIS, F. *Women in Marital Conflict*. New York. Family Service Association of America, 1949.

HOLLIS, F. *Casework: A·Psychosocial Therapy*. New York. Random House Press, 1964.

HOLLIS, F. 'Explorations in the development of a typology of casework treatment'. *Social Casework*, **48**, 3, 1967, 335—341.

HOLLIS, F. 'The coding and application of a typology of casework treatment'. *Social Casework*, **48**, 4, 1967, 489—97.

HOLLIS, F. 'A profile of early interviews in marital counselling'. *Social Casework*, **49**, 1, 1968, 35—43.

HOLLIS, F. 'Continuance and discontinuance in marital counselling and some observations on joint interviews'. *Social Casework*, **49**, 2, 1968, 167—174.

HOLT, R.R. 'Two influences on Freud's scientific thought: a fragment of intellectual biography'. In R.W. White (ed.) *The Study of Lives: Essays on personality in honour of H.A. Murray*. New York. Atherton Press, 1963.

HOLT, R.R. 'Freud's cognitive style'. *American Imago*, **22**, 1965, 163—179.

HOLT, R.R. 'Sigmund Freud'. *International Encyclopaedia of the Social Sciences*, 1968 edn. Vol. 6.

HOLT, R.R. and Freund, E.P. *Psychoanalysis and Contemporary Science*. London. Collier-Macmillan, 1972.

HOOK, S. (ed.) *Determinism and Freedom in the Age of Modern Science*. New York. University Institute of Philosophy, 1957.

HOOK, S. (ed.) *Psychoanalysis, Scientific Method and Philosophy*. New York. University Institute of Philosophy, 1958.

HOWARTH, H.E. 'The present dilemma of social casework'. *Social Work*, **8**, 2, April 1951, 527.

HOWARTH, H.E. 'Present trends in psychiatric social work'. *Social Work*, **3**, 1, January 1944, 16—20.

HUGHES, E.C. *Men and Their Work*. Glencoe, Illinois. The Free Press, 1958.

HUNT, Arthur. 'Enforcement in probation casework'. In E. Younghusband (ed.) *New Developments in Casework*.

HUTTEN, Joan. 'Psychodynamic approach to casework'. *Social Work Today*, **2**, 22, 1972, 5.

INSTITUTE FOR THE STUDY AND TREATMENT OF DELINQUENCY. *The Problem Family*. Report of a conference, 1957.

IRVINE, E.E. 'Renaissance in British casework'. *Social Work*, **13**, 3, July 1956, 187.

IRVINE, E.E. 'Some implications of Freudian theory for casework'. *The Almoner*, **9**, 2, 1956, 39—44.

IRVINE, E.E. 'Transference and reality in the casework relationship'. *British Journal of Psychiatric Social Work*, **3**, 4, 1956, 1—10. Also in *Relationship in Casework*. London. Association of Psychiatric Social Workers, 1963.

IRVINE, E.E. 'Social work literature in Great Britain'. *The Indian Journal of Social Work*, **25**, 4, 1965, 309—320.

IRVINE, E.E. 'A new look at casework'. In E. Younghusband (ed.) *New Developments in Casework*. London. George Allen & Unwin, 1966.

IRVINE, E.E. 'Education for social work: science or humanity?' *Social Work*, 1970, 3—6.

IRVINE, E.E. Review of Dicks, H.V. *Fifty Years of the Tavistock Clinic*. *Applied Social Studies*, **3**, 1, 1971, 61—2.

IRVINE, E.F. *A Pioneer of the New Psychology: Hugh Crichton-Miller*. Chatham. W. and J. Mackay & Co. Ltd., 1963.

ISAACS, S. See Brierley, S. (afterward Isaacs).

JACKSON, J.A. (ed.) *Professions and Professionalization*. Cambridge. Sociological Studies **3**, 1970.

JAHODA, M. *Freud and the Dilemmas of Psychology*. London. The Hogarth Press, 1977.

JAMES, William. *Principles of Psychology*. London. Macmillan & Co., 1910.

JANET, P. 'Psycho-analysis'. 17th International Congress of Medicine. London, 1913. *Proceedings*, Section 12, 13—64.

JANCHILL, Sister Mary P. 'Systems concepts in casework theory and practice'. *Social Casework*, **50**, 2, February 1969, 74.

JARRETT, Mary. 'The psychiatric thread running through all social work'. *Mental Hygiene*, **3**, 2, 1919, 210—219.

JEHU, D., HARDIKER P. and YELLOLY, M. and SHAW, M. *Behaviour Modification in Social Work*. London. John Wiley & Sons Ltd., 1972.

JOINT COMMITTEE ON METHODS OF PREVENTING DELINQUENCY. *The Commonwealth Fund Program for the Prevention of Delinquency*. New York. 1923.

JOINT UNIVERSITY COUNCIL FOR SOCIAL STUDIES AND PUBLIC ADMINISTRATION. *A Review of Work during the years 1918—1944*.

JONES, Ernest. *Papers on Psycho-Analysis*. London. Bailliere, Tindall & Cox, 1913.

JONES, Ernest. 'Psychoanalysis'. *Mental Hygiene*, **1**, 5, 1932.

JONES, Ernest. 'Reminiscent notes on the early history of psychoanalysis in English-speaking countries'. *International Journal of Psychoanalysis*, **26**, 1945, 8—10.

JONES, Ernest. 'Freud and his achievements'. *British Medical Journal*. 5th May 1956, 997—1000.

JONES, Ernest. *Sigmund Freud: Life and Work*. 3 Vols. London. The Hogarth Press and the Institute of Psycho-Analysis, 1953—7.

JONES, Ernest. *Free Associations. Memoirs of a Psychoanalyst*. London. The Hogarth Press and the Institute of Psycho-Analysis, 1959.

JONES, Gareth Stedman. *Outcast London*. Oxford. Clarendon Press, 1971.

JONES, H. (ed.) *Towards a New Social Work*. London. Routledge & Kegan Paul, 1975.

JONES, K. *Mental Health and Social Policy, 1845—1959*. London. Routledge & Kegan Paul, 1960.

JONES, K. *The Teaching of Social Studies in British Universities*. London. Bell, 1964. Social Administration Research Trust: Occasional Papers in Social Administration No.12.

JOSEPH, Betty. 'Psychoanalysis and social casework'. *Social Work*, **8**, 4, 1951, 589—599.

JUNG, C.G. 'Sigmund Freud in his historical setting'. *Collected Works*, **15**, 33—40.

JUNG, C.G. *Analytical Psychology*. London. Bailliere, Tindall & Cox, 1917.

JUNG, C.G. *Modern Man in Search of a Soul*. London. Routledge & Kegan Paul, 1961.

JUNG, C.G. Forward to Neumann, Erich. *Depth Psychology and a New Ethic*. London. Hodder and Stoughton, 1969.

JUNG, C.G. *Aion*. London. Routledge & Kegan Paul, 1959.

KADUSHIN, A. 'The Knowledge base of social work'. In A.J. Kahn (ed.) *Issues in American Social Work*.

KAHN, (ed.) *Issues in American Social Work*. New York. Columbia University Press, 1959.

KANFER, F.H. 'Issues and ethics in behavior manipulation'. *Psychological Reports*. **16**, 1965, 187—196.

KASIUS, C. (ed.) *Principles and Techniques in Social Casework. Selected Articles, 1940—50*. New York. Family Service Association of America.

KASIUS, C. (ed.) *Social Casework in the Fifties. Selected Articles, 1951—60*. New York. Family Service Association of America, 1962.

KATZ, E. 'Interpersonal Influence'. *Encyclopaedia of the Social Sciences*, 1968, edn.

KATZ, E. and Lazarsfeld, P.F. *Personal Influence: The Part played by People in the Flow of Mass Communications*. New York. Free Press of Glencoe, 1955.

KAUFMAN, W. (ed.) *Existentialism from Dostoevsky to Sartre*. London. Thames & Hudson, 1957.

KEELING, Dorothy. *The Crowded Stairs*. London. National Council of Social

Service, 1961.

KEENLEYSIDE, M. 'Development in casework method'. *Social Work*, **15**, 4, 1958, 516−521.

KEIR, Gertrude. 'A History of child guidance'. *British Journal of Educational Psychology*, **22**, 1, 1951, 5.

KEITH- LUCAS, A. 'The political theory implicit in social casework theory'. *American Political Science Quarterly Review*, **47**, 4, 1953, 1076−1091.

KELLNER, R. 'The evidence in favour of psychotherapy'. *British Journal of Medical Psychology*, **40**, 1967, 341−358.

KENDALL, K.A. 'Dream or nightmare? Future of social work education'. *Social Work Today*, **3**, 16, 1972.

KENWORTHY, M.E. 'Psychoanalytic Concepts in mental hygiene'. *The Family*, **7**, 7, 1926, 213−223.

KIDNEIGH, J.C. 'History of American Social Work'. In *Encyclopaedia of Social Work*, New York. National Association of Social Workers, **15**, 1965, 3−19.

KLEIN, C.S. 'Ego psychology'. *International Encyclopaedia of the Social Sciences* (1968 edn.) Vol. 13.

KLEIN, M. *Contributions to Psychoanalysis, 1921−1945*. London. The Hogarth Press and the Institute of Psycho-Analysis, 1948.

KLEIN, M. *Love, Guilt and Reparation*. London. The Hogarth Press and the Institute of Psycho-Analysis, 1951.

KLEIN, M. *New Directions in Psychoanalysis*. London. Tavistock Publications, 1955.

KLEIN, M. *Envy and Gratitude: a study of unconscious sources*. London. Tavistock Publications, 1957.

KLEIN, M. *Our Adult World and other essays*. London. William Heinemann, 1963.

KLEIN, Philip. *From Philanthropy to Social Work*. San Francisco. Jossey-Bass Inc. 1968.

KOESTLER, A. *The Yogi and the Commissar*. London. Jonathan Cape, 1945.

KOCH, Sigmund (ed.) *Psychology: A study of a Science*. Vols. 1−6. New York. McGraw-Hill, 1959−63.

KOHLER, W. *The Mentality of Apes*. London. Routledge & Kegan Paul, 1925.

KRIS, E. 'On preconscious mental processes'. *Psychoanalytic Quarterly*, **19**, 1950, 540−560.

KRIS, E. 'On some vicissitudes of insight in psychoanalysis'. *International Journal of Psycho-Analysis*, **37**, 1956, 445−455.

KUHN, T.S. *The Structure of Scientific Revolutions*. Chicago. University of Chicago Press. 2nd edn. 1970.

LAING, R. 'An examination of Tillich's theory of anxiety and neurosis'. *British Journal of Medical Psychology*, **30**, 2, 1957.

LAING, R.D. 'The psychotherapeutic experience'. In *The Politics of Experience*. London. Penguin Books, 1967, 39−48.

LAING, R.D. *The Divided Self*. London. Pelican Books, 1965.

LAIRD, John. 'Is the conception of the unconscious of value in psychology?' *Mind*. October, 1922.

LANDIS, D. and TAUBER, E.S. (eds.) *In the Name of Life: Essays in honour of Erich Fromm*. New York. Holt, Rinehart and Winston, 1971.

LANGER, S. *Mind: An Essay on Human Feeling*. Baltimore. Johns Hopkins Press, 1967.

LAPIERE, R. *The Freudian Ethic*. London. George Allen & Unwin, 1959.

LEDERMANN, Rushi, S. 'The significance of feeling in the therapeutic relationship'. *British Journal of Psychiatric Social Work*, **2**, 9, 1954, 12.

LEE, Porter, and Kenworthy, Marion. *Mental Hygiene and Social Work*. New York. The Commonwealth Fund, 1929.

LEES, Ray. *Politics and Social Work*. London. Routledge & Kegan Paul, 1972.

LEES, Ray. 'Politics and social deprivation'. *Social Work Today*, **2**, 18, 1971, 3.

LEIGHTON, Neil. 'Society at work: the myth of self-determination'. *New Society*, 23 February, 1967.

LEONARD, P. 'The application of sociological analysis to social work training'. *British Journal of Sociology*, **19**, 4, 1968, 375.

LEONARD, P. *Sociology in Social Work*. London. Routledge & Kegan Paul, 1966.

'LESSONS FROM JUNG ABOUT CASEWORK'. Letter. *Charity Organisation Quarterly*, **20**, 1927, 356—366.

LEUBUSCHER, C. 'Training for social service as a branch of university education'. In *Training for Social Work*. Nuffield College. Oxford University Press, 1946.

LEVINE, M. and Levine A. *A Social History of Helping Services*. New York. Appleton-Century-Crofts, 1970.

LEVITT, Morton (ed.) *Readings in Psychoanalytic Psychology*. London. Staples Press, 1959.

LEWIS, Aubrey. 'Sigmund Freud: 1856—1939'. In Lewis, A. *The State of Psychiatry*. London. Routledge & Kegan Paul, 1967.

LIDZ, T. *The Person*. New York. Basic Books, 1968.

LOCH, C.S. 'The work of the School of Sociology'. *Charity Organisation Review*, 1907, 41—56.

LOCH, C.S. 'Charity and Charities'. *Encycl. Brit.*, 11th edition.

LOEWENSTEIN, R.M. 'The problem of interpretation'. *Psychoanalytic Quarterly*, **20**, 1951, 1—14.

LOEWENSTEIN, R.M. 'Some remarks on the role of speech in psychoanalytic technique'. *International Journal of Psycho-Analysis*, **37**, 6, 1956, 460—467.

LOMAS, P. 'Psychoanalysis: Freudian or Existential?' In C. Rycroft (ed.) *Psychoanalysis Observed*.

LOMAS, P. *True and False Experience*. London. Allen Lane, 1973.

LONERGAN, B.J.F. *Insight. A Study of Human Understanding*. London.

Longmans Green & Co., 1957.

LONDON, P. *The Modes and Morals of Psychotherapy*. New York. Holt, Rinehart & Winston Inc., 1964.

LOWRY, F. (ed.) *Readings in Social Casework, 1920—1938*. New York. Columbia University Press, 1940.

LOWREY, L.G. and Smith, G. (eds.) *The Institute for Child Guidance, 1927—1933*. New York, 1933.

LUBOVE, R. *The Professional Altruist*. Cambridge, Mass. Harvard University Press, 1965.

MACADAM, E. 'Training for social work'. *Charity Organisation Review*, **28**, 1910, 72.

MACADAM, E. *The Equipment of the Social Worker*. London. George Allen & Unwin, 1925.

MACADAM, E. *The New Philanthropy*. London. Unwin Bros. Ltd., 1934.

MACADAM, E. *The Social Servant in the Making*. London. George Allen & Unwin, 1945.

MACINTYRE, A.C. *The Unconscious*. London. Routledge & Kegan Paul, 1958.

MACLAY, David. *Treatment for Children: the work of a child guidance clinic*. London. Allen & Unwin, 1970.

MACQUARRIE, J. *Existentialism*. Harmondsworth. Penguin Books, 1973.

MACRAE, D.G. 'Darwinism and the social sciences'. In S.A. Barnett (ed.) *A Century of Darwin*. Heinemann, London, 1958.

MACRAE, D.G. 'Class relationships and ideology'. *Sociological Review*, **6**, 1958, 261—272.

MAHRER, A.R. *The Goals of Psychotherapy*. New York. Appleton-Century-Crofts, 1967.

MANNONI, O. *Freud: The Theory of the Unconscious*. London. Pantheon Books, 1971.

MARCUSE, H. *Eros and Civilization. A philosophical enquiry into Freud*. London. Allen Lane, 1969. Reprinted Sphere Books, 1970.

MARKHAM, V. *Return Passage*. London. Oxford University Press, 1953.

MARKS, I.M. and Gelder, N.G. 'Common ground between behaviour therapy and psychodynamic methods'. *British Journal of Medical Psychology*, **39**, 1966, 11—23.

MARMOR, J. 'Psychoanalytic therapy as an educational process: Common denominators in the therapeutic approaches of different psychoanalytic schools'. In J.H. Masserman (ed.) *Science and Psychoanalysis*, Vol. **5**, New York. Grune & Stratton, 1962.

MARSHALL, T.H. *Social Policy*. London. Hutchinson University Library. 4th edn. 1975.

MARSHALL, T.H. *Citizenship and Social Class*. Cambridge University Press, 1950.

MARSHALL, T.H. *Sociology at the Crossroads*. London. Heinemann, 1963.

MARSHALL, T.H. 'The basic training for all types of social work'. In *Training for Social Work*. Nuffield College. Oxford University Press, 1946.

MARX, J.H. 'A multidimensional conception of ideologies in professional arenas: The case of the mental health field'. *Pacific Sociological Review*, **12**, 2, 1969, 75.

MASON, E.M. 'The centenary of Freud'. *British Journal of Psychiatric Social Work*, **3**, 4, 1956, 12–14.

MAURICE, C.E. *The Life of Octavia Hill as revealed in her letters*. London. Macmillan & Co., 1913.

MAY, Rollo, ANGEL, E. and ELLENBERGER, H.F. (eds.) *Existence*. New York. Basic Books, 1960.

MAY, R. and BASESCU, S. 'Existential Psychology'. *International Encyclopaedia of the Social Sciences* (1968 edn.) Vol. 13.

MAYER, J.E. and Timms, N. *The Client Speaks*. London. Routledge & Kegan Paul, 1970.

McDOUGALL, K. 'The future of casework in England today'. *The Almoner*, **5**, 6, 1952, 243–250.

McDOUGALL, W. *Psycho-analysis and Social Psychology*. London. Methuen & Co., 1936.

MELTSOFF, J. and Kornreich, M. *Research in Psychotherapy*. New York. Atherton Press, 1970.

MENNINGER, K. *Theory of Psychoanalytic Technique*. London. Imago Publishing Co., 1958.

MEYER, C.H. *Social Work Practice: A Response to the Urban Crisis*. London. Collier-Macmillan Ltd., 1970.

MEYER, C.H. 'Practice Models: The New Ideology'. *Smith College Studies in Social Work*, **43**, 2, February 1973, 85–98.

MEYER, H.J. 'Professionalization and social work'. In A.J. Kahn (ed.) *Issues in American Social Work*, 319–340.

MEYER, H.J. 'Social Work'. In *The Encyclopaedia of the Social Sciences*, Vol. 14, 1968.

MEYER, V. and Chesser, E.S. *Behaviour Therapy in Clinical Psychiatry*. London. Penguin Books Ltd., 1970.

MILES, T.R. *Eliminating the Unconscious. A behaviourist view of psycho-analysis*. Oxford. Pergamon Press, 1966.

MILLER, E.J. and RICE, A.K. *Systems of Organisation*. London. Tavistock Publications Ltd., 1967.

MILLER, James G. 'Toward a general theory for the behavioural sciences'. *American Psychologist*, **10**, 1955, 513–531.

MILLER, James G. *Living Systems*. New York. Wiley & Sons, 1972.

MILLER, James G. 'A general systems approach to the patient and his environment'. In A. Sheldon et al. (eds.) *Systems and Medical Care*. Cambridge. MIT Press, 1971.

MILLER, S.M. and Riessman, F. *Social Class and Social Policy*. New York and London. Basic Books, 1968.

MILLERSON, G.L. *The Qualifying Associations: A study in professionalisa-*

tion. London. Routledge & Kegan Paul, 1964.

MILLS, C. Wright. 'The professional ideology of social pathologists'. *American Journal of Sociology*, **49**, 2, 1943, 165—180.

MINOGUE, K.R. *The Liberal Mind*. London. Methuen & Co., 1963.

MISHRA, R. 'Welfare and industrial man'. *Sociological Review*, **21**, 4, 1973, 535—560.

MITCHELL, Juliet. *Psychoanalysis and Feminism*. London. Allen Lane, 1974.

MOFFATT, J. *Concepts in Casework Treatment*. London. Routledge & Kegan Paul, 1968.

MONEY-KYRLE, R.E. 'The world of the unconscious and the world of commonsense'. *British Journal for the Philosophy of Science*, **7**, 1957, 86—96.

MONGER, M. *Casework in ·Probation*. London. Butterworth's. 2nd. edn. 1972.

MONGER, M. *Husband, Wife and Caseworker*. London. Butterworth's, 1971.

MOODIE, W. *Child Guidance by Team Work*. London. Child Guidance Council (not dated).

MOODIE, W. 'The child guidance clinic'. *The Magistrate*, **2**, 1930, 391—392.

MOODY, R.L. 'A Conflict of Disciplines and Personalities'. *British Journal of Educational Psychology*, **22**, 3, 1951, 155.

MOORE, A. 'Psychoanalysis, man and value'. *Inquiry*, **4**, 1961, 53—65.

MORRIS, C. 'Public health during the first months of the war'. *Social Work*, **1**, 3, 1940, 186.

MORRIS, C. (ed.) *Social Casework in Great Britain*. London. Faber & Faber, 1950.

MOWAT, C.L. 'Charity and casework in late Victorian London: the work of the Charity Organisation Society'. *Social Service Review*, **31**, 3, 1957, 258.

MOWAT, C.L. *The Charity Organisation Society*. London. Methuen & Co., 1961.

MOWRER, O.H. ' "Sin": The lesser of two evils'. *American Psychologist*, **15**, 1960, 301.

MOWRER, O.H. 'Too little and too late'. *International Journal of Psychiatry*, **7**, 1, 1969, 536—55.

MULLEN, E.J. 'Differences in worker style in casework'. *Social Casework*, **50**, 6, 1969, 347—353.

MULLEN, E.J. 'Casework communication'. *Social Casework*, **49**, 1968, 546—551.

MULLEN, E.J. and Dumpson, J.R. (eds.) *The Effects of Social Intervention*. San Francisco. Jossey-Bass, 1972.

MUNROE, Ruth. *Schools of Psychoanalytic Thought*. New York, Holt, Rinehart & Winston, 1955.

MURPHY, G. *A Historical Introduction to Modern Psychology*. London. Kegan Paul & Co., 1939. Rev. edn. Harcourt, Brace & Co., 1949.

MURPHY,· G. 'The current impact of Freud on American psychology'. In B. Nelson (ed.) *Freud and the Twentieth Century*. London. George Allen &

Unwin, 1958.

MYERS, F.W.H. 'Review of Breuer and Freud's "Preliminary Communication" '. London. *Proceedings of the Society for Psychical Research*, 1893.

MYERS, F.W.H. *Human Personality and its Survival of Bodily Death*. London. Longmans & Co., 1903.

MYERS, F.W.H. *Essays*. London. McMillan, 1908.

NACHT, Sacha. 'The curative factors in psychoanalysis'. *International Journal of Psycho-Analysis*, **43**, 1962, 206—211.

NACHT, Sacha. 'The non-verbal relationship in psychoanalytic treatment'. *International Journal of Psycho-Analysis*, **44**, 1963, 328—333.

NEILSON, W.A. 'The Smith College Experiment in training for psychiatric social work'. *Mental Health*, **3**, 1, 1919, 59—64.

NELSON, B. *Freud and the Twentieth Century*. London. George Allen & Unwin, 1958.

NELSON, B. 'The future of illusions'. In *Man in Contemporary Society*, (ed.) Contemporary Civilization Staff of Columbia College. New York. Columbia University Press, 1956.

NELSON, B. 'Phenomenological psychiatry: Daseinsanalyze and American existential analysis'. *Psychoanalysis and the Psychoanalytic Review*, **48**, 1961—2, 3—23.

New Trends in European Social Work: The Impact of Casework. Essays dedicated to Marguerite Pohak. Printed in Austria (not dated).

NEW YORK ACADEMY OF MEDICINE. *Freud and Contemporary Culture*. New York, 1957.

NICHOLL, M. RIVERS, W.H.R. and JONES E. 'Why is the 'unconscious' unconscious'. *British Journal of Psychology*, **9**, 1918, 230—256.

NUNBERG, H. 'On the theory of the therapeutic results of psychoanalysis'. *International Journal of Psycho-Analysis*, **18**, 1937, 161—169.

OWEN, D. *English Philanthropy*, 1660—1960. Cambridge, Mass. Harvard University Press, 1965.

PARAD, H.J. (ed.) *Ego Psychology and Dynamic Casework*. New York, Family Service Association of America, 1958.

PARAD, H.J. and MILLER, R.R. (eds.) *Ego-oriented Casework: Problems and Perspectives*. New York. Family Service Association of America, 1963.

PARKER, R.A. 'Social ills and public remedies'. In W.A. Robson (ed.) *Man and the Social Sciences*. London. The London School of Economics and Allen & Unwin, 1972.

PARKES, C. Murray. *Bereavement: Studies of grief in adult life*. London. Tavistock Publications Ltd., 1972.

PATTERSON, C.H. 'Relationship therapy and/or behavior therapy?' In *Psychotherapy — Theory, Research and Practice*, **5**, 4, 1968, 226—233.

PAUL, C.L. *Insight versus Desensitization in Psychotherapy*. Stanford University Press, 1966.

PEAR, T.H. 'The Analysis of some personal dreams, with reference to Freud's theory of dream interpretation'. *British Journal of Psychology*, **6**, 1914,

281—303.

PENTONY, R. 'Value change in psychotherapy'. *Human Relations*, **19**, 1966. 39—46.

PERLMAN, H. *Casework, A Problem-solving Process*. Chicago. University of Chicago Press, 1957.

PERLMAN, H.H. 'Freud's contribution to social welfare'. *Social Service Review*, **31**, 2, 1957, 192—202.

PERLMAN, H.H. 'Social casework'. In *Encyclopaedia of Social Work*. New York. National Association of Social Workers, **15**, 1965, 704—715.

PETERS, R.S. 'Freud's theory'. *British Journal for the Philosophy of Science*, **7**, 25, 1956, 4—12.

PETERS, R.S. *The Concept of Motivation*. London. Routledge & Kegan Paul, 1958.

PETERSON, D.R. and LONDON, P. 'A role for cognition in the behavioural treatment of a child's eliminative disturbance'. In L.P. Ullman and L. Krasner (eds.) *Case Studies in Behaviour Modification*, 289—295.

PINCUS, A. and MINAHAN, A. *Social Work Practice: Model and Method*. Peacock Publications, 1973.

PINKER, R. *Social Theory and Social Policy*. London. Heinemann Educational Books Ltd., 1971.

PLANT, R. *Social and Moral Theory in Casework*. London. Routledge & Kegan Paul, 1970.

PLATT, A.M. *The Child Savers. The Invention of Delinquency*. Chicago and London. University of Chicago Press, 1969.

POLLAK, O. *Integrating Sociological and Psychoanalytic concepts: an exploration in child psychiatry*. New York. Russell Sage Foundation, 1956.

POPPER, K.R. *Conjectures and Refutations*. London. Routledge & Kegan Paul, 3rd edn. 1969.

POPPLESTONE, G. 'The ideology of professional community workers'. *British Journal of Social Work*, **1**, 1, 1971, 85—104.

POWDERMAKER, F., LEWIS, H.T. and TOURAINE, S. 'Psychopathology and treatment of delinquent girls'. American Journal of Orthopsychiatry, **7**, 58, 1937.

PRICE, John Rea. Review of Lees, R. *Politics and Social Work*. *British Journal of Social Work*, **3**, 2, 1973, 288.

PRICE-WILLIAMS, D. 'The place of psychology in social work'. *Case Conference*, **3**, 2, June 1956, 50; **3**, 3, July 1956, 82; **3**, 4, September 1956, 110.

PUMPHREY, M.W. 'Mary Richmond's process of conceptualization'. *Social Casework*, **38**, 8, 1957, 399—406.

PUMPHREY, R.E. and M.W. *The Heritage of American Social Work*. New York. Columbia University Press, 1961.

PUMPIAN-MINDLIN, E. (ed.) *Psychoanalysis as Science*. Stanford, California. Stanford University Press, 1950.

PUMPIAN-MINDLIN, E. 'The position of psychoanalysis in relation to the biological and social sciences'. In E. Pumpian-Mindlin (ed.) *Psycho-*

analysis and Science.

RABLIN, R. 'Is the unconscious necessary?' *International Journal of Psychiatry*, **8**, 2, 1969, 570–583.

RAPAPORT, D. 'The scientific methodology of psychoanalysis'. In M.M. Gill (ed.) *The Collected Papers of David Rapaport*. New York. Basic Books, 1967.

RAPAPORT, D. and GILL, M. 'The points of view and assumptions of metapsychology'. *International Journal of Psycho-Analysis*, **40**, 1959, 153–162.

RAPAPORT, L. 'Social Casework: an appraisal and an affirmation'. *Smith College Studies in Social Work*, **39**, June, 1969.

RATCLIFFE, T.A. 'Relationship therapy and casework'. *British Journal of Psychiatric Social Work*, **5**, 1, 1956, 4.

RAVEN, Alice. 'The use of psychology in social work'. *Charity Organisation Quarterly*, **14**, July 1925.

RAYNER, E.V. *Human Development: an introduction to the psychodynamics of growth, maturity and ageing*. London. George Allen & Unwin, 1971.

REES, H.R. 'UN Seminar on the teaching and supervision of social casework in Europe'. *The Almoner*, **4**, 8, 1951, 357.

REES, J.R. and ROBINSON, Doris. 'Modern psychiatry and social work'. *Hospital Almoners Association Year Book*, 1930.

REEVES, J.W. *Thinking about Thinking: Studies in the background of some psychological approaches*. London. Secker & Warburg, 1965.

REID, William J. 'A study of caseworkers' use of insight-oriented techniques'. *Social Casework*, **48**, 1967, 3–9.

REID, William J. and Epstein, Laura. *Task-centered Casework*. New York. Columbia University Press, 1972.

REID, M. 'Social work in search of a radical profession'. *Social Work*, **15**, 2, April 1970, 13–28.

REYNOLDS, Bertha C. *An Uncharted Journey*. New York. Citadel Press, 1963.

RICE, A.K. *The Enterprise and its Environment*. London. Tavistock Publications Ltd., 1963.

RICH, Margaret E. *A Belief in People: A History of Family Social Work*. New York. Family Service Association of America, 1956.

RICHFIELD, J. 'An analysis of the concept of insight'. *Psychoanalytic Quarterly*, **23**, 1954, 390–408.

RICHMOND, Mary E. *Social Diagnosis*. First Published 1917. New York. Free Press paperback edn. 1965.

RICHTER, Melvin. *The Politics of Conscience. T.H. Green and His Age*. London. Weidenfeld & Nicholson, 1964.

RICOEUR, P. *Freud and Philosophy: An Essay on Interpretation*. New Haven and London. Yale University Press, 1970.

RIEFF, P. *Freud: The Mind of a Moralist*. London. Gollancz, 1960.

RIESMAN, David. *Individualism Reconsidered*. Glencoe, Illinois, The Free Press, 1954.

RIVERS, W.H.R. *et al.* 'Instinct and the unconscious'. *British Journal of Psychology*, **10**, 1919, 1042.

ROBERTS, F.D. *Victorian Origins of the British Welfare State*. New Haven. Yale University Press, 1960.

ROBERTS, R.W. and NEE, R.H. *Theories of Social Casework*. Chicago. University of Chicago Press, 1970.

ROBERTSON, Alex. 'Penal policy and social change'. *Human Relations*, **22**, 6, 547—563.

ROBERTSON, James and Joyce. 'Young children in brief separation: a fresh look'. *The Psychoanalytic Study of the Child*, **26**, 1971, 264—315.

ROBERTSON, James and Joyce. 'Quality of substitute care as an influence on separation responses'. *Journal of Psychosomatic Research*, **16**, 1972, 261—265.

ROBERTSON, James and Joyce. 'Substitute mothering in family crisis'. In R. Gosling (ed.) *Support, Innovation and Autonomy*. London. Tavistock Publications, 1973.

ROBINSON, Virginia P. *A Changing Psychology in Social Casework*. Chapel Hill. University of North Carolina Press, 1930.

ROBINSON, Virginia P. *Jessie Taft: Therapist and social work educator*. Philadelphia. University Press, 1962.

RODGERS, B.N. and Stevenson, J. *A New Portrait of Social Work*. London. Heinemann Educational Books, 1973.

ROGERS, C.R. 'The interpersonal relationship: The core of guidance'. *Harvard Educational Review*, **32**, 1962, 416—429.

ROGERS, C.R. 'Autobiography'. In E.G. Boring and G. Lindsey (eds.) *A History of Psychology in Autobiography*. New York. Appleton-Century-Crofts, 1967.

ROGERS, C.R. *Client-centered Therapy*. Boston. Houghton Mifflin Co., 1951.

ROGERS, C.R. 'The characteristics of a helping relationship'. *Personnel Guidance Journal*, **37**, 1958, 6—16.

ROGERS, Everett, C. *The Diffusion of Innovations*. New York. Free Press, 1962.

ROOFF, M. *A Hundred Years of Family Welfare*. London. Michael Joseph, 1972.

ROSENFIELD, I. *Freud: Character and Consciousness*. New York. University Books Inc., 1970.

ROXBURGH, M.J. 'The First Fifty Years: Episode three, 1939—1953'. *The Almoner*, **6**, 8, 1953, 373—381.

RUBIN, G.K. 'General systems theory: An organismic conception for teaching modalities of social work intervention'. *Smith College Studies in Social Work*, June 1973.

RUBINSTEIN, B.B. (ed.) *Psychoanalysis and Contemporary Science*. London. Collier-Macmillan, 1973.

RUITENBECK, H.M. *Psychoanalysis and Existential Philosophy*. New York E.P. Dutton & Co., Inc., 1962.

218

RUTTER, M. *Maternal Deprivation Re-assessed*. Harmondsworth. Penguin Books Ltd., 1972.

RYCROFT, C. (ed.) *Psychoanalysis Observed*. London. Constable, 1966.

RYCROFT, C. *A Critical Dictionary of Psychoanalysis*. London. Nelson, 1968.

SAINSBURY, E. *Social Diagnosis in Casework*. London. Routledge & Kegan Paul 1970.

SALZBERGER-WITTENBERG, I. *Psycho-Analytic Insight and Relationships: A Kleinian Approach*. London. Routledge & Kegan Paul, 1970.

SALZMAN, Leon. 'Review of Wyss: *Depth Psychology, A Critical History*'. *Psychiatry and Social Science Review*, **1**, 12, 1967.

SANDLER, J. *On the Communication of Psychoanalytic Thought*. Leiden. University Press, 1969.

SANDLER, J., Dare, C., and Holder, A. *The Patient and the Analyst*. London. George Allen & Unwin, 1975.

SARGENT, W. 'Psychiatric treatment'. *The Atlantic Monthly*, July 1964.

SARTRE, J.P. 'Existentialism is a humanism'. In Kaufman, W. (ed.) *Existentialism from Dostoevsky to Sartre*.

SAUL, L.J. 'The goals of pyschoanalytic therapy'. In A.H. Mahrer (ed.) *The Goals of Psychotherapy*. New York. Appleton-Century-Crofts, 1967.

SCHAFER, R. *Language and Insight*. New Haven. Yale University Press, 1978.

SCHATZMAN, M. 'Paranoia or persecution: the case of Schreber'. *Salmogundi*, Spring, 1972, 38–65.

SCHMIDEBERG, M. 'Reality therapy with offenders'. *British Journal of Criminology*, **5**, 1965, 168–182.

SCHMIDEBERG, M. 'Reply to Dr. Holden'. *British Journal of Criminology*, **6**, 1966, 99–100.

SCHMIDEBERG, M. 'How relevant is insight?' *British Journal of Criminology*, **7**, 1967, 243–4.

SCHMIDEBERG, M. 'A contribution to the history of the Psychoanalytic movement in Britain'. *British Journal of Psychiatry*, **118**, 1971, 61–8.

SCHMIDEBERG, M. 'The psycho-analytic movement in Britain: a posthumous endorsement'. *British Journal of Psychiatry*, **122**, 1973, 115.

SCHON, D.A. *The Displacement of Concepts*. London. Tavistock Publications, 1963.

SCHONBAR, R.A. 'Interpretation and insight in psychotherapy'. *Psychotherapy: Theory, research and practice*, **2**, 2, 1965, 78–83.

SCHUR, M. *Freud: Living and Dying*. London. Hogarth Press and the Institute of Psychoanalysis, 1972.

SEARLE, C.R. *The Quest for National Efficiency*. Oxford. Basil Blackwell, 1971.

SEDGWICK, P. 'R.D. Laing: Self, symptom and society'. In R. Boyers (ed.) *Laing and Anti-psychiatry*. London. Penguin Books, 1972.

SEED, Philip. *The Expansion of Social Work in Britain*. London. Routledge & Kegan Paul, 1973.

SEGAL, H. 'The curative factors in psychoanalysis'. *International Journal of*

Psycho-Analysis, **43**, 1962, 212—217.

SEGAL, H. *Introduction to the Work of Molanie Klein*. London. William Heinemann Ltd., 1964.

SHAKOW, D. and RAPAPORT, D. 'The Influence of Freud on American Psychology'. *Psychological Issues*, Vol. IV, **1**, Monograph 13, New York. International Universities Press Inc. 1964.

SHAPIRO, D.A. 'Empathy, warmth and genuineness in psychotherapy'. *British Journal of Social and Clinical Psychology*, **8**, 1969, 350—361.

SHAPIRO, T. 'On the uses of abuses of "unconsciousness" '. *International Journal of Psychiatry*, **8**, 2, 1969, 579—584.

SHENFIELD, B. 'Social casework in Great Britain'. *The Almoner*, **6**, 5, 1953, 226—233.

SHERMAN, Murray H. (ed.) *Psychoanalysis in America: Historical Perspectives*. Springfield, Illinois. Charles C. Thomas, 1966.

SHILS, E. 'The concept of function of ideology'. *International Encyclopaedia of the Social Sciences*, **7**, 1968, 66—76.

SHOBEN, E.J. 'The therapeutic object. Men or machines?' *Journal of Counseling Psychology*, **10**, 1963, 264—268.

SHOR, J. 'The ethics of Freud's psychoanalysis'. *Midstream*, Winter 1959.

SHRUBSALL, F.O. 'Notes on the investigation and treatment of 'difficult' children in the United States of America'. *Mental Welfare*, **8**, 2, 1927.

SIEGLER, M., Osmond, H. and Mann, H. 'Liang's Models of Madness'. *British Journal of Psychiatry*, **115**, 1969. Reprinted in R. Boyers (ed.) *Laing and Anti-Psychiatry*.

SILCOCK, T.H. 'Training social workers in universities'. *Universities Quarterly*, **4**, 2, February 1950, 168—176.

SILVERMAN, D. 'Clerical ideologies: a research note'. *British Journal of Sociology*, **19**, 3, 1968, 326.

SIMEY, T.S. 'Social Research and Social Casework'. In *The Boundaries of Casework*, London. Association of Psychiatric Social Workers, 1956, 60—69.

SIMON, Justin. 'Toward a psychoanalytic definition of social casework'. *Social Service Review*, **36**, 1, 1962, 1—12.

SINFIELD, Adrian. *Which Way for Social Work*? London. Fabian Society, 1969. Fabian Tract No. 393.

SIPORIN, M. 'Situational assessment and intervention'. *Social Casework*, **53**, 2, February 1972, 91—109.

SKYNNER, A.C.R. *One Flesh: Separate Persons*. Constable 1977.

SLATER, E. 'Freud: A philosophical assessment'. *British Journal of Psychiatry*, **120**, 1972, 455—7.

SLUCKIN, A. *The Impressionable Age*. Leicester University Press, 1967.

SMALLEY, R. *The Practice of Social Work*. New York. Columbia University Press, 1967.

SMITH, Gilbert and Harris, Robert. 'Ideologies of need and the organisation of social work departments'. *British Journal of Social Work*, **2**, 1, 1972,

27–45.

SMITH, Marjorie. *Professional Education for Social Work in Britain: an historical account*. London. George Allen & Unwin, 1965.

SNELLING, J.M. 'The United Nations Seminar on the teaching and supervision of social casework'. *The Almoner*, **5**, 10, 1953, 432–439.

Social Casework: Generic and Specific. New York. American Association of Social Workers, 1929.

JOINT UNIVERSITY COUNCIL FOR SOCIAL STUDIES. *Social Study and Training at the Universities*. P.S. King & Co., 1918.

SOCIOLOGICAL REVIEW MONOGRAPHS. Keele. University College of North Staffordshire.
   No. 1.   Problems arising from the teaching of personality development, 1958.
   No. 2.   Problems arising from the teaching of personality development, 1959.
   No. 3.   Moral issues in the training of teachers and social workers, 1960.
   No. 6.   The Canford Families, 1962.

SOROKIN, P. *Society, Culture and Personality*. New York and London. Harper & Bros., 1947.

SOUTHARD, E.E. and JARRETT, M.C. *The Kingdom of Evils*. London. George Allen & Unwin, 1922.

SPECHT, H. 'The deprofessionalization of social work'. *Social Work*, **17**, 2, 1972, 3–15.

SPIEGEL, John P. 'A model for relationships among systems'. In Roy R. Grinker (ed.) *Towards a Unified Theory of Human Behaviour*.

SPITZ, R.A. and WOLF, K.M. 'Anaclitic depression: an enquiry into the genesis of psychiatric conditions in early childhood'. In *The Psychoanalytic Study of the Child*, 1953.

STEFFLRE, B. *Theories of Counseling*. New York. McGraw-Hill, 1965.

STEINBERG, Hannah (ed.) *The British Psychological Society, 1901–61*. London. The Society, 1961.

STENGEL, H. 'The origins and status of dynamic psychiatry'. *British Journal of Medical Psychology*, **27**, 1954, 193–199.

STENGEL, H. 'Freud's impact on psychiatry'. *British Medical Journal*, 5th May 1956, 1000-1003.

STORR, A. 'The concept of cure'. In Rycroft, Co. (ed.) *Psychoanalysis Observed*. London. Constable, 1966.

STRACHEY, J. St. Loe. 'American Juvenile courts and childrens' courts in England'. *The Magistrate*, **1**, 10, March 1926, 117–8.

STRACHEY, J. 'The nature of the therapeutic action in psychoanalysis'. *International Journal of Psycho-Analysis*, **15**, 1934, 127–59.

STRACHEY, J. Introduction to *The Ego and the Id*. Standard Edn. of the Works of Sigmund Freud, 19.

STRAUSS, A. *et al*. *Psychiatric Institutions and Ideologies*. New York. Free Press of Glencoe, 1964.

221

STREAN, H. *Social Casework — Theories in Action*. Metuchen, N.J. Scarecrow Press, 1971.

STRUPP, H.H. 'An objective comparison of Rogerian and psychoanalytic techniques'. *Journal of Consulting Psychology*, **19**, 1955, 1—8.

STRUPP, H.H. 'A multidimensional comparison of therapist activity in analytic and client-centred therapy'. *Journal of Consulting Psychology*, **21**, 1957, 301—308.

STRUPP, H.H. and BERGIN, A.E. 'Some empirical and conceptual bases for coordinated research in psychotherapy'. *International Journal of Psychiatry*, **7**, 37, 1969.

STUDT, Eliot. 'Social work theory and implications for the practice of methods'. *Social Work Education Reporter*, **16**, 2, June 1968, 22—46.

SULLIVAN, C.T. *Freud and Fairbairn: Two Theories of Ego-psychology*. Pennsylvania. The Doylestown Foundation, 1963.

SUTHERLAND, J.D. 'Clinical psychology'. *Universities Quarterly*, **4**, 2, 1950.

SUTHERLAND, J.D. 'Psychological medicine and the National Health Service: The need for an integrated approach to research'. *British Journal of Medical Psychology*, **25**, 1952, 71—85.

SWIFT, Sarah H. *Training in Psychiatric Social Work at the Institute for Child Guidance*, 1927—1953. New York. The Commonwealth Fund, 1933.

SZASZ, T. 'On the theory of psycho-analytic treatment'. *International Journal of Psychoanalysis*, **38**, 1967, 166—182.

SZASZ, T. 'The concept of transference'. *International Journal of Psychoanalysis*, **44**, 1963, 432—43.

SZASZ, T. 'Bootlegging humanistic values through psychiatry'. *The Antioch Review*, **22**, 3, 1962, 341—349.

SZASZ, T. *The Myth of Mental Illness*. London. Paladin Books, 1972.

TAFT, Jessie. *Otto Rank, A biographical Study*. New York. Julian Press, 1958.

TAFT, Jessie. 'The qualifications of the psychiatric social worker'. *Mental Hygiene*, **3**, 3, 1919, 427—435.

TAFT, Jessie. *The Dynamics of Therapy in a Controlled Relationship*. New York. Macmillan, 1933.

TAFT, Jessie. 'The Dane case'. *Social Work*, **6**, 3, July 1949, 316.

TAWNEY, R.H. *Equality*. London. George Allen & Unwin, 1931.

THARP, R.C. and WETZEL, R.J. *Behaviour Modification in the Natural Environment*. New York and London. Academic Press, 1969.

'The Role of the Psychiatric Social Worker'. *British Medical Journal*, July 29th, 1950.

THOMAS, E.J. 'Selecting knowledge from behavioural science'. In *Building Social Work Knowledge*. New York. National Association of Social Workers, 1964, 38—48.

THOMAS, E.J. (ed.) *The Socio-behavioral Approach and Applications to Social Work*. New York. Council on Social Work Education, 1967.

THOMAS, E.J. (ed.) *Behavioral Science for Social Workers*. New York. Free Press, 1967.

THOMAS, E.J. 'Selected Sociobehavioral techniques and principles: an approach to interpersonal helping'. *Social Work*, **13**, 1, January 1968, 12−26.

THOMAS, E.J. *Behavior Modification Procedures in Social Work*. New York. Aldine, 1974.

THOMPSON, Clara. 'The role of the analyst's personality'. *American Journal of Psychotherapy*, **10**, 1956, 347−367.

THOMSON, R. *The Psychology of Thinking*. England. Penguin Books Ltd., 1959.

TILLICH, P. *The Courage to Be*. London. Fontana Library, 1962.

TILLICH, P. 'Existential philosophy'. *Journal of the History of Ideas*, **5**, 44, 44−70.

TILLICH, P. 'The philosophy of social work'. *Social Service Review*, **36**, 1, March, 1962, 13−16.

TIMMS, N. 'Theory and practice in social work education'. *Case Conference*, **5**, 7, January 1959, 167−173.

TIMMS, N. *Psychiatric Social Work in Great Britain, 1929−1962*. London. Routledge & Kegan Paul, 1964.

TIMMS, N. 'Theorizing about social casework'. *British Journal of Psychiatric Social Work*, **5**, 2, 1959.

TIMMS, N. *Social Casework: Principles and Practice*. London. Routledge & Kegan Paul, 1964.

TIMMS, N. *The Language of Social Casework*. London. Routledge & Kegan Paul, 1968.

TITMUSS, R.M. *Problems of Social Policy*. London. HMSO, 1950.

TITMUSS, R.M. 'The administrative setting of social service'. *Case Conference*, **1**, 1, May 1954, 5−11.

TOREN, N. *Social Work: The Case of a Semi-profession*. Beverley Hills, California. Sage Publications, 1972.

TOWLE, C. *The Learner in Education for the Professions*. Chicago. University of Chicago Press, 1954.

TOWLE, C. 'New developments in social case work in the United States'. *British Journal of Psychiatric Social Work*, **3**, 2, 1955, 4−12.

TOWLE, C. *Generic trends in training for social work*. London. Association of Social Workers, 1956.

TOWLE, C. Preface to Hollis, F. *Casework, A Psychosocial Therapy*. New York, Random House, 1964.

TREDGOLD, A.F. 'Review of *A Critical examination of Psychoanalysis*, by A. Wohlgemuth'. *Studies in Mental Inefficiency*, **5**, 3, 1924.

TRUAX, C.B. 'Reinforcement and nonreinforcement in Rogerian psychotherapy', *Journal of Abnormal and Social Psychology*, **71**, 1, 1966, 1−9.

TRUAX, C.B. and CARKHUFF, R.R. *Toward Effective Counseling and Psychotherapy*. Chicago. Aldine Publishing Co., 1967.

TROTTER, W.H. *Instincts of the Herd in Peace and War*. London. T. Fisher Unwin, 1916.

ULLMAN, L. and KRASNER, L. *Case Studies in Behaviour Modification*. New York. Holt, Rinehart & Winston, 1965.

UNITED NATIONS, *Training for Social Work: Third International Survey*. United Nations. Department of Economic and Social Affairs. New York, 1958.

URWICK, E.J. *A Philosophy of Social Progress*. London. Methuen & Co., 1912.

URWICK, E.J. *The Social Good*. London. Methuen & Co., 1927.

URWICK, E.J. *The Values of Life*. Toronto. University Press, 1948.

URWICK, E.J. 'The development of training'. *Charity Organisation Review*, 36, 1914.

URWICK, E.J. 'Social education of today and yesterday'. *Charity Organisation Review*, **14**, 1903, 254.

WAELDER, R. *Basic Theory of Psychoanalysis*. New York. International Universities Press Inc., Paperback edn. 1964.

WAHLER, R.G. and POLLIO, H.R. 'Behavior and insight: a case study in behavior therapy'. *Journal of Experimental Research in Personality*, **3**, 1968, 45−56.

WALKER, N. 'Freud and homeostasis.' *British Journal for the Philosophy of Science*, **7**, 1956−7, 61−72.

WALKER, N. *A Short History of Psychotherapy*. London. Routledge & Kegan Paul, 1957.

WALLACH, M.S. and STRUPP, H.H. 'Psychotherapists' clinical judgements and attitudes toward patients'. *Journal of Consulting Psychology*, **24**, 1960, 316−323.

WASSERMAN, H. 'Social Work Treatment: an essay review'. *Smith College Studies in Social Work*, February, 1975.

WEBB, B. *My Apprenticeship*. London. Longmans & Co., 1950.

WEBB, S. and B. *English Poor Law History*. Part II 'The Last Hundred Years'. London. Longmans Green & Co., 1929.

WEISBERGER, Eleanor B. 'The current usefulness of psychoanalytic theory to casework'. *Smith College Studies in Social Work*, **37**, 2, 1967, 106−118.

WELFARE, Marjorie U. 'Dame Evelyn Fox'. *Social Service*, **28**, April 1955, 172−175.

WHITAKER, D.S. 'The processes by which change occurs and the role of insight'. In M. Pines and T. Spoerri (eds.) *Proceedings of the 6th International Congress of Psychotherapy*. Basel. Karger, 1965, 126−141.

WHITAKER, D.S. and Lieberman, M. *Psychotherapy through the group process*. New York. Atherton Press, 1964.

WHITAKER, D.S. and LIEBERMAN, M 'Assessing the 'affective message' in interpersonal behavior'. *Perceptual and Motor Skills*, **18**, 1964, 163−4.

WHYTE, W.H. *The Unconscious Before Freud*. London. Social Science Paperbacks, 1960.

WILENSKY, H.L. and LEBEAUX, C.N. *Industrial Society and Social Welfare*. New York. The Free Press. (1958), 1965.

WILENSKY, H.L. 'The professionalisation of everyone'. *American Journal of Sociology*, **70**, 2, 1964, 137—158.

WILLIAMS, Gertrude. *The State and the Standard of Living*. London. P.S. King & Son, 1936.

WILLS, W, David. *The Hawkspur Experiment. An informal account of the training of wayward adolescence*. London. George Allen & Unwin, 1941.

WILLS, W. David. *Homer Lane: A biography*. London. George Allen & Unwin, 1964.

WILSON, A.T.M. 'The development of a scientific basis in family casework'. *Social Work*, **4**, 3, July 1947, 62—69.

WILSON, A.T.M., Menzies, I. and Eichholz, E. 'The Marriage Welfare Subcommittee of the Family Welfare Association'. *Social Work*, **6**, 1, 1949, 258.

WILSON, A.T.M. 'A note on some current problems of the social services'. *Social Work*, **8**, 1, January 1951, 504.

WILSON, Roger 'Aims and methods of a department of social studies'. *Social Work*, **6**, 4, October 1949, 353.

WINNICOTT, C. *Child Care and Social Work*. Hitchin. Codicote Press, 1964.

WINNICOTT, C. 'The development of insight'. In *Problems Arising from the Teaching of Personality Development*. Sociological Review Monograph, No. 2, Keele. University College of North Staffordshire, 1959.

WINNICOTT, D.W. 'On transference'. *International Journal of Psychoanalysis*.

WINNICOTT, D.W. and BRITTON, C. 'The problem of homeless children'. In *Children's Communities*. New Education Fellowship Monograph No. 1, 1944.

WINNICOTT, D.W. and BRITTON, C. 'Residential management as a treatment for difficult children'. *Human Relations*, **1**, 1947, 87—97.

WINNICOTT, D.W. 'On transference'. *International Journal of Psycho-Analysis*, **37**, 1956, 386—388.

WINNICOTT, D.W. *The Child, The Family and the Outside World*. London. Tavistock Publications Ltd., 1957.

WINNICOTT, D.W. *Collected Papers: Through Paediatrics to Psycho-analysis*. London. Tavistock Publications Ltd., 1958.

WINNICOTT, D.W. *The Family and Individual Development*. London. Tavistock Publications, 1969.

WINNICOTT, D.W. *The Maturational Processes and the Facilitating Environment*. London. Hogarth Press, 1965.

WISDOM, J.O. 'Review of *New Directions in Psychoanalysis*'. *British Journal for the Philosophy of Science*, **7**, 167—8, 105—110.

WISDOM, J.O. 'Testing an interpretation within a session'. *International Journal of Psychoanalysis*, **48**, 1967, 44—60.

WITMER, H.L. *Psychiatric Clinics for Children*. New York. Commonwealth Fund, 1940.

WOHL, Anthony S. 'The bitter cry of outcast London'. *International Review of*

Social History, **13**, 2, 1968, 222—5.

WOHLGEMUTH, G.A. *A Critical Examination of Psycho-Analysis*. London. G. Allen & Unwin, 1923.

WOLBERG, L.R. *The Techniques of Psychotherapy*. London. Heinemann, 2nd edn. 1967.

WOLF, E. 'Learning theory and psychoanalysis'. *British Journal of Medical Psychology*, **39**, 1966, 1—10.

WOLMAN, B.B. 'Evidence in psychoanalytic research'. *Journal of the American Psychoanalytic Association*, **12**, 1964, 717—733.

WOLMAN, B.B. (ed.) *Psychoanalytic Technique: A Handbook for the Practising Analyst*. New York. Basic Books Inc., 1967.

WOLMAN, B.B. (ed.) *Historical Roots of Contemporary Psychology*. New York Harper & Row, 1967.

WOLMAN, B.B. *The Unconscious Mind*. Englewood-Cliffs. New Jersey. Prentice-Hall, 1968.

WOLPE, J. *Psychotherapy by Reciprocal Inhibition*. Stanford, California. Stanford University Press, 1958.

WOLPE, J. Slater, A. and Reyna, L.J. (eds.) *The Conditioning Therapies*. New York. Holt, Rinehart & Winston, 1965.

WOODARD, C. 'The COS and its place in history'. *Social Work*, **18**, 4, October 1961, 12—16.

WOODROOFE, K. Charles Stewart Loch. *Social Work*, **18**, 4, October 1961, 2—10.

WOODROOFE, K. *From Charity to Social Work in England and the United States*. London, Routledge & Kegan Paul, 1962.

WOOLF, L. *Beginning Again*. London. The Hogarth Press, 1964.

WOOTTON, B. *Social Science and Social Pathology*. London. George Allen & Unwin, 1959.

WOOTTON, B. 'Daddy knows best'. *The Twentieth Century*, October 1959, 248—261.

WOOTTON, B. *Social Science and Social Pathology*. London. George Allen & Unwin, 1959.

WOOTTON, B. 'The image of the social worker'. *British Journal of Sociology*, 11, **4**, 1960, 373—385.

WYSS, Dieter. *Depth Psychology. A Critical History*. London. George Allen & Unwin, 1966.

YOUNG, A.F. and ASHTON, E.T. *British Social Work in the Nineteenth Century*. London. Routledge & Kegan Paul, 1956.

YOUNG, G.M. *Victorian England: Portrait of an Age*. London. Oxford University Press, 1936. Paperback edn. 1960.

YOUNGHUSBAND, E.L. *Report on the Employment and Training of Social Workers*. Edinburgh. Carnegie UK Trust, 1947.

YOUNGHUSBAND, E.L. *Social Work in Britain*. Edinburgh. Carnegie UK Trust, 1951.

YOUNGHUSBAND, E.L. *Basic Training for Social Work — its place in the*

Curriculum. London. Association of Social Workers, 1953.

YOUNGHUSBAND, E.L. Introduction to Biestek, F. *The Casework Relationship*. (British edition). London. George Allen & Unwin, 1961.

YOUNGHUSBAND, E.L. (ed.) *Social Work and Social Change*. London. George Allen & Unwin, 1964.

YOUNGHUSBAND, E.L. (ed.) *New Developments in Casework*. London. George Allen & Unwin, 1966.

YOUNGHUSBAND, E.L. (ed.) *Education for Social Work*. London. George Allen & Unwin, 1968.

YOUNGHUSBAND, E.L. 'Social work with individuals'. In A.V.S. Lochhead (ed.) *A Reader in Social Administration*. London. Constable, 1968.

ZALD, Mayer N. *Social Welfare Institutions: A Sociological Reader*. London. John Wiley & Sons Inc., 1965.

ZEITLYN, B.B. 'The therapeutic community — fact or fantasy?' *British Journal of Psychiatry*, **113**, 503, 1967, 1083—1086.

ZETZEL, E. 'Current concepts of transference'. *International Journal of Psychoanalysis*, **37**, 1956, 369—376.

ZILBOORG, G. 'The emotional problem and the therapeutic role of insight'. *Psychoanalytic Quarterly*, **21**, 1952, 1—24.

ZILBOORG, G. 'Freud in the perspective of medical history'. In I. Galston (ed.) *Freud and Contemporary Culture*. New York. International Universities Press, 1957.

ZILBOORG, G. and Henry G.W. *A History of Medical Psychology*. New York. W.W. Norton & Co., 1941.

ZINBERG, N.E. 'Psycho-analytic training and psycho-analytic values'. *International Journal of Psycho-Analysis*, **48**, 88, 1967, 88—96.

Index

Ackerman, N., 25
almoners, 48—51, 108—109
American Association of Medical Social Workers, 60
American Association of Psychiatric Social Workers, 60
American Association of Social Workers, 60
anxiety, 18—19
Aristotelian Society, 32
Association for Behavioural Psychotherapy, 171
Association of Genera and Family Case-workers, 110
Association of Psychiatric Social Workers, 50, 54, 57, 104, 111
Association of Psychotherapists, 143
Attlee, C.R., 40, 43, 44, 45, 127
Austin, L., 64
Aves, G., 95

Balint, M., 14, 16, 131
Barnett, S., 37, 38, 39, 40—41, 42
behaviour modification, 138, 146
behavioural methods, 146—151, 166, *see also* behaviour modification
Bernheim, H., 7
Beveridge, W.H., 40, 41, 43
Beveridge Committee, 71
  Report, 82
Binswanger, L., 19—20, 21
Bion, W.R., 24
Birmingham Education Committee, 47
Boehm, W., 144
Booth, C., 37
Bosanquet, B., 38, 39
Bosanquet, H., 37
Boss, M., 19
Bowlby, J., 14, 56, 75—79, 80, 85, 152, 154, 155, 164
British Association of Psychotherapy, 24
British Federation of Social Workers, 58, 60, 88
British Medical Association, 35
British Psychoanalytical Society, 5
British Psychological Society, 32
Britton, C., 84—85, 95
Brown, C., 46, 54, 55, 60
Brown, W., 29, 32
Brown, W.P., 56

Buber, M., 18
Burke, N., 52
Burt, C., 55
Butler, K., 50, 52
Butrym, Z., 110

Carnegie Reports, 92—94, 100
Carnegie United Kingdom Trust, 92, 94, 103
Carr-Saunders, A., 43
casework, *see* social casework
Catholic Marriage Advisory Council, 82
Central Association for Mental Welfare, 47, 49, 51
Central Training Council in Child Care, 84, 85, 104
Charity Organisation Society, 36—38, 42, 43, 44, 70—71, *see also* Family Welfare Association
  Reconstruction Committee, 81
  Quarterly, 58—59
child care, 84, 152—153
  training, 83—85
child development, 74—79, 152—153
child guidance, 2, 46—53, 55, 56, 75—76, 130
  clinics, 51—52, 69
  psychoanalytic influences, 56, 57, 87
Child Guidance Council, 47, 50, 51, 52
Child Guidance Training Centre, 54
Child Treatment Research Unit, 147
Child Welfare League of America, 60
Children Act 1948, 84
Children's Country Holiday Fund, 44
Children's Departments, 83, 84
Citizens' Advice Bureaux, 81
Clark, J.M., 27
Commonwealth Fund, 47, 49, 51, 52, 54, 59, 69
community work, 3, 114
Cooper, D., 17
Craggs, K., 52
Crichton-Miller, H., 31, 33, 34, 49, 50
criminology, 85—86
crisis theory, 134
  and social work intervention, 154
Crowley, R., 52
Curtis Committee, 84

dream analysis, 7, 8, 130, 143, 157, 160

228

229

230

World Health Organisation, 77